COPYRIGHT ACT AND DIGITAL MILLENIUM ACT

Emerging Thrust Areas in Library and Information Science

PUSHPLATA SRIVASTAVA
Librarian, Kanya Mahavidyalaya Arya Samaj,
Bhoor, Bareilly (U.P.)

Ess Ess Publications
New Delhi

COPYRIGHT ACT AND DIGITAL MILLENIUM ACT
Emerging Thrust Areas in Library and Information Science

ISBN: 978-81-7000-753-1

First Published 2015

Published by:
Ess Ess Publications
4831/24, Ansari Road,
Darya Ganj,
New Delhi-110 002.
INDIA
Phones: 23260807, 41563444
Fax: 41563334
E-mail: info@essessreference.com
www.essessreference.com

Cover Design by *Patch Creative Unit*

Printed and bound in India at Salasar Imaging Systems.

Contents

Preface

The Title symbol © that is found in all books has been an object of affection for me since quite a long time. Why and how should such a small symbol be so significant has always been an interesting issue. This book is a result of my curiosity and interest in ©.

In this globalized and digital era, infringement of copyright is an important issue which requires considerable thinking and how the librarians can play their role in resolving the problems arising out of infringement of copyright and also how far it is transferable and up to which extent it can be used for advancement and development of knowledge society needs attention. Preventing infringement of copyright in today's world of information explosion and the role of a librarian in doing so is discussed in this book.

The present book is a short and brief commentary on the above subject . The important enactments dealing with this subject can be enumerated in brief as follows:

"Copyright: History and Development, Copyright Act 1957, Duration And Infringement, Copyright Office and Copyright Board, Universal Copyright Act, Digital Millennium Copyright Act (DMCA), International Copyright Act, Intellectual Property Right, Conclusion And Suggestions." Useful appendices has been added to improve the book further.

The concept of Intellectual Property Rights (IPR) and its branches such as; Trade Mark, Patents, Copyright, The Design Act etc. is developing fast in library networking which is a big and challenging issue.

I have tried to consider Digital Millennium Copyright Act (DMCA), World Intellectual Property Organization (WIPO Treaty), Sonny Bono Copyright Term Extension Act (CTEA), Technology Education and Copyright Harmonization Act (TEACH) etc. in my book and also what developments are made by the Government/society in this respect.

I have made some suggestions for advancement and development of protection and preservation of copyright. The entire study tells us that librarians and information professionals have an important role in protecting the rights of copyright holders. It is really true that librarians and informational professionals are to become the information intermediaries between generators and the receivers of information in the real sense of the word.

This book should be useful to librarians, information scientists, educationists, and the persons working in revenue, law, judiciary, advocates, students of law, police departments, business executives and even for a common man. However, its success remains in the fact how effectively copyrights are protected in our day to day life by a common man.

I want useful and constructive suggestions to improve this book further.

Pushplata Srivastava

Acknowledgements

The present study was possible with the help of many an erudite minds but the person I am most grateful and indebted to is none other than my guruji Retd. Prof. N. R. Satyanarayana, Department of Library and Information Science, Babasaheb Bhimrao Ambedkar University, Lucknow, who at all hours has given his most precious time in reading my book and offering his invaluable suggestions at every step.

My study is based on various national and international seminars, conferences and workshops held at Allahabad University of Allahabad, National Botanical Research Institute, Lucknow, Central Drug Research Institute, Lucknow, M.J.P. Rohilkhand University Bareilly, National Research Development Corporation, Rishikesh, Dehradun and 55th Indian Library Association, Greator Noida.

I am thankful to Mr. Anand Narain Shukla, Mr. Somesh Chandra, Dr. Kuhu Dutta Gupta & Dr. Asha Chaubey who have helped me in many ways.

This book could not have been completed with the whole hearted co-operation and support from all my well wishers.

I am heartily grateful to my mother and sister whose

encouragement resulted in this book seeing the light of the day. It is with their blessings that I could complete this venture.

— Author

I. Copyright Rules.

   i. Copyright Act (1957).
   ii. Copyright Amendment Act, 1992, 1994, 1996.
   iii. Copyright Society.
   iv. Digital Millennium Copyright Act (1998).
   v. Application for Registration of Copyright.
   vi. Statement of Particulars.
   vii. Second Schedule to the Copyright Rules, 1958. Enlisting various fee payable under Copyright Act, 1957.
   viii. Role of Judiciary in the effective protection of Intellectual Property Rights.
   ix. The Gazette of India Part II, Ministry of law and Company Affairs (Legislative Department). (Copyright (Amendment) Act, 1999
   x. The Gazette of India Part II-Section-1. Ministry of Law and Justice Legislative Department. The Copyright Amendment Act,2012

Na Chouraharyama, Na Cha Rajaharyam,
Na Bhratrabhajyam, Na Cha Bharakari,
Vyaye Krite Vardhate Eva Nityam,
Vidya Dhanam, Sarva Dhanam Pradhanam.

"Bhartruhari"

"Education, Knowledge and Wisdom are invaluable for a complete intellectual and spiritual development of man The invaluable wealth or treasure of knowledge can neither be stolen by a thief nor can it be usurped by a king, nor can it be divided among brothers as a common inherited property, nor it is ever tiresome or burdensome; rather, the more it is spent or utilized, the more it increases in amount and size. Hence, Knowledge or learning is the supreme and the best of all wealth and treasures available is world."

1

Copyright : History And Development

INTRODUCTION

Copyright, branch of law granting authors the exclusive privilege to reproduce, distribute, perform or display their creative works. **The *main purpose*** of this study is the creating awareness about copyrights among artistic, producers and general public, who is unwitting violator of copyright assumes great importance. Copyright law is to encourage authors to invest efforts in creating new works of art and literature.

Copyright Act 1957 is based the Indian environment and Digital Millennium Copyright Act 1998 basically based in United States environment.

Copyright is one branch of the larger legal field known as intellectual property, which also includes trademark and patent law. Copyright law is the legal foundation protecting the work of many major industries, including book publishing, motion- picture production, music- recording and computer software development. These industries account for considerable economic activity in the United States, making copyright law a field of enormous economic importance.

Not every work of authorship is eligible for copyright, to qualify for copyright protection work must be original. The law considers a work to be original if it is recorded in some permanent format. The work original include writing it down, storing it on a computer floppy disk or compact disc (CD), recording it on video tape or sculpting it in marble. If a poet thinks of a new poem and recites it to an audience without writing it down, copyright does not protect the poem because it is not fixed. To be original, the work must not be copied from previously existing material and must display at least a reasonable amount of creativity. For *example*, if an author writes the words "the sky is blue" on a piece of paper, copyright does not protect the words because they lack sufficient creativity. Because short phrases and titles are not protected by copyright, but in some situation trade- mark law may protect them.

Copyright only protects the words, notes or images that the creator has used. It does not protect any ideas or concepts. Such as, a scientist publishes an article explaining a new process for refining oil, the copyright prevents others from copying the words of that article. It does not, however, prevent anyone else from using the process described to refine oil. To protect the process, the scientist must obtain a patent. Other example, if a novelist writes a book about a man obsessed about killing a whale, other people may write their own books on the same subject, as long as they do not use the exact words.

Copyrights are a set of exclusive rights granted by law to the creators and producers of forms or creative expressions such as literary, artistic, musical, and cinematographic works. These rights bestow on the copyright owner the control over the use of his works like their reproduction and distribution for a limited duration.

HISTORY OF COPYRIGHT

The concept of copyright is very ancient. The laws granting these rights are of comparatively recent origin. Their genesis can be traced to the chaotic market conditions in culture industries created by advancements in technology following the industrial revolution. There was a felt need to have proper norms to regulate the new business opportunities in the creative arts. Laws protecting copyright have been introduced as a response to the wide spread commercial exploitation of literary works as a result of technological developments in printing methods.

Before the invention of the printing press in Europe in the 15th century, copyright law did not exist. Books were expansive and difficult to produce and few people know how to read, so there was little need for copyright protections. By the mid- 1500s, however, books had become cheaper and more widely available in Europe. To reduce the risk of rival printing politically dangerous books, the royal government of England granted a publishing monopoly to a group of book publishers, who all belonged to a guild called the Stationer's Company.

The first Copyright Act in England is 8 Anne c. 19. The preamble states that printers, booksellers and other persons were frequently in the habit of printing, reprinting and publishing "books and other writings without the consent of the authors or proprietors of such books and writings, to their very great detriment and too often to the ruin of them and their families." "For preventing, therefore, such practices for the future and for the encouragement of learned men to compose and write useful book's, it is enacted that the author of any book or books already printed, who have not transferred to any other the copy or copies of such book or books in order to print or reprint the same, shall have the sole right and liberty of printing such book or books for the term of one and twenty years, and that the author of any book or books already composed, and not printed and published, or that shall hereafter be composed and his assignee or assignees, shall have the sole liberty of printing and reprinting such book or books for the term of fourteen years, to commence from the day of first publishing the same and no longer."

Prehistory of Copyright

Authors, patrons and owners of works throughout the ages have tried to direct and control how copies of such works could be used once disseminated to others. Mozart's patron, Baroness Von Waldstatten, allowed his compositions created for her to be performed, while Handel's patron, George I. Jealously guarded "Water Music"

During the centuries following the destruction of the Roman Empire, European literary undertakings were confined almost entirely to the monasteries. The Roman usage, under which authors could dispose of their works to booksellers and the latter could be secure of some commercial control of property purchased, was entirely forgotten.(In Ken Follet's novel 'The Pillors of the Earth a character is astonished to meet a woman who actually owns books, which were normally owned only by churches and monasteries.)

Before legal and economic restrictions on print ownership came into being, one would occasionally find an author's or archivist's book curse inscribed in a given volume. Beyond this, however, two major developments in the fourteenth and fifteenth centuries seem to have provoked the development of modern copyright. *First*, the expansion of mercantile trade in major European cities and the appearance of the secular university helped produce an educated bourgeois class interested in the information of the day. This helped spur the emergence of a public sphere, which was increasingly served by entrepreneurial stationers who produced copies of books on demand. *Second,* Gutenberg's development of movable type and the development and spread of the printing press made mass reproduction of printed works quick and much cheaper than ever before. Before printing, the process of copying a work could be nearly as labor ever intensive and expensive as creating the original, and was largely relegated to monastic scribed. It appears that publishers, rather than authors, were the first restrictions on the copying of printed works. Given that publishers commonly now obtain the copyright from the authors as a condition of mass reproduction of a work, one of the criticisms of the current system is that it benefits publishers more than it does authors. This is one of the chief arguments in favor of peer-to-peer file sharing systems, making an analogy with the changes wrought by printing. .

An interesting attempt at copyright in the early modern period was the notice attached to the Ha-Shirim asher li- Shelomo, a setting of the Psalms by the composer Salomone Ross, which happened to be the first music to be printed with a Hebrew type-face text (1623).

In India too modern copyright law emerged consequent to the spread of printing technology. It is true that while the history of printing of books in India goes back to 1557, that of copyright law is only little more than a hundred and fifty years old. This was because the early printing activities were mostly non- commercial and Christian Missionary driven. But once commercial publishing picked up, need for a copyright law to protect the interests of authors and publishers was felt. This led to the enactment of Indian Copyright Act of 1847 on December 15, 1847. This Act made the English law applicable to the area under the control of the British East India Company.

Subsequently, when Britain enacted the Copyright Act, 1911, "the first British legislation to bring the various copyrights within a single text," it was considered appropriate to have a new legislation of India too. Thus was promulgated the Indian Copyright Act of 1914 which was a slightly modified version of the British Copyright Act, 1911, adapting it to the requirements of India. This law remained in force till 1958 when the present Indian Copyright Act of 1957 had come into force.

The vagaries and compulsions of history dragged India into the legal regime of Great Britain for about a hundred years. This has had certain advantages so far as copyright protection was concerned. Great Britain had been one of the founder members of the Berne Convention; its laws on copyright had kept abreast of the international treaties and state of technological in this area. This naturally ensured that the Indian law was also on par with the same. Thus at the time of its independence India had a copyright law which was fully compatible with the international treaties on copyright and the technologies in the cultural industries at that time.

New challenges posed by developments in the technological field, necessary amendments had been carried out in the Act. The influence of new technologies is visible in the amendments made in 1983, 1984 and 1994. For example, the 1983 amendment in law inserted new sections and definitions in the Act to take care of broadcasting technology, reprographic technologies and so on. In order to tackle the menace of increased piracy of copyrighted works due to the introduction of new techniques of printing, recording and fixation of broadcast programmed, amendments were made in the Act in 1984. The situation created by various technological developments that had taken place in the world in the 1980s and early1990s was a prime reason for the comprehensive amendments in 1994.

While the contours of copyright law has always been drawn by the developments in the technological world, the emergence of digital technologies towards the concluding decades of the twentieth century as the defining paradigms of new age communication raised a whole new set of challenges to copyright regimes. The traditional notions of the basic concepts of copyright such as rights of reproduction and distribution have become in adequate and even irrelevant in the digital era. A host of intangibles have arisen in the world of 'property incorporeal.' All works can now be digitalized whether they comprise texts, images, sound or diagrams and once digitalized the various elements such as images are all 'equal and can be merged, transformed, manipulated or mixed to create and endless variety of new works. Earlier rights of reproduction and distribution affected tangible physical copies only of a work. The new technologies brought in non-material reproduction and distribution. Physical reproductions were replaced by digital reproduction. While initially the intellectual property right community got be wildered at these developments, slowly they learnt the tricks of the new game and found out ways to regulate the rights in the new media.

The concerted effort of the international community to respond to the challenges of digital technologies mostly took place under the aegis of World Intellectual Property Organisation (WIPO). This special agency of the United Nations Organisation responsible for the promotion of the protection of intellectual property throughout the world began in 1989 to examine the revisions needed in the multilateral conventions, specifically in the Berne Convention for the protection of literary and artistic works (the Berne Convention) (1886) in the light of the new technologies and concluded two new treaties in a diplomatic conference in December, 1996 namely the WIPO Copyright Treaty (WCT) and the WIPO Performances and Phonograms Treaty (WPPT). These treaties are popularly known as Internet treaties as they are intended to address the issue so copyright protection on the Internet. The World Wide communication system made possible by advancements in digital technologies. The

WCT and WPPT addressed the issues in three ways, namely;

1. By clarifying the existing provisions in the Berne Convention and in International Convention for the Protection of Performers. Producers of Phonograms and Broadcasting Organisations (the Rome Convention) 1961 and in some cases, reaffirming the interpretations already generally adopted.
2. Giving new interpretation to the existing provisions widening their scope and,
3. Adding new provisions on rights and obligations. While the negotiations in WIPO had been going as, the Uruguay Round of Multilateral Trade Negotiations had concluded the Agreement on Trade Related Aspects of Intellectual Property Rights (TRIPS) in 1994. This Agreement though covered only two products of the new technology, namely, computer software and databases.

The major challenges to copyright generated by advancements in digital technologies in the recent years, the provisions in the TRIPS Agreement and the WCT having a bearing on those issues and the position of Indian law.

The Berne Convention

The result of the conferences at Berne in 1885 and 1887 this system was simple and made more general by the treaty known as *"The Berne Convention," signed on 5 September, 1887.* The contracting parties were the British empire, Belgium, France, Germany, Italy, Spain, Switzerland, Tunis and Haiti, Luxemburg, Monaco, Norway and Japan have since joined. Austria and Hungry have a separate convention with Great Britain, concluded on 24th April, 1893. The bases was the Berne Convention was that authors first published in one of them, should enjoy in each of other countries of the union the same rights as the law of that country granted to native authors.

Berne Convention Countries, which have accepted to the 1971 Text of the Convention

Albania, Argentina, Australia, Austria, Bahrain, Barbados, Belarus, Bolivia, Botswana, Brazil, Bulgaria, Cameroon, Central African Republic, Chili, China, Colombia, Congo, Cuba, Cyprus, Denmark, Egypt, Guinea, Finland, France, Germany, Ghana, Greece, Guatemala, Guinea, Hungry, Iceland, Italy, Iceland, Indonesia, Japan, Russian Federation, U.K., U.S.A., Spain etc. 116 countries are involved and accepted the convention.

Berne Convention Countries, which are yet to ratify/ accept to the 1971 Text of Convention

The Countries are Belgium, Canada, Chad, fiji, Ireland, Israel, Lebanon, Liechtenstein, Madagascar, New Zealand, Pakistan,_Romania.

UK COPY RIGHT LAW

Most people are not interested in copyright for its own sake of as an academic subject. They simply want to be able to copy material with the confidence that they are doing so lawfully. The problem is that copy right law is extremely complex and does not provide the certainty that every one wants. There are two key reasons such as;

1. There are a number of key words and phrases in the (UK) Copyright Designs and Patents Act 1988 that are left undefined. They, include original, substantial, reasonable, fair dealing and copying for a commercial purpose.
2. In the legal system to England and the Wales, case law plays an important part. Legal cases present specific problems out of which a point of law is extracted. The point of law is known as appreciate. It is necessary to take into account both statute law and any relevant case law.

Authorization is needed for any copying of material that is protected by copyright or database right. That authorization could be in the form of statute or getting the direct permission of the rights holder by entering into a contract or licences.

There is no need that the every time to get the direct permission of the rights holder. *For example*: if we are sure that our copying falls within one of the permitted copyright acts, then this is, by definition, a lawful use of a work. Although it has not been authorized by the publisher. The problem is the copying really does fit within a copyright exception and that a court takes the same view.

When we contact the rights holder directly for the permission to copy we should provide them with as much information as for as possible about what it is we want to copy for the following details;

- Author and title of the extract you wish to reproduce;
- Author and title of the publication in which the extract;
- Appears; Pages range;
- Date of publication and in the case of journals, the volume and the issue number;
- The number of copies to be made.
- In the copy content we have think about this term, that what we know and want to do in terms;
- How many people are sending the materials to
- The status to the people. Such as, In-house, employees, freelance or client.
- Location of the people;
- The purpose for the copying is done. (Such as; Article, newspaper, magazine)

UNITED STATE COPY RIGHT ACT

Act of the United States, known as the Act of March, 1891, which replaced the Act of July, 1870 and which is still in force, constituted the most important modification in copyright law since the original Act of 1790. Under all acts proceeding it, copyright had been granted to "citizens or residents of the United States," In the United states a some what similar question as to perpetual common law copyright arose in the classic case of Wheaton V. Peters, decided by the Supreme Court in 1834. The court held that copyright in the published work was solely a creature of statute, so that the proprietor was required to comply with the statute or his work entered the " public domain— that is became public property, which any one could in its or in its or freely use in its original form.

Development of United State

The adaptation of the constitution in 1789 was Congress vested (by Article I, section 8) with the power to protect literary property and the investigations. Formerly, the separate states had enacted their own copyright statutes. The subject matter of literary protection under the new law federal act of 1790 did not go beyond maps, charts and books. Foreign authors were not eligible for protection until the passage of the Chance Act 1n 1891.

In the intervening century, Charles Dickens and other leading English authors had been freely pirated by U.S. publishers. The American authors complained bitterly that their own books were being ignored by many U.S publishers in favor of royalty- free English works. There was strenuous petitioning over the years by such American literary giants as 'Twain', one fellow, Holmes, Emerson and Whittier. American authors were adversely affected by the unfair competition of the large and accessible number of English work in the U.S. " Public domain." This coupled with the creation in Europe of the Berne Union (Which opened the door to European

Copyright for Americans) led to the Chace Act.

Between the passage of the Act of 1790 and the previous major revision in 1909, the protect able subject matter expanded considerably. The Congress added prints (1802); musical compositions (1831); the right of public performance in dramatic compositions (1856), which had previously been protected only against printed copies. Photographs (1805); works of fine art, the right of translation, and the right to dramatize non- dramatic literary works (1870); and the right of the performance in public of musical compositions (1897).

The 1909 act extended the control of the " Proprietor"(the author, his assignee or his heirs to the right to make any other version of a literary work. *For example*, an abridgment) and the right to convert a drama into a non dramatic work. Proprietors of musical works were protected against unauthorized recording.

Through codification and reenactment in 1947 as title 17 of the U.S. code, the 1909 act added new protective categories of works (lectures, sermons and address prepared for oral delivery; models or designs for works of art; reproductions of the works of art; and drawings or plastic works of a scientific or technical character), In 1952 the copyright proprietor of a non dramatic literary works was given control over public renditions for profit and the making of transcriptions or records.

In 1971, Congress established a limited copyright in sound recordings that were first recorded and issued beginning Feb. 15, 1972 and before Jan 1, 1975 for the purpose of protecting them against unauthorized duplication and piracy. In 1974 with general revision still mired in hearings. Congress eliminated the Jan.1.1975, cut off date, thus making the new right a permanent part of the copy right law.

The long- awaited general revision of the copyright law enacted Oct. 19, 1976, radically altered the American

Copyright system. The federal statute preempted state common law copyright. It also adopted the "author's life-plus 50 years" term of the protection for new works and existing unpublished works not previously copyrighted (with some exceptions and qualifications). It brought cable television, juke boxes and public broadcasting use of certain copyrighted works within the new act but subject to new forms of compulsory licensing (Under a Copyright Royalty Tribunal). Other provisions prohibited library photocopying except under specified conditions, instituted a new mechanism for terminating transfers of copyrights, phased out the manufacturing clause" (which deals with books and periodicals by U.S. citizens and residents or in the English language), and liberalized the system of copyright notice that had for too long punished American creators protecting them.

Copyright Law in CANADA

Canadian Copyright law is governed by the Copyright Act, which protects original literary, artistic, musical and dramatic works. A partial list of work which are entitled to copyright protection in Canada includes; books, newspapers, dictionaries, manuals, catalogues, sculptures, magazines, pamphlets, computer software, paintings, drawings, designs, trademarks, Architectural works, engravings, photographs, films, videos, scripts, maps, lyrics and musical works.

One of the very significant rights granted to the owner of Canadian copyright in a work is the exclusive right to reproduce the work, in any material form whatever. *For Example*, the owner of copyright in a book has the right to stop others from making copies of the books, (or any substantial part of the books), whatever the copying is by way of a computer image/text scanner.

In addition to acquiring the exclusive right to copy the work, the owner of copyright in a work also receives an entire "bundle" of rights, some of which are specific to the type of work in question. *For example*; in the case of dramatic work, copyright includes the right to convert the dramatic work into a novel.

In the case of computer software, it includes the right to rent the software to others. Each different type of work has its own bundle of copyrights. Copyright comes into existence automatically, at the time the work was created, and in the case of most works, it continues until the end of the calendar year in which the author of the work dies, and continues for an additional period of 50 years. There are some notable exceptions of this rule however. One such objection related to photographs, which are protected by copyright from the time of the photograph was taken up, until the end of the calendar year in which the photograph was taken, and of an additional period of 50 years. The time of photographs is include when the date of the photographs was taken, and not include the date of the expire of Photographers.

"Moral" rights are also protected under Canadian Copyright Law. Moral rights included the author's right to be associated with the work by name, or pseudonym and the right to remain anonymous, and include the author's right to the integrity of the work.

Moral rights to depend on the author of a work. The copyright in the work has been sold. Moral rights continue to exist in a work or the same length of the time as other copyrights in work in question.

Harmonization of Copyright Law and Procedure : Milestones

Details of convention are as under;

1886 Berne Convention for protection of literary and artistic work.

1952 Universal Copyright Convention.

1961 Rome Convention –Performer's Producer's of Phonograms and Broadcasting Organizations.

1971 Geneva Convention-Producer's of Phonograms against unauthorized duplication of their Phonograms.

1972 Brussels Convention- Distribution of Programme-Carrying Signals transmitted by Satellite.

1976 WIPO Copyright Treaty.

1996 WIPO Performance and Phonogram Treaty.

Copyright Protection : New Works

Protection for a work created after Jan.1, 1978, begins at the time of the creation and lasts for the author's life and 50 years after the death of a author If it is joint work, the 50 years is measured from the death of the last survivor of the joint author's. For anonymous and pseudonymous works and works made for hire, the copyright endures for 75 years from first publication, of 100 years from creation which ever expires first. Copyright in works created but not published or copyrighted before Jan.1, 1978 subsists from Jan.1, 1978 and endures at least for the terms accorded new works, the copyright in such works shall not expire before Dec. 31, 2002 , and if published before Dec.31,2027.

A transfer or license of copyright executed by the author of a work after Jan.1,1978, other than by will, be subject to termination under certain circumstances during five year period beginning 35 to 40 years from the date of execution.

Major Copyright Libraries

Date Estd.	*Deposit Library*	*Location*
1602	Bodleian Library	Oxford
1972	British Library	London
Unknown	Cambridge University	Cambridge
1800	Library of Congress	Washington, D.C.
1591	Library of Trinity College	Dublin

1953	The National Library, India	Kolkata
1960	National Library of Australia	Canberra
1965	National Library of Newzealand	Wellington
1925	National Library of Scotland	Edinburgh
1907	National Library of Wales	Aberystwyth

Sources : Microsoft® 2006.©1993-2005 Microsoft corporation.
 10

REFERENCES

- Britannica Encyclopaedia 9th ed., 6th vols, London: Adam and Charles. Black Adinburgh, 1904, 356-362.
- Britannica Encyclopaedia. 10th ed., xxvii vols. London: Adam and Charles. Black Adinburgh, 1904, 239-240.
- Britannica, Micropaedia Ready Reference, Encyclopaedia of Britannica. 15th ed., 3 vols. Chicago: Britannica, 2003, 616-617.
- Chamber's Encyclopaedia. "A Dictionary of Universal Knowledge for the people" rev. ed., 10 vols. London: W and R. Edinburgh, 1880.
- Cornish, W R . Intellectual Property. Delhi: Universal, 2003,
- David, Bainbridge. Intellectual Property. 5th ed. Singapore: Pearson, 2003, 5-6, 27-34.
- Encyclopaedia Americana. 7th vol. Danbury: Grolier Incorporated International, 1988, 772-776.
- Government of India. A Hand Book of Copyright Law. New Delhi: Ministry of HRD, 1999.
- Government of India. The Copyright Act, 1957. Delhi: India Government, 1998, 171-173.
- James, T C. Indian Copyright Law and Digital Technologies. *"Selective Study Material on IPR from NRDC Depository. IP Consultancy and Management Division". New Delhi: Kailash Colony Extension. CD-ROM 2001. E –mail: cmgaind@nrdc .in. 1,2*
- Levene, Siman. Rev. Microsoft ® Encarta ® 2006 © 1993-2005, Microsoft Corporation.
- Narayana, P. Intellectual Property Law. 2 ed. Calcutta: Eastern Law, 1997, 215-220.
- R R, and T D. ed. India 2004. New Delhi: Government of India, 2004, 220-221.

- Srivastava, P L. Copyright Act 1957 and Digital Millennium Act: Role of Librarians in Compliance of the Provisions of Copyright Act. "Granthalaya Vigyan. " 36, 1-2, Jaipur: Kaula ,2005, 54-60.
- Tripathi, R C. The Emerging IPR Regime in Electronics and Information Technologies" *Selective Study Material on IPR from NRDC Depository. IP Consultancy and Management Division" New Delhi: Kailash Colony Extension .CD ROM 2002. . E-mail:cmgaind@nrdc.in.*
- Saxana, Priti. Private Creation Entitling Public Protection with Special Reference for Protection of Neighbouring Rights in India. "National Seminar on Changing Dimensions of Copyright and Other Neighbouring Rights 9-10th Oct. 2004. Bareilly: 2004,3-4.
- Tripathi, Amrendra, N. Emergence of Copyright New Delhi: Dhir and Dhir Associates.
- Received from *"http:// en. Wikipedia.org/ wiki/ History_ of _copyright_law.*

2

Copyright Act (1957) : A Profile

INTRODUCTION

The advent of knowledge society replacing agricultural and industrial societies has resulted in the emergence of new forms of property, which is resulted of human intellectual property has come to play a vital role in the lives of human beings.

Copyright is a unique kind of intellectual property and its importance is growing day by day. It is the human beings who have the capacity of creativity. They can be authors, composers, artists and designers for creating or producing original works.

Copyright, branch of law granting authors the exclusive privilege to reproduce, distribute, perform, or display their creative works. The *aim* of *copyright law is to encourage authors to invest effort in creating new works of art and literature.* Copyright is one branch of the larger legal field known as intellectual property, which are also includes; Trade Mark and Patent Law.

Copyright law is the legal foundation protecting the

work of many major industries, including book publishing, motion- picture production, music recording and computer software development. These industries account for considerable economic activity in the United States, Making copyright law a field of enormous economic importance.

Every work of authorship is not eligible for copyright. To qualify for copyright protection, a work must be both fixed and original. The law considers a work to be fixed if it is recorded in some permanent format. Acceptable ways of fixing a work include writing it down, storing it on a computer floppy disk or compact disk (CD), recording it on videotape or sculpting it in marble. If *a poet thinks of a new poem and recites it to an audience without writing it down, copyright does not protect poem because it is not fixed.* To be original, the work must not be copied from previously existing material and must display at least a reasonable amount of creativity. For example, if an author writes the words "the sky is blue" on a piece of paper, copyright does not protect the words because they lack sufficient creativity. Short phrases and titles are usually not protected by copyright, but in some circumstances they may be protected by Copyright /Trade Mark Law.

Copyright only protects the words, notes or images that the creator has used. It does not protect any ideas or concepts revealed by the work. If, for *example*, a *Scientist publishes an article explaining a new process for refining oil*, the copyright prevents others from copying the words of that article. It does not, however, prevent anyone else from using the process described to refined oil. To protect the process, the scientist must obtain a patent, similarly, if a novelist writes a book about a man obsessed about killing a whale, other people may write their own books on the same subject, as long as they do not use the exact words.

COPYRIGHT : MEANING AND DEFINITION

The word *"Copyright"* and the phrase" *Intellectual Property"* are the interchangeable, but in actually copyright law is one arm of the intellectual property triumvirate. The other two arms are Patents and Trademark Law. There has always been much philosophical legal debate over the validity of the term. "Intellectual Property" as it relates to other types of property *such as* - personal and real. Suffice to say that intellectual property and as such copyright can be transferred to another person or entity and can also be part of an estate and disposed of by a will or trust. It is recognized property and such as a valuable commodity.

"Copyright, a common law, is defined as the right to prevent publication. Statutes have extended the definition to include the right to prevent others from multiplying copies. Copyright is now defined as 'the sole right in the case of unpublished works to produce any literary, dramatic or musical work of any substantial part of a work in any material form whatever, provided the author is qualified to hold copyright."

"The exclusive statutory right of authors, composers, playwrights, artists, publishers of distributors to publish and dispose of their works for a limited time . In the United States, for 28 years, with privilege of one renewal for an additional 28 years. The common law property rights in unpublished works continue in effect until publication with or without copyright to secure copyright for, as a book or work of art copyrightable."

"Copyright is usually described as 'literary and artistic work' i.e. original creations in the field of 'literature and arts' The works may be expressed in words, symbols music and picture. Indian law protects original literary, dramatic, musical and artistic work; cinematograph film and sound recordings, broadcasting, cable relay and telecasting rights are some of the new branches of copy rights."

"Copyright mean's the exclusive right to do or authorize some one 'to reproduce' the work in any material form including its storing in any medium to release copies on the work to the public not being copies in circulation; to perform in public or communicate it to public; to make any cinematographic. Indian law also protects copyright in translation/adoption of a work. Copyright law protects only expression i.e. the form in which the ideas are expressed. It does not protect the ideas, themes, plots, historical and violation of copyright is confine to the form, manner and arrangement thereof. Where there is only one way to express an idea, the expression and idea will merge with each other and there will be no protection- to protect the expression will be to protect the idea itself."

The syllabi issued by the Board of Secondary Education containing guidelines for authors and publishers of text book cannot be taken as original works being the product of labour, skill and capital of some men engaged by the board. The work of a cine artist his performance as an actor in a cinema is not protected; it is the film that enjoys protection along with its sound track.

The *main object* of the copyright is to secure the author from the knowledge and the capital used and for made as well as encourage him bestow an bundle of rights conferred by copyright.

"Copyright is the exclusive right that protects an author, composer or artist from having his work recorded, performed, displayed, translated, distributed or reproduced by way of copies, phonorecords, or other versions (derivative works) except with his permission, subject to specified limitations. This intangible property right comes into existence automatically on creation of an original musical or dramatic composition; a novel, poem, or work of non fiction; a painting; or a map- to name but a few of the intellectual productions that qualify for such legal protection."

Copyright is a right given to or derived from works and it is not a right in novelty only of ideas. The increased incident of copying compelled the law makers to make law to check such incidents. In India the earliest statue law on copyright is the Indian Copy Right Act, 1847. This Act was enacted in new form in 1914. The Act of 1914 protected the interests of creators of original works and prescribed penalties for infringement of Copyright.

EMERGENCE OF COPY RIGHT IN 'IT' (INFORMATION TECHNOLOGY) TERM

In the digital environment the meaning of copy is to read data from a source, leaving the source data unchanged and to write the same data elsewhere in a physical form that may differ from that of the source. For example; to copy a deck of punched cards onto magnetic tap. The degree of editing that may be carried out at the same time depends upon the circumstances in which the copying is performed. In word processing, the reproduction of selected recorded text from storage or from a recording medium to another recording medium.

Copyright in IT TERM

Legal protection of the expression of an idea from being copied or used without the permission of the author. Copyright has been virtually unenforceable in cyberspace, where thousands of perfect copies of an author's writing or software can be mass- mailed to thousands of people with a few effortless keyboard commands. Most Software agreements require a separate purchase for every computer that the programme will be installed on. Large software vendors have successfully used large corporations for pirating-illegally copying software. Nevertheless, since copying programmes is quick and easy, many users have not complied the rules. The expansion of digital transmission and the most difficulty of preventing copyright misuse have challenged creators to develop new ways of minimizing the unpaid use of their works.

Meaning of Copy Right

The Copy Right Act, 1957 of India describes the provisions with respect to nature of copyrights and section 14 deals with meaning which is reproduced here under;

For the purpose of this Act, copyright means the exclusive right, subject to the provisions to the Act, to do or authorize the doing of any of the following acts in respect of a work or any substantial part thereof, namely;

(a) in the case of a **literacy, dramatic or musical work**, not being a computer programme-

  (i) to reproduce the work in any material form including the storing of it in any medium by electronic means;

  (ii) to issue copies of the work to the public and not being copies already in circulation;

  (iii) to perform the work in public, or communicate it to the public;

  (iv) to make any cinematograph film or sound recording in respect of the work;

  (v) to make any translation of the work;

  (vi) to make any adaptation of the work; and

  (vii) to do, in relation to a translation or an adaptation of the work, any of the acts specified in relation to the work in sub-clauses (I) to (vi);

(b) in the case of **a Computer Programme:**

  (i) to do any of the acts specified in clause (a); and

  (ii) to sell or give on hire, or offer for sale or hire, any copy of the computer programme, regardless of whether such copy has been sold or given on hire on earlier occasions.

The scope of copyright protection extends to the protection of the form and not the idea. Copyright would therefore vest in the computer programme itself and not in the idea that the programme represents.

According to Copyright Act 1957, the scope of the term literary work has been stated to 'include computer programmes, tables, and compilations including computer databases, In the short time a computer programme is written out on a piece of paper, copyright subsists in the work, in the same way as it would in respect of any other literary work. However, what is not so clear is whether copyright law could be extended to cover computer programmes, which exist merely in magnetic or electronic form or as special circuits etched on to a silicon chip. With the amendment of the Copyright Act 1957, in 1994. The meaning of computer programme is means ' *a set of instructions expressed in words, codes, schemes of in any other form, including a machine readable medium, capable of, causing a computer to perform a particular task or achieve a particular result.'*

The definition of a computer programme in the Copyright Act 1957, would include all representations of computer programmes, regardless of whether, they are reduced to writing or in machine - readable form.

The copyright in a computer programme made or published in the U.S.A. For *Example*; The copyright protection is available to the computer programme, if it had been made or published in India. This would be hint that any programme developed in any of these treaty countries would automatically become copyright material in India and that the owner of the copyright in U.S.A. would be label to enforce the same rights under the Copyright Act1957 as any other person who developed the software programme in India.

The copyright in a computer programme made or published in the United States of America, for example; would receive the same protection as would have been available to that programme, if it had published in India.

This would imply that any programme developed in any of these treaty countries would automatically become copyright material in India and that the holder of the copyright in U.S.A. would be label to enforce the same rights under the Copy right Act 1957 as any other person who developed the software in India.

Under section 13 of Copyright Act, 1957 (For short Act) the copyright subsists **in three classes of work** :

- Original literary, Dramatic, Musical and Artistic works; Cinematography films, and
- Sound recording.

For the purposes of this act "copyright" means the exclusive Right, by virtue of and subject to the provisions of, this Acts;

Literary, dramatic and musical work to do and authorise the doing of any of the following acts, namely ;

- to reproduce the work in any material form;
- to publish the work;
- to perform the work in public;
- to produce, reproduce, perform or publish any translation of the work; to makes any cinematograph film or a record in respect of the work;
- to communicate the work by (Broadcast) or to communicate to the public by a loud-speakers or any other similar instrument the(Broadcast) of the work,
- to make any adaptation of the work;
- to do in relation to a translation or an adaptation of the work any of the acts specified in relation to the work in clause (I to (vi);

In the case of an **artistic work,** to do or authorize the doing of any of the following acts;

- to reproduce the work in any material form ;
- to publish the work,

- to include the work in any cinematograph film;
- to makes any adaptation of the work;
- to do in relation to an adaptation of the work any of the acts specified in relation to the work in clause (i) to (iii);

In case of **Cinematograph film** ;

- to make a copy of the film;
- to cause the film, in so far as it consists of visual images, to be seen in public and it consists of sounds, to be heard in public.
- to make any record embodying the recording in any part of the sound track associated with the film by utilizing such sound track;
- to communicate the film by (Broadcast)

In case of **Sound Recordings;**

- to make any other record embodying the same recording;
- to cause the recording embodied in the record by (Broadcast).

Copyright is not confined to a literary repetition, but includes various modes in which the matter of any publication may be adopted, transferred with more or less colorable alteration. Showing of video film over cable T.V. Network to subscribers amounts to broadcasting of film or communicating it to a section of the public when unauthorized it amounts to infringement of copy right.

The present law on copyright in India is the Copyright Act, 1957.The basic feature of this act the provisions of Two international conventions on copyright. The Berne Convention and the Universal Copyright Convention. India is a member of both the conventions. The copyright Act, 1957 has been amended in 1983, 1984, 1992, 1994 and 1999. These amendments have been in corporate due to changed circumstances.

Indian Copyright Act 1957

So far as Indian regime of neighboring rights is concerned, India has, to some extent, a positive correlation between neighboring rights and developing technologies. Need is only the implementation and enforcement of these rights be revised in view of developments in the enforcement technology. The Copyright Act, 1957 has 79 sections divided in 14th chapters. *See for further information in details about Copyright 1957 Appendix IInd.*

Indian Law Dealing With Copyright

The Indian Copyright Act was first passed in 1957. A few amendments were made in 1983 & in 1988. However keeping in view with the latest developments in the field of technology, especially in the field of computers and digital technologies. The new amendment Act called Copyright (Amendment) Act, 1994. (38of 1994) was passed and this made Indian Copyright Law is one of the toughest in the world. This included the definition of " Computer Programme" also in its ambit. It clearly explains the rights of Copyright Holder, position on rentals of software, the rights of the user to make backup copies and the heavy punishment and fines on infringement of Copyright of software. It is also make it illegal to make or distribute copies of copyrighted software without proper or specific authorization.

Copyright Act 1957 as amended in 1983, 1984, 1992, 1994 and 1999.

A number of amendments to Copyright Act, 1957 were affected in 1983 mainly to avail of the benefits arising from the revision of the Berne Convention and Universal Copyright Convention, to which India is an adherent. Further amendments were also affected in 1984 with the main object of discouraging and preventing the widespread piracy prevailing in video films and records.

The amendment made in the Act in 1992 extended the term of copyright protection from the life time of the author plus 50 years to the life time of author plus 60 years.

The Copyright Act was further amended in 1994 mainly to define more clearly the term computer and computer programs. The amendments mainly relate to;

(a) Making adequate provision for the special nature of computer programs and the protection of computer generating works.

(b) Extending to authors, resale share in respect of original copies of their paintings. Sculptures and drawings and original manuscripts of literary and dramatic or musical works.

(c) Including within the scope of copyright in artistic works, the right to display the work in public.

(d) Promoting collective administration rights through copyright societies in the interests of both the owners of rights and the general public.

(e) Dealing more effectively with the infringement of copyright and related works.

(f) Further improving the functioning of the Copyright Board.

(g) Simplifying and improving the law relating to copyright and related rights, in the interests of the general public, in particular of the user as well as the owners of such rights.

Copyright Act, 1957 (As modified up to 9th June 1994) "Literary work" includes computer programs, tables and compilations including computer database under section 2 (0) [1]. here "Computer" includes any electronic or similar device having information e a particular processing capabilities—under section 2 (ffb) [2].

"Computer Program" means a set of instructions expressed in words, code, schemes or in any other form, including a machine readable medium, capable of causing a computer or perform a particular task or achieve a particular result—section 2 (ffc)[2].

The Copyright (Amendment) Act 1999 makes it free for purchaser of gadget/ equipment to sell it onwards if the item being transacted is not the main item covered under Copyright Act. This means computer programmer is built in integral part of a gadget/equipment can be freely transacted without permission of copyright owner. This amendment also ensures fair dealing of broadcasting gaining popularity with the growth of the Internet. *For further information about Copyright Amendment Act, see Appendix II (2).*

Main Changes in the new Amendment Act: Now ***"Literary work"*** includes "***Computer" and "Computer Programme***" also.

Computer programs

According to National Research Development Corporation "Computer programs are generally understood as a set of instructions capable, when incorporated in a machine-readable medium, of causing a machine having information-processing capabilities to indicate, perform or achieve a particular function, task or result.

The issue of appropriate intellectual property rights regime for protecting computer programs had exercised the international community for quite long. Arguments were advanced in favour of and against patent regime and copyright regime and even a sue generic system to protect computer software. Discussions at the Uruguay Round of Multilateral Trade Negotiations finally put a seal on these debates when the Agreement on Trade Related Aspects of Intellectual Property Rights (TRIPS) incorporated the provisions "Computer programs, whether in source or object code, shall be protected as literary works under the Berne Convention". This was subsequently reiterated in WCT when it stated, "protection applies to computer programs, whatever may be the mode or form of their expression".

Even though it was only in the TRIPS Agreement of 1994 that a clear position emerged about protecting computer programs as literary works under the copyright laws. India's was one of the early legislations, which had extended copyright protection to computer programs much before that agreement. This was in consonance with Berne Convention definition of literary and artistic works as including "every production in the literary, scientific and artistic domain, whatever may be the mode or form of this expression." In 1984 an inclusive definition of 'literary works' was inserted in the Copyright Act to include computer software. Subsequently, in 1994 the definition was further clarified to include "computer programs, tables and compilations including databases."

In Section 2(ffc) of the Act *'computer programs'* has been defined as *"a set of instructions expressed in words, codes, schemes or any other form, including a machine-readable medium, capable of causing a computer to perform a particular task or achieve a particular result."* In the case of computer the Act gives an inclusive definition namely, *"computer includes any electronic or similar device having information processing capabilities"*. These are technology neutral definitions and thus capable of absorbing future developments in digital technologies."

According to Encyclopedia of Information Technology

"The definition of a computer program in the Copyright Act,1957, would include all representations of computer programs, regardless of whether they are reduced to writing or in machine -readable form.

Ordinary, the copyright in any work would not subsist unless that work is either first published (1) in India (or where published out of India, if the author was a citizen of India on the date of publication) or in the case of an unpublished work, other than a work of architecture, the author is on the date of making the work, a citizen of or domiciled in India. However, the Central Government has the power to extend the benefit of the Act to works fist published in other countries by an appropriate notification in the Official Gazette.

In this regard, the Central Government passed the International Copyright Order in 1958. Accordingly to this order, the provisions of the Copyright Act, 1957 (with the exception of the rights of the broadcasting organizations and performers and all those rights that would pertain to Indian works) would apply to works published in any of the Berne Convention, Universal Copyright Convention or Phonograph Convention countries that were specified in the Schedule the order. The International Copyright Order, 1991, subsequently superseded this order. The Government of India has recently passed the International Copyright Order, 1998.

The copyright in a computer program made or published in the United States of America, for example would receive the same protection as would have been available to that programme, if it had been made or published in India. This would imply that any program developed in any of these treaty countries would automatically become copyright material in India and that the holder of the copyright in United States of America would be label to enforce the same rights under the Copyright Act, 1957, as any other person who developed the software in India."

The Act categorized 'computer program' as being part of the class provisions for computer programs. Thus in Section 14(b), the act bestows upon computer programs all the rights enjoyed by literary works and in addition, sale and rental rights. Through an amendment in 1993, the Act provided that commercial rental rights would not apply in respect of those computer programs where the program itself is not the essential object of the rental. This is in accordance with Article 11 of the TRIPS

Agreement Since digital technology are now being used in the wide spectrum of areas affecting daily life such exception is considered appropriate as, otherwise, one may end up paying for technologies that one had no intention of using in the first place. Keeping in view the requirements of the software industry and the need for giving an impetus to development of digital technologies in the country, the 1999 amendment to the Copyright Act also completed recompilation of reverse engineering of a computer program in certain circumstances.

It is also interesting to note that the Act separately defines the author of a computer-generated work "as the person who causes the work to be created". This removes any doubts about the legal authorship of a computer program where a number of persons are engaged, as is the normal case.

The laws, taking into account the special features of computer programs as distinct from other literary works, particularly the affect of its use, has made the knowing "use" of the infringing copy of a computer program an offence under the Act for which mandatory minimum punishments are prescribed.

Databases

Another groups of works, which were affected in major way by the development of the digital technologies is databases. In the digital context,

'Database means a collection of independent works, data or other materials arranged in a systematic or methodical way and capable of being individually accessed by electronic or other means.

Manual collection and development of database were very cumbersome and time-consuming processes. Digital technologies made development of databases much easier and user friendly then in the past. Traditionally databases were protected as compilations under literary works. In a computer database there are two structural paths: the program, which is used to control or manage the data and data itself. The program, no doubt gets protected as literary work. Doubts persisted among many about protection for the content part, despite the provisions on compilations in the Berne Convention. Therefore the TRIPS Agreement categorically provide that compilations of data or other materials, whether in machine readable or other form, which by reason of the selection or arrangement of their contents constitute intellectual collections shall be protected as such.

The WCT also reaffirmed the position in Article 5. The crucial element in the above is the insistence on the database qualifying as an 'intellectual creation' which is in fact the fundamental principle Copyright Protection. The database should be the result of an original intellectual effort and should not have been copied from some other work or database.

The norm of 'originality' is not prescribed in any copyright treaty and it generally depend upon on the case law position that is available in a country. In countries where the courts insisted upon a high level of 'originality' for copyright protection, many databases were wanting in 'originality' although much investment had been made in the making of it. This was a major issue in the Feist Publications v, Rural Telephone Service Company Case in the USA. The US Supreme Court, while reaffirming that most, although not all. Commercially significant databases satisfy the 'originality' requirement for protection under Copyright, emphasized that this protection is necessarily thin.

Computer databases are specifically covered by the definition of literary works in the Indian Act and thus all original computer databases enjoy protection in India. Since the standard of originality accepted by the courts for entitlement of copyright protection is aloe one, almost all compilations enjoy Copyright Protection. Expending of labour and skill in the creation is the only criterion that is applied to judge the eligibility of a work for Copyright Protection and based on that computer databases enjoy protection in India.

The problem posed by the Feist Judgment in the USA may not be materially relevant in India because of the liberal interpretation of originality adopted by the Indian courts. Be that as it may, as more and more databases get created with massive investments and parallel databases on related topics get generated with lots of common material, questions may arise as to the use that can be made of Copyright material to establish and maintain a database on the originality of newly created and constantly changing databases. Self-perpetuating and automatically upgrading databases on computer networks may also be leaving questions mark on the effectiveness of copyright protection in preventing misappropriations of such data.

One problem that confronted the copyright community during the run-up to the Diplomatic Conference, which finalized the WCT, was the protection of non-original databases. Preparation of any database in a digital format involves considerable investment, both in financial and physical resources. But when a database is compiled purely or wholly of non-copyrightable material, the problem of protecting the same arises.

Multimedia Works

Digital Technologies have created works with much more versatility than in the past. A work may now consist of literary, artistic, musical and dramatic elements and may also include a phonogram and a cinematographic film. The user can interact with the work in a way a past generation could not do. He can make changes and alterations and even can create new work out of an existing one. Multimedia works by their basic premises are works combining different elements, such as text, sound, still visuals, and moving images, of different classes of works. The resultant work defies existing classification. If the rights for all classes of works were the same, then perhaps, this would not have been a major issue. But the law as it stands in India, distinguishes between different classes of works in the matter of rights. *For example*, the rights in a literary work and those in a cinematographic film are different. There is no rental right in a literary work, whereas there is such a right in a cinematographic film. The authorship may raise another problem, as the criterion of authorship is different between literary, dramatic, musical and artistic works on the one hand and cinematographic film and sound recordings on the other hand. There is a view that multimedia works being a digital product be classified as computer programs. Since there are separate provisions for rights and authorship of a computer program as distinct from literary works in the Copyright Act, this could be a possible solution. However, issues may arise on the retention of separate Copyrights in the works incorporated in the multi-media, in terms of section 13 of the Act and the rights of performers in the product. At present large number of multimedia combining pre-existing works creates works. The problem will get accentuated when more and more multimedia works will be created as new complex ones. The classification of multimedia works is an issue, which needs to be looked into in-depth.

Copyright Ownership, Assignment and Works for Hire

Generally, the first author of the work called principal author is designated as the owner of the copyright in the work. The Copyright Act, 1957, specifies the owner of the copyright to assign the copyright to other person. The assignment of the copyright must be made through a written deed of assignment and indicate clearly the rights being assigned. The Act also mention the right of the owner to license the right. The issue of ownership of software developed under a contract of employment is an issue that is critical today information technology industry. According to the Act, it is clear that the author of the work will be first owner of the copyright in the work in all circumstances, except where specially provided for in the statute.

According to the section 17 of the Act the provisions are the author of a work shall be first owner of the copyright provided that-

(a) In the case of a *literary, dramatic or artistic work* made by the author in the course of his employment by the proprietor of a news paper, magazine or similar periodical under a contract of service of apprenticeship, for the purpose of publication in a news paper, magazine or similar periodical, the said proprietor shall in the absence of any agreement to the country, be the first owner of the copyright in the work in so far as the copyright relates to the publication of the work in any newspaper, magazine or similar periodical, or to the reproduction of the work for the purpose of its being so published, but in all other respects the author shall be the first owner of the copyright in the work;

See for further information more details in Appendix I Chapter IVth.12 Section 17 © of the Act express, the factor of employment establishes a prima facie a assumption that the copyright the works developed be the employee vest with employer.

Under Section 17 the publisher of an encyclopedia cannot issue an article written for an encyclopedia and paid for accordingly, as a separate work, (1848)17 LJ Ch 210 (214)

U/section 17c where the employment is in terms that the copyright shall belong to he proprietor of the journal in which the work is published as an article the proprietor cannot publish the same separately, expect as a part of the journal to which the article was contributed.(1860) 70 ER 766 (767).

Articles secured for and published in a journal do not become the copyright of the publishers of the journal when the authors of such article have not been paid for. (1846) 16 LJ C h 140 (144).

Author of a work shall be the first owner of the copyright therein. AIR 1967 Ker 234 (235): 1967 Cri IJ 1517 (2). Under section 17 (13).Under section17 (13) where two different pharmaceutical companies were marketing an ointment with similar looking packages and similar sounding names with difference of only a alphabet in the spellings. The company which had started manufacture of the product at an earlier point of time than the other and which had a well- established market had a clear claim to the copyright in the product as against the other. (1990) I Kant LC 257(267).

Under Section17 (14) The question papers are not 'Government work' as defined in S.2 (k) and hence proviso (d) to section 17 does not confer ownership of the copyright in such papers on the Board or on the Government and the copyright belongs to the paper- setters in the absence of assignment under section 18 or a contract giving up the claim for copyright. AIR 1967 ALL 91(93).

Question papers set by paper-setters appointed under Bihar School Examination Board Act (7 of 1952)- Paper setters are first owners of copyright in question papers. AIR 1966 Pat 33(36,37): 1966 Cri LJ 54.

Owner has the sole and exclusive right over the work done. None of the provisions of the Copyright Act lays down any conditions for the exercise of such right and preventing the infringement of it. Registration of such rights under S.44 of the Copyright Act is not a condition precedent for availing remedy. Sections 13 and 17 which confer and recognize the copyright do not lay down any condition that registration is mandatory. AIR 1981 All 200 (203(204) 1986 Cri LJ 522 (524): (1985) 2 Andh WR352. 13

The Information Technology Act, 2000

It hardly address itself to the broader problems of protection and enforcement of IPR. The Act provides for investigation, trial and punishment for certain offences like tempering with the computer source documents, hacking of computer system piracy, etc.

Object of copyright law

According to act ' Copyright law is in essence, concerned with the negative right of preventing the copying of physical material existing in the field of literature and arts. Its object is to protect the writer and artist from the unlawful reproduction of his material. (1969) 71 Bom LR 777:'

COPY RIGHT : Introduce Several New Features

India which is a signatory of two International Conventions the 'Berne Convention (1886) and The 'Universal Copyright Convention' (1952) was governed by the copyright act of 1914 (formulated on the patterns of British copyright act (1911) till it established its own copyright act in 1957, repeating the earlier act of 1914 and coming into force from 1958.

The law of copyright was first concerned only with preventing the unlawful reproduction of copies of books but was extended for the first time to include films and broadcasts. Along with the copyright office under control of the Registrar of copyright (MOE), a quasi judicial body known as the copyright board was also set up into the disputes regarding copyright infringements. The copyright board was reconstituted for a term of 5 years with effect from 22nd Feb 2001.

Copyright amendments were made in 1983, 1984 to keep in step with the technological developments and for enhancing penalties for infringement of copyright, combat large scale piracy etc. In lieu of the constantly changing technologies and communication medias as-radio, cable, satellite etc. The copyright problems associated with the above, a working group was assigned the task to study a provisions of the early acts which came up with a copyright amendment act in 1994.

This was a wonderful document which clearly spelt out the law as;

- Statement of works enjoying protection of law.
- Definition of a person enjoying such protection.
- Nature and extent of protection.
- Assignment of copyright
- Exception outside the purview of copyright
- Legal remedies available to a copyright owner.
- Statutory arbitration in cases of dispute.

Sections 13 (1), 14,17,18,19 & 19 (A), 22-29, 30, 32 and several others are of great importance to us. Copyright amendment of 1991 extended the term of copyright for all kinds of intellectual works such as ; anonymous, or pseudonymous works, cinematograph films, mechanical contrivances, photographs etc. from 50 to 60 years (from the date of first publication and later after the death of the authors). Amendments also changed these definitions time and again to include new concepts in the literary work category ad computer software, the performers right (audio- video records of live performance etc paintings, sculptures, drawing and their resale share right. The copyright act was further amended in 1999 (came into force on 15th Jan.2000).

- A cinematograph film will have a separate copyright a part from its various components, namely, story, music etc.
- Under the existing law, the sole right to produce a translation of a work first published in India is extinguished after ten years, unless a translation thereof is produced within that period. The draft bill makes the right co-extensive with other rights

arising out of copyright.

- Provision is made for the issue of a general or special licence for public performances of any work by means of a radio receiving set or a mechanical contrivance.
- A licence may be issued to any library to make one copy of any book in which copy right subsists and which is not available for sale.
- Provision is made for regulating the activities of performing rights societies and also for controlling the fees, charge or royalties to be collected by them.
- Copyrights are conferred on broadcasting authorities in respect of programmes broadcast by them.
- International Copyright relations which are based on International treaties, will be regulated by specific orders to be made by the Central Government.
- A fair dealing with any work for the purposes of radio summary or judicial proceeding will not here after constitute an infringement of copy right

FAIR USE

The term 'Fair use' is used in USA, however the same concept is better known as 'fair dealing' in U K. Fair use is the permissible use of copyrighted works for the purpose and permits partial or limited reproduction. Although, the definitions have not been clear, it is expected that the court would decide what is fair.

This principle is of special interest to information professionals since we as the intermediaries (Information providers) have in deciding with what amount of information could be provided to be beneficiaries. True there are several guidelines but the interpretations can be many. Though, this can be closely linked with the' reprographic' facilities provided in almost all the information today, the same can also be down loaded through the net and provided to their clientele.

Guide Line of Fair Use

***Dr. P.S.G.Kumar* (2002)** has given us several bench marks which can serve as the guiding indicator;

- The effect of copying on the potential market for the work.
- Nature of work and the number of copies made out of the original;
- The purpose for which copying has been done along with purpose and character of use research and other Academic activities;
- Extent of copying used in relation to the work as a whole etc. Society of authors in association with the writers guild and Publishers Association has stated certain norms for the extent of copying, including books and periodical materials. The norms are as under;
- A maximum of a chapter or 5% (whichever is less) can be copied from a literary work.
- Up to 10% (Not more than 20 pages or 2 pages in brief) can be copied from short books, reports, standards, pamphlets etc.
- One copy of a short story, poem etc or 5 % (which ever is less).

The details of the norms regarding the copying of books, periodicals, and other non- book material is explained in various sections of the copy right Act.

COPY RIGHT In Computer Software

In 1999, amendment of the Copyright Act, 1957 was created new rental right of computer programme, the traditional 'Fair Dealing' has been eliminated and radical new penalties have been imposed for infringing programmes. In Napster case, Napster facilitated a free music system open to public over internet and pleaded

'Fair use the court held that "Repeated and exploitative copying of copyrighted work even if the copies are not offered for sale may constitute commercial use. Section 52 of the Indian copyright act, 1957 does not cover 'Home Taping' under the provision of fair dealing.S.52 (1) (i) allows of sound recording and films without the permission of the author, only for domestic purposes.

The exclusive right to reproduce the work in any material form, to reproduce the work in any medium by electronic means extends to computer programmes and also digital copies of such work, therefore, a computer programme license does not have a right to lend or otherwise transfer programme copy, unless authorized by the copyright owner.

The Government of India have taken several steps to enforce software copyright protection. Some of the salient points are described below:

- IPRs software is covered under Copyright Law violation of which attracts both fine and imprisonment.
- IT Act, 2ooo has provision to deal with unauthorized copying of software.
- To create awareness, Government has been supporting anti- piracy campaign of NASSCOM.
- Instructions have been issued to Government Departments to use only the legal copy of the software.

Government has set up a Copyright Enforcement Advisory Council under Ministry of HRD, Book Promotion and Copyright Division.

- Organization of seminars/workshops to create greater awareness about Copyright Law among the enforcement personnel and general public are organized repeatedly.
- Creation of separate Cells in police headquarters is

taking up to deal with the problem.

- Custom duty on software has been made zero.

New Challenge of computer programme

Under the 'New Copyright Treaty', computer software and computer programmes in any mode or form of expression are protected as literary words. Under the' Performances and Phonograms Treaty', a new right called the 'Right of Transmission' (which is specific for electronic records) has been added to the existing rights of reproduction, public performance and communication. As it clear from the relevant clause,' The copyrights treaty;

- Brings copyright into the digital age: Established a "Win-win" situation for both creators and users.
- Promotes creativity and jobs, Protect world wide authors. Internet piracy is international piracy.

IPR laws are different from one country to another country. In order to fully exploit the GII (Global Information Infrastructure) commission urges international harmonization of IPR legislations. The GIIC has recommended that the existing IP laws be revised to order to adapt to the future development of technology. With respect to software, the GIIC has opined that Governments examine the feasibility of issuing patents for software, through multilateral organizations.

Copyright Act and other Countries

The following countries are following the Copyright Acts;

- United States code title 17 (S.Ia).
- United Kingdom Act 1911, (S.I(2) and United Kingdom, 1956, Act SS, 6-10.
- Ghana Copyright Act, 1961 (S.5)(1).
- Draft Mode Copyright law for Africa in Article 2.
- Norwegian Copyright law, 1961 (S.17).

- Finish Copyright law 1961 (S.17).
- Swedish Copyright law 1960 (S.12).
- Danish Copyright law 1961.
- Newzealand Copyright law 1962.
- United Arab Republic Copyright law 1956.
- United States Draft Copyright law.

COPYRIGHT IN FOREIGN STATES

France

Copyright in France is recognized in the most ample manner. Two distinct rights are secured by law, first the right of reproduction of literary works, musical composition and works of arts, and second, the right of reproduction of dramatic works and musical compositions. The period is for the life of the author and fifty years after his death. After the author's death the surviving consort has the usufructuary enjoyment of the rights which the author has not disposed of in his life time or by will, subject to reduction for the benefit of the author's protected heirs it any. The author may dispose of his rights in the most absolute manner in the forms and within the limits of the Code Napoleon. Piracy is a crime punishable by fine or not less than 100 not more than 2000 francs; in the case from 25 to 500 franc piracy also form the ground for a civil action of damages to the amount of the injury sustained – the produce of the confiscation, if any, to go towards payment of the indemnity (Penal Code, Art,425- 429).

The following statements regarding copyright in other European countries are abridged from Copinger's law of copyright;-

Prussia

Copyright endures for the author's life and heirs have a term of Thirty years from his decease. When a copyright is assigned without any special stipulation, the publisher cannot issue more than one edition without the author's written permission. He may issue a reprint, on paying the author half the some paid for the first issue.

Austria

By treaty with Sardinia, Tuscany and the Papal States, gives copyright for Thirty years after author's death.

Halland And Belgium

Copyright formerly perpetual now limited to the life of the author and 20 years thereafter.

Denmark And Sweden

Copyright formerly perpetual, now limited to Thirty years in the former and the twenty in the lattes; if the publication is allowed to lapse, copyright felt to the state.

Russia

The author's life and Twenty Five years and Ten years more if an edition is published within Five years of the end. SPAIN The period is the author's life and Fifty years thereafter.

Germany

The author's life and Thirty years after.

Greece

Copyright is for Fifteen years from publication.

Property is unpublished musical compositions, lectures, sermons works of art are governed by the same principles that apply in the case of dramatic productions. There is no statute as in England, regulating the author's rights in manuscript lectures. The writer of an unpublished letter, whether possessing literary value or not, may prevent at common law its unauthorized publication by, unless publication is necessary to protect the latter against injurious representations made by the former.

COPY RIGHT AND LICENSING ISSUES

The measure changes, speed and ease to electronic communication and copying are both threatening the basic concept of copyright. Copying no longer just means

Photo copying and not all countries (even when they have signed one or other of the major copyright conventions) appear able to control copying or even to accept that control is necessary.

NEEDS OF LICENSING

Large-scale piracy of major reference works, whether in print and non- print form such as; CD-ROM and on- line digital copyright, together with a complete disregard for the rights of creators and performers of films and musical recordings to some nations. The control to piracy we needs the licensing.

Licensing users to copy is the logical conclusion and several countries now have systems that allow authors and publishers to share the proceeds of legal, limited copying.

The owner of the copyright in any existing work or the prospective owner of the copyright in any future work may grant any interest in the right by licence in writing signed by him duly authorized agent.

Provided that in the case of a licence relating to copyright in any future work, the licence shall be take effect only when the work comes into existence.

Where, a person to whom a license relating to copyright in any future work is allowed under this section dies before the work comes into existence his legal representative shall, in the absence of any provision to the contrary in the licence, be entitled to the benefit of the licence.

Where, licence was not granted to the club by the

authors, the publisher's note in the drama reserving all rights in the club neither confers ownership nor amount to assignment of licence by the authors to the cub. AIR 1967 Assam 70 (73) (DB).

According to Compulsory Licence Copyright Act under section 31;

If at any time during the term of copyright in any Indian work which has been published a complaint is made to the Copyright Board that the Owner of copyright;

(a) has refused to republish or allow the republication or has refused to allow the performance in public of the work, and by reason of such refusal the work is withheld from the public; or

(b) has refused to allow communication to the public by (Broadcast) of such work or in the case of a record the work recorded in such record, on terms which the complainant considers reasonable; the Copyright Board, after giving to the owner of copyright in the work a reasonable opportunity of being heard and after holding such inquiry as it may deem necessary, may if it is satisfied that the grounds for such refusal are not reasonable, direct the Registrar of Copyright to grant to the complainant a licence to republish, perform and communicate the work to the public. As the case, may be subject to payment to the owner of copyright of such compensation and conditions as the Copyright Board may determine; the Registrar of Copyrights shall grant the licence to the complainant in accordance with the directions of the Copyright Board, on payment of such fee as may be prescribed. The expression "Indian work" include-

- an a artistic work, the author of which is a citizen of India,
- a cinematograph film or a record made or manufactured in India.

Licence in unpublished Indian Work

What place in the case of an Indian work referred to in sub- clause (iii) &(1) of section 2, the author is dead or cannot be available, the owner of copyright in such work cannot be found, any other person may apply to the Copyright Board for a licence to published.

Where a licence is granted, Registrar of copyright may, by order or direct, the applicant to deposit the amount of the royalty. Legal representative to claim royalty at any time.

In case of the publish translations any person may apply to the CRB for a licence of a literary work and in printed or non- print forms of reproduction in any language, period of 7th year from the first publication of the work. Every applicant for a licence to deposit with the Registrar of copyrights such fee as may be prescribed.

In the case of royalties of copies to the translation work sold. To the public calculated at such rate as the CRB may to take action to each case will be decided and permitted.

THE SOLE RIGHT OF TRANSLATION

The object of the provisions of section4 (1) of the copyright Act (1914) was to confer on the author the sole right of translation for a period of Ten years. If it was omitted to be exercised the result would be that at the end of the ten years period the statutory rights to copyright would not be include the sole right of translation. The right to the copyright in the translation move from the very terms of section 1 of the English Act of 1911, because the translation itself would be an origin literary work. Section 4 is no bar to the statement of such a right. AIR 1959 Mad 410(426).

Termination of Licences

According to the under section 32 B If at any time after the granting of a licence to the translation of work in any language under sub section (1A) the owner of the copyright in the work or any person authorized by him publishers a translation of such work in the same language at a price reasonably related to the price normally charged in India for the translation works of the same standard on the same, the licence so granted shall be terminated.

Copyright In On-Line User Education

The creators of copyrighted works, user must be have a basic understanding of the principles regarding intellectual property in the online users education. In the present time on line users infringing copyright are greater simply because of the venue- nearly every activity has copyright The creators considerations. Users need to take full advantage of the privileges copyright afford.

Copyright In Electronic Resources

In the present time electronic resources are more popular. As an increasing number of publishers move to electronic format, the number of licences grows proportionately. In universities, these licences may be negotiated by someone.

Electro copying and electronic publishing are areas that sometimes course great difficulty because "copying" is easy, quick and often impossible to detect. Users feel they want immediately obtain to information (on a network) for example; While creators feel that a system must be devised to monitor use, limit exploitation, control misuse and reward them for copying works they have created.

Legislation and contracts specifically controlling or licencing all forms of electronic use do not exist in any satisfactory form. It has been said that "the answer to the machine is in the machine." A system of electronic authorization or coding may be possible, as in the European Union's CITED (copyright in transmitted electronic documents) project. The system set up under the European Union's ESPRIT programme, is a means of controlling, policing and providing remuneration in respect of work stored in digital form. 18

Many unique identifiers are under development in Europe and the U.S. The Serial Item and contribution Identifier (SICI) gives a unique code to journal articles, while PII((Publisher Item Identifier) in the U.S. has been developed by scientific and technical publishers. There are various "Gate keeper" systems that restrict on-line and can charge users or subscriber's on a credit card or account bases, including a smart-card that must be "Swiped" before copying or networking is allowed. Very large amount of copyright material is also now available on the Internet. There are some effective ways so far for protecting this many regard the creation of sites on the www (World Wide Web) as a way of promoting sales of their more valuable copyright material, through on journal subscriptions or marketing books and CD-ROMs.

Important of Copyright for the Users

Copyright has direct implications for on-line users not only are they users of copyrighted works, but as students, they are creators. Everyday activities such as forwarding an attachment to a fellow student, posting an entry to a discussion group, downloading a journal article from a database, present or writing a paper for a course, all carry copyright considerations. The chances of infringing copyright in the online environment are very simple.

The consumers of copyright works, then students must become say about what is not permissible not only to avoid infringement of other's works, to protect their contributions in this information age. If information is the currency of the information age, then students must be encouraged to create knowledge, they forged a closes relationship between knowledge and to create new knowledge. In the 21th century needs workers that are reflective thinkers and creators of knowledge. Librarians have talked much and worked hard to promote the skills of information literacy. Why? Because students need skill to effectively locate, evaluate and finally use information effectively to create new knowledge. That is the target of information literacy and it is a essential of the mission of higher education.

Users know about copyright

Users should have an awareness of the exclusive rights Allowed to authors. Copyright is in fact a bundle of rights and includes the rights to;

- Reproduction the work
- prepare derivative work
- distribute copies of the work to the public.
- perform the work publicly.

It is very important to know that what students need & what those rights are by copyright are exclusive not absolute. The rights of copyright are restricted some exceptions and limitations. The students to exchange ideas, build knowledge and connect new links between knowledge, students need access to information. Really online students are at greater risk of violating copyright laws simply due to the delivery method of the course. The web is in fact a publication medium for online students, allowing for easy reproduction, distribution and publication of information. The librarians know that engagement with the content of a course is what higher education is all about. It is the heart of an intellectual life, and is an objective of every course taught, whether face to face or online

The students must have an awareness of both the rights and responsibilities they have when dealing with copyrighted works. The TEACH Act 2002 impacts online educators more directly than online students.

The Impact of Copyright

According to the Jill Hurst- Wahl, MLS Syracuse University's School of information Studies

Copyright impact us everyday, yet, it is a concept most people know very little about. As an adjunct senior instructor at Syracuse University, I tend to cover a bit about copyright in every course. (It is usually quite an eye-opener for the students.)When I taught a class on digitization, Copyright was a very important topic and one that reared its ugly head for weeks as students came to terms copyright. When we take a book, for example, and digitize it, we have made a copy. If that book was published before 1923, it is in the public domain and anybody can make a copy of it legally. However, if the book was published after 1923, then copyright law comes into play. The U.S. copyright law give the following rights to the owner of the work:

- to reproduce the work in copies or phono-records;
- to prepare derivative works based upon the work;
- to distribute copies or phone-records of the work to the public by sale or other transfer of ownership, or by rental, lease or lending;
- to perform the work publicly, in the case of Literary, musical, dramatic and choreographic works, and motion pictures and other audiovisual works;. And
- In case of sound recordings, to perform the work publicly by means of a digital audio transmission.

As a person who wants to make a copy of a copyrighted work, you must consider if your use will be fair. Fair use considers:

- the purpose and character of the use, including, whether such use is of commercial nature or is for non- profit educational purposes;
- the nature of the copyrighted work,
- Amount and substantiality of the portion used in

relation to the copyrighted work as a whole; and

- The effect of the use upon the potential market for or value of the copyrighted work.

Each of these four factors must be considered when deciding if the use is fair or not. For example, if the copy takes away potential income (e.g., sales or copyright fees) from the owner of the work, then the use is not fair.

Impact of Information Technology on copyrights

Information Technology (especially digitization) has made the process of copying, publishing and distributing digital copies very inexpensive. New forms of media have been created.

On the electronic side of IT, microscopic integrated circuit technology became extremely valuable and so called "mask works" (for creating the functional layers of semi conductors) were found to be not subject to copyright because of their functional nature. A new type of statutory protection was created, outside of copyright, to protect these expensive art works from illegal copying.

Digital audio tapes (and later media) spawned an entirely new way of making and distributing copies of sound recordings, including copyrighted music. New methods were created for collecting and sharing the royalty revenue and for protection against booting copies. New laws were created to cover digital piracy, copy protection and the information related to copies (the author, date, owner, license terms etc)., eve www profiteroles in the early 1990s, made nearly everyone with a computer a potential publisher. On the flip side, every "web browser" automatically downloads a copy of "web page", as part of its normal operation to display the information the author has published, under a newly "implied license" to make copies, at least for personal use.

As faster network speeds became economical and

protocols more efficient, the new channels were quickly filed with new media: online music, video, photographs. A new wave of treaties and statutes will attempt to rationalized the royalties with modern copying and distribution means.

Reproduction of Copyrighted Works by Educators and Librarians

Library is a storehouse of knowledge. Readers from different areas of society and varied requirements on different topics visit libraries. Librarianship involves acquisition, Storage and retrieval of information sources. With the developments, in science and technology, the information sources acquired in libraries are not limited with print media like books and periodicals but audio-visuals, sound recordings and optical/digital/magnetic disks are also considered as information sources. Libraries acquire all such material and make them available to the users.

Many educators and librarians ask about the reprography and photocopying provisions of the copyright law. The copyright office cannot give legal advice and opinions on what is permitted or prohibited. However, we have published in this circular basic information on some of the most important legislative provisions and other documents dealing with reproduction by librarians and educators.

Also available is the 1983 report of the register of copyrights on library reproduction of copyrighted works (17 U.S.C.108). The report and seven appendixes can be purchased in microfiche or paper copies be written request from the National Technical Information Service (NTIS), U.S. Department of Commerce, 5285 Port Royal Road, Springfield, VA 22161 or by calling the Sales Desk at (703)487-4650. The Fax number for placing orders is (703) 321-8547. The TTY number for placing orders is(703) 487-4639. When ordering, please include the following NTIS Accession Numbers: PB 83 148239ACY, Entire set; PB83148247 ACY, Report Only; PB83148254 ACY.

The 1988 Five year report of the Register of copyrights on Library reproduction of copyrighted works is also available from NTIS Accession Number PB88 212014ACY.

The **reproduction of copyrighted** works by ***educators, librarians and archivists*** for a variety of uses, including:

- Reproduction for teaching in educational institutions at all levels. And
- Reproduction by libraries and archives for purposes of study, research, I interlibrary exchanges and archival preservation.

Under the copyright law reproduction are *Two forms:*

- The making of copies: by photocopying, making microform reproductions, videotaping, or any other method of duplicating material and
- The making of phonorecords: by duplicating sound recordings, taping of the air, or any other method of recapturing sounds.

Reproduction

Read together with the relevant definitions in section 101. the right " to reproduce the copyrighted work in copies or phonorecords" means the right to produce a material object in which the work is duplicated, transmitted, imitated, reproduce or otherwise communicated, either directly or with the aids of machine or device." As Under the present law, a copyrighted work would be infringed by reproducing it in whole or in any substantial part, and by duplicating it exactly. Variations from the copyrighted work would still be an infringement as long as the author's "expression" rather than merely the author's "ideas" are taken. An exception to this general principle, applicable to the reproduction of copyrighted sound recordings, is specified in section 114.

"Reproduction" under clause (1) of section 106 is to be distinguished from "display" under clause (5) For a work to be "reproduce." Its fixation in tangible form must be "Sufficiently permanent or otherwise communicated for a period of more than transitory duration." Thus, the showing of images on a screen would not be a violation of clause (1), although it might come within the scope of clause (5).

The Right of Reproduction

The right of reproduction means that no person shall make one or more copies of a work or of a substantial part of it in any material form including sound and film recording without the permission of the copyright owner. The most common kind of reproduction is printing an edition of a work. Reproduction occurs in storing of a work in the computer memory.

Rights-Conferred by Copyright Act

Many rights are conferred to the copyright holder by virtue of its owner. Sometimes copyright holder does not share their work for public good. In that circumstances advancement of the society are stopped. For this purpose compulsory licensing system is being used which brings balance between monopoly of owner and advancement of the knowledge of society. Copyright is one of the key element in development as creativity and newness is inherent in it. The object behind copyright law is to advance the progress of society and to benefit the people at large.

There are different types of copyrights—

1. Statutory Rights
2. Monopoly Rights
3. Negative Rights

4. Multiple Rights
5. Economics Rights
6. Moral Rights
7. Neighbouring Rights
8. Performer's Right

Statutory Rights

Section 14 of copyright Act 1957 defines copyright. The statutory rights means the exclusive right to do or authorize others to do certain acts in relation to;

- Literary work;
- Artistic work;
- Cinematography film and
- Sound recording

The right must be such which can be legally protected and judicially enforceable. Sec. 14 (1) © of the copyright act permits the owner of the copyright of cinematography film to do certain things Copyright is a creation of the statute.

Monopoly Rights

It is a monopoly right of the owner to restrain others from exercising that rights under the provisions of the Act.

Negative Right

Copyright is a right in negative manner that it restrains others from exploiting the work of the owner for their own benefit without the consent or license of the author. It never confers any positive on the author.

Multiple Rights

Copyright is a bundle of rights. It depends upon categories of works. i.e.;

- cinematograph and Sound recording.

- literary dramatic and musical works are grouped together.

Economic Rights

Rights conferred Under Sec. 14 are economic rights exploitation of the work by the author, by exercising these rights may bring economic benefit. The author may exploit himself or authorize other to exploit one or more of the rights for consideration. It may be in the form of royalty.

Moral right

Those are not defined in statute. But it is a right of an author to decide whether to publish the work or not. It is for author to claim authorship of a published work.

The right of integrity Sec. 57 of the amended Act provides author's special right. Such as ;

1. To claim authorship of the work.
2. To restrain or claim damages.

The author of a work has the to claim authorship of the work and to restrain or claim damages in respect of any distortion, mutilation, modification or other acts in relation to the said work which is done before the expiration of the term of copyright if such distortion, mutilation, modification or other act would be prejudicial to his honour or reputation. Moral rights are available to the authors even after the economic rights are assigned.

Neighbouring Rights

Sec. 52 of the Act enables other persons to exercise the rights comprised in a copyright for specific purposes under specific circumstances without infringement – Rights like the right of public performance the recording right, broadcasting rights are the rights which can be termed as neighboring rights.

Performer's Right

Prior to 1994 there was no protection of the rights

of the performer such as; musician. Actors, dancers. Sec. 38 has been introduced in the Act 1957. These rights are called performer's right.

A performer has been given exclusive rights to do the followings —

- Making sound recording or visual recording of performance.
- Reproduction of a sound recording or visual recording of performance.
- Broadcasting of the performance.
- Communication of the performance to the public otherwise than by broadcasting.

In a person reproduction a sound recording or visual recording without the consent of the performer for different purpose as referred under sec. 39, it will be an infringement of performers right.

Sec. 39 of the Act states about certain exceptions to the infringement of performer's right.;

- When a sound recording or visual recording is made for the purpose of bonafide teaching or research of a performance in the reporting of current events or for bonafide review teaching or research.
- There is a fair dealing of excepts of a performance in the reporting of current events, review, teaching, research.
- Other Acts with any necessary adaptations and modification which do not constitute infringement of copyright under sec. 52 of the Act.

Thus, legislation is in favour of protection of performer's right. It is an art which can be said result of devotion, mediation of the performer. Therefore non can be allowed to interfere with it. *For further information about Copyright Societies see the sec.33 Chapter VII Appendix III.*

Importance of Copyright Act: Publication of Books And Libraries

In the growing intellectual activity around the world, the copyright law has come to play an important role in the worlds of modern communication. *Kala Thairani* (1998) say that, 'The basic aim of this branch of law is to promote the cultural development of the society by affording legal protection to the rights of authors of creative works as well as those concerned with the dissemination of such works to the public in order to prevent unauthorized appropriation.' It is in the above context that, information professionals have to assume greater responsibilities by acting as a negotiator to transfer the information as well as the technology to their clients .

The history of copyright reflects the development of technology. Copyright develops as the means by which 'works' i.e. materials deserving copyright protection reach the public. At the beginning was the invention of the printing press which gave copyright its impetus. The protection of printed materials against unauthorized reproduction was the main concern of copyright and the right to protect such reproduction, the reproduction right, was the basic and the main right.

The next right which became important for literary works was the translation right. Until the second half of the nineteenth century the printing press was the sole technology involved in taking literary works of all kinds to their public. In the case of dramatic and musical works the routine of the work to its public was live performance and in the case of artistic works, exhibition.

In the second half of the nineteenth century technology added photographs, sound recordings and silent films and in the twentieth century films with sound tracks, radio and television. By these additions the copyright scene was entirely transformed. Two new problems arose. The first was to decide what rights authors were to have in these new uses of their work. The second was to decide whether in the terminology of copyright, these new 'materials' needed and deserved copyright protection, in the terminology of the 'droit d'auteur' where they constituted. 'works ' to be protected . It became fairly clear by the first decade to the twentieth century that photographs, cinematograph films and sound recordings deserved and needed copyright protection.

Author's Works

A ***work*** means any of the following, namely, a literary, dramatic, musical or artistic work, a cinematograph film, or a sound recording.

"Work of ***Joint authorship***" means a work produced by the collaboration of two or more authors in which the contribution of one author is not distinct from the contribution of the other author or authors.

The ***classes*** of works are;

- Original literary, dramatic, musical and artistic works.
- Cinematograph films and
- Sound recordings.

An *artistic works* means;

A painting, a sculpture, a drawing (Including a diagram, map, chart or plan) , a photograph whatever or not any such work possesses artistic quality.

- A work of architecture and
- Any other work of artistic craftsmanship.

"Musical work" means a work consisting of music and includes any graphical notation of such work but does not include any words or any action intended to be sung. Spoken of performed with the music. A musical work need not be written down to enjoy copyright protection.

"Sound Recording" Means a recording of sounds from which sounds may be protected regardless of the medium on which such recording is made or the method by which the sounds are produced. A phonogram and a CD –ROM are also sound recordings.

"Cinematograph film" means any work of visual recording on any medium produced through a process from which a moving image may be produced by any means and includes a sound recording accompanying such visual recording and "Cinematograph" shall be construed as including any work produced by any process analogous to cinematography including Video films.

- An ***"Indian work"*** means a literary, dramatic or musical work,
- The author of which is a citizen of India;
- The first published in India;
- The author of which, in the case of an unpublished work is, at the time of making of the work, a citizen of India.

"Government work" means a work which made or published by or under the direction or control of,

- the government or any department of the government,
- any legislature in India,
- any court, tribunal or other judicial authority in India.

The ***Common Works*** of copyrights are as under—

IPR accordingly revision in the act on those fronts has been more interstitial than in relation to copyright. Nonetheless there has been a flow of important case law, so there is new dimension and material at many points of the dissertation.

In International context the impulse behind the new International economic order, our curiosity that by developing countries, has to be hesitated. The tensions generated by this movement have meant the surrender of attempts to revise the Rome and Berne copyright convention. More recently, reaction again it has taken from pressure within the current round of GATT negotiations to secure a much improved level of recognition and enforcement of Intellectual Property Rights.

- Copyright and their implementation in letter and sprit have acquired international dimensions specially in view of the expansion and the leading role of publishing industry in the economic, political and cultural development of the world system. Copyright is a very interesting subject but has been neglected since long by the academicians creation of the works .
- Fixation of the work;
- Publication of the work;
- Categories of works and subject matters of copyright.

IMPORTANCE OF PUBLICATION OF BOOK

Publishing is the main work of the publication of books.

Meaning of Publication

For the purpose of this act," *publication" means;*

In the case of a *literary, dramatic, musical or artistic* work, the issue of copies of the work, either in whole or in part to the public in manner sufficient to satisfy the reasonable requirements of the public having regard to the nature of the work.

(b) In the case of ***cinematograph film***, the sale or hire or offer for sale or hire of the film or copies thereof to the public;

(c) In the case of ***record***, the issue of records to the public in sufficient quantities;

But does not except as other wise expressively provided in this act, include,_

(i) In the case of a literary, dramatic or musical work, the issue of any records recording such work;

(ii) In the case of a work of sculpture or an architectural work of art, the issue of photographs and engravings of such works.

Number of copies required to constitute publication will very from place to place and from language to language. (AIR 1990 (NOC) 178 (Kant).

COPY RIGHT AGREEMENT

In April, The British Library signed a new agreement with the Copy right Licensing Agency (CLA). Under the agreement the British Library will pay copyright fees at the rates set by publishers and the authors. The BLDSC will continue to charge a rate set at the average fee. But we are looking at introducing a system eventually which will charge the fee at the rate set by each publishers. As a result of the agreement, the library is extending its policy of requiring certain groups of customers to use the copyright fee paid service for all their requests. In addition, we have taken the opportunity to define more clearly the names of the services we offer overseas. We now offer a library privilege photocopy services where documents are provided under the library provisions of UK Copyright Law and a copyright fee paid for photocopy service where documents are provided under the terms of our agreement with the CLA.

Where certain foreign books are imported under copyright, Issue of copies for public distribution is publication within the meaning of S. 3 of the Copyright Act 14 of 1957.

For the purposes of this Act, a work published in India shall be deemed to be first published in India, not with standing that it has been published simultaneously in some other country, unless such other country provides a shorter term of copyright for such work; and a work shall be deemed to be published simultaneously in India and in another country if the time between the publication in India and the publication in such other country does not exceed thirty days or such other period as Central Government may, in relation to any specified country.

COPY RIGHT ENFORCEMENT AND INTERNET

Internet is the most suitable medium for global trade and exchange of services. The services available in the Internet include software, entertainment, information products and professional services. However, many business houses are still wary of conducting extensive business in Cyberspace because of the lack of a predictable legal environment governing transactions. Such result in concerns about IPP, privacy, security and other matters. Commerce on Internet involves the sale and licensing of IP. To promote an effective environment, sellers must know that their Intellectual Property will not be pirated and buyers must know that they are obtaining authentic products and not pirated copies. For this reason on, international agreements that establish clear and effective copyright, patents and trade mark protection are necessary to prevent piracy and fraud. While technical means of protection such as an encryption can help prevent piracy, an adequate legal framework also is necessary to penalize piracy and fraud and to provide legal remedies when these crimes are committed. Indian Government should improvise the IPR laws according to international agreements, in such a way that our national interests are protected and preserved.

The computer's ability to share date with other computers over a network linked through telephone has led to a major telecommunication revolution. A computer network is network consisting of a central computer (server) and a number of remote stations that report to it.

The documents stored in the electronic form as soft copies, which could be retrieved at any point of time and visualized in the monitor. Electronic data consists of text, images, voice and programmes. The present day data transmitted is far superior in terms of speed , quality, visuals, utility, impact and convenience. Internet is global in nature. It is a fact that the growth and speed of Internet has become an important yardstick for measuring the growth and strength of any economy. The growth of Internet in India show in the Table given as under;

Growth of Internet Internet connection user (in Million)

—March, 2002 8.0 million 18

December, 2003 11.0 million 23

World Wide Web

World Wide Web is a huge collection of hyper- text pages in the Internet. The concept of WWW developed by the European Laboratory for physics. A hyper- text based, distributed information system in which users create, edit or browse- hyper- text links connect information in separate html pages situated at different Internet sites. One can explore these pages using a web browser. Web Browser is a software application used to locate and display web- pages. A web client application that enables hyper- text documents and establishes links to other html documents in the Internet.

Internet is a network of computer networks

A combination of number of smaller networks which use different networking protocols.

Strength of users on the Internet

The world largest computer network consisting of over 20 million users spread over 200 different countries. The Internet is growing at a phenomenal rate of 10-15 percent per month.

The **Internet** has generated a lot of hype in the past decade and that has encouraged the people who run the current information and entertainment industries to look at least as much of a threat as an opportunity. The Internet sometimes gets characterized as giant copying machine that facilitates widespread and undetectable copyright infringement. That's about 50% hype- the Internet facilitates widespread copying, but it also facilitates detection of copying. The Internet also gets painted as the next new thing that will replace conventional newspapers, television and phonograph records in our lives. We can see how that notion might bother newspaper publishers and television networks and record companies. The internet gets promoted as a new market we will use of sell everything from computer software to vacation homes and while that may be an attractive idea, it's far from clear that the current market leader in the sales of computer software and vacation homes are going to be the new market leaders in the new medium.

The Internet new thing such as radar screen and it's big and it's scary and everybody wants a piece of it. The commercial lawyers scurry off to redraft the uniform commercial code to cover electronic contracts, and the civil liberties lawyers worry about strong encryption and sexually explicit Usenet news. In the early 1990s, the dominant players in the entertainment and information industries got cracking on reforming the copyright law to make the Internet safe for then leading copyright owners.

The copyright owner discussed that the U.S. currently dominated the world in film, music, television, computer software and databases and if the Internet were not made safe for copyright owners, either all the people in all the other countries would get together and steal all our stuff or U.S. copyright owners would decline to put their stuff on the Internet and the U.S. might lose the advantage of world leadership on this new medium.

When we get to the down and dirty of formulating actual proposals for legislation, interested parties first tactic is to claim that extant copyright law already gives them whatever it is they want.(When it came to the Internet, it was a little hard to square this with the claim that unless Congress did something, U.S. industries would stay out of the online market, but that claim already proving to be demonstrably false). The dynamics of the copyright negotiation make it important to claim that we want already. If we want Internet service provider to be held liable for their subscriber's infringing activities; For examples; it will be easier to accomplish that if we claim that current law tell us such liability.(If we would be willing to bargaining towards a suitable narrow limitation), Than to demand that congress impose that liability in the first instance. But Congress had enacted the current copyright law more than 20 years earlier, so it would have been hard to discuss that congress had the Internet in mind. To make the case that copyright law already provided the enhanced protection they wanted copyright owners needed some statutory language to hang their new improved interpretation.

Some peoples are oppose and claimed that the copyright statute gives copyright owner. The exclusive right to reproduce protected works in "copies", subject only to the exceptions enumerated in the statute. A computer works by reproducing things in its volatile Random Access Memory (RAM) and anything that exists in volatile memory could, any portion of a work in any computer's RAM is a reproduction in a copy within the meaning of the statute. There are no enumerated exceptions for Internet related uses, that the copyright owner has the legal right to control, enjoy or collect money for every single appearance of a work in the memory of any computer anywhere. Since the reproduction right is the "fundamental" copyright right. This is the useful of science & useful arts.

COPY RIGHT LAW TO BE MADE DIGITAL- FRIENDLY

The center is planning to amend the copyright law to tackle the problems possessed by the arrival of digital technology. India has fully complained to Trade Related Intellectual Property Rights (TRIPS), about changes which have become necessary due to the growth of information technology and imperatives of globalization. The advanced countries like the US are confronted with copyright related problems arising out of advent of digital technology, The Education Secretary, Mr. M.K. Kaw, inaugurated a meeting of State Nodal Officers dealing with copyright matter at New-Delhi on 12 June,2001, in the first conference at the central level to understand the difficulties faced by States in enforcing the copy right law and arrest in violations.

Regarding the efforts of the challenges of digitalizing, the government is equally keen to tighten up copyright norms pertaining to copy right print and other media. The centre has asked states to stress the copy right enforcement machinery by setting up special cells and specialized training to the police and other officers dealing with copyright violations. Although India is well a head of other nations. Mr. Kaw said, that more is needed to be done. Early detection of crime and prompt prosecution of violators would help keep copy right infringements in check.

Mr. Kaw suggested the challenging particularly with regard to the copy right enforcement machinery. Copy right violations are becoming more complex and continuing unabated leading to huge revenue losses. Criminal administration has to be modernized and made more effective. Periodic review of copyright law is essential. The centre had tried to provide a theoretical exercise by setting up IPR chairs in five universities. It has also held several seminars to sensitized the user, service provider and society.

WORLD BOOK AND COPY RIGHT DAY 2004 & MESSAGE OF THE DIRECTOR- GENERAL OF UNESCO

Every 23 April, World Book and Copy Right Day is being celebrated all over the world. Several million people and many countries are involved in this day. The aim of it promotion of books, copyright and in joint reflection on their irreplaceable roles in education, culture and the sciences through out the world. The message of the Director General of UNESCO on the occasion of "World Book and Copy Right Day, 23 April, 2004 has been as under—

"As a window on the diversity of cultures and a bridge between civilizations, as carriers of value, knowledge, the aesthetic sense on the world of them imagination, books are above all works of the mind creativity and culture of human beings, which thereby enrich the heritage intangible of humanity, copy right moral and patrimonial protection for intellectual works and their creators—provides the legal frame works conductive to the full development of these valuable resources.

In addition, books are both as cultural products and as traded goods, the raison **d't re** of an entire sector of the economy that the publishing. Copyright, which protects the legal use of works of the mind, also plays a crucial role in the creation, production and dissemination of knowledge which is the fruit of human creativity.

With their complex nature, books are therefore playing an increasingly important part in people's lives and in the blossoming of their societies. For this reason, for the protection and the promotion of books and copy right, it is necessary to, constitute a unique challenge for the progress of democracy.

In this context, I call upon policy - makers, economic operators and other actors in civil society. I invite them to promote public awareness of the unique role of the book and of the need to uphold respect for copyright. Thanks to the decision of the International community, World Book and Copyright Day, exists for that purpose. It is still in 2004, an occasion not to be missed "

Celebration of The World Book And Copy Right Day & Padmashree Prof. Kaula's Efforts In Establishing National Book Musium At Delhi:

The International World Book and Copyright Day was celebrated On 25 April 2004 by Ranganathan Society for Book Culture, Library And Informatics Studies in collaboration with prof. P.N. Kaula Endowment for Library and Information Science and National Botanical Research Institute(NBRI) at Lucknow. The programme included a Panel Discussion cum Seminar on the " Value of Books Reading , Copyright and Libraries." Prof. R.L. Raina .Library, IIM, Lucknow was the main speaker of the function. He spoke on essence of copyright and consortium growth in India. He also emphasized the application of technology in information generation process and retrieval. He also referred to the copyright law that needs its modification in the light of electronic development and digital device. Prof. P.N. Kaula in his presidential address stated the role of UNESCO in promoting Book Culture and Libraries. He said that UNESCO had laid down the essential elements in the value and use of books by bring out a Charter of Book. At the end in his speech Prof. Kaula suggested that Government of India should take a lesson from Russia, Turkey, Cuba and some other Latin American countries in banishing Illiteracy. He desired that awareness be created in the participants in bring the digital drive among our society. In rural and urban areas and try to remove barriers for giving every one the benefit of promotion of knowledge, information & wisdom

NATIONAL SEMINAR ON COPYRIGHTS : EMERGING ISSUES IN INDIA

The School of Management and Social Sciences, Thaper Institute of Engineering and Technology, Patiala organized recently a National Seminar on ' Copyrights : Emerging Issues in India.' The seminar was sponsored by Ministry of Human Resource Development, Government of India. Dr. Neelima Jerath, Joint Director, Punjab State Council of Science and Technology in her inaugural address highlighted the importance of the intellectual property rights in developing countries like India, the protection provided by copyrights to the efforts of writers, artists, designers, dramatics, musicians, architects etc.

Dr. S C Saxena, Director of the Institute in his Presidential remarks Emphasizes the importance of copyrights in the period of globalization. He is also highlighted that creating awareness about copyrights among artistic producers and general public. Who is the unwitting violator of copyright assumes great importance.

Public Awareness on Copyright

About 27 percent of copyright owners and sellers of copyright products placed the main responsibility on the end users. About 61 percent of the respondents belonging to this category. It will be said that in general public awareness of copyright in India is poor. The opinion of the 26 percent persons are satisfactory where as the rest (Only about 12 percent said that it is excellent or good.

The discussions put forward by the right holders of copyright product have been contradicted by the end users.

From the responses of the end users it was observed that 81.5 percent of them are aware of phenomenon of copyright violations. About 73 percent of the end users were also of the view that one should not buy pirated products even it is available at a lower price because it is harmful to the interests of right holders and the society. The majority of the answering (About 78 percent) also admitted that they were aware of the punishment for copyright violation.

It has been found that public is generally aware of the fact that copyright violation is not a desired thing. They also admit that anything created/made/produced by some body is not to be duplicated, copied and commercially exploited by others. The survey of software end users belonging mostly to the organizations from both service as well as manufacturing sectors. The computer personnel whether by using one legal software in more that one independent computer machine, would amount to copyright violation. It found that a majority (about 59 percent) out of 87 persons mentioned that it is not a violation.

Public Awareness of copyright by various Target Group

Target Group	*Rating of Awareness (%)*				
	Excellent	*Good*	*Satisfactory*	*Poor*	*Total No of Responses*
Film Producers	Nil	56	24.1	70.4	54(100.0)
Video Film Pro.	91	-	9.1	81.8	22(100.0)
Music Companies	—	28.6	14.3	57.1	14(100.0)
Book publishers	—	7.9	20.2	71.9	89.9(100.0)
Public performers	1.0	9.2	24.4	65.3	98(100.0)
Video Cassette Sellers	2.4	20.5	26.5	50.6	83(100.0)
Music Cassettes Sellers	6.6	8.1	38.2	47.1	136(100.0)
Computer software Sellers	1.0	11.9	22.9	64.2	109(100.0)
Total No. of Respondents	15(2.5)	64(10.6)	158(26.1)	368(60.8)	605(100)

Source : NPC survey

Educationists can also be launched at the school and college levels since students are the major consumers of the goods produced by copyright industry. Piracy is not an occurrence that can be tackled through any short cut in the short term. This should be a long term effort to educate students of schools and colleges. Piracy related matters could be part of school or college curriculum especially for the students of electronics who may be exposed to implications and methods of software piracy.

COPYRIGHT: LIBRARIANS AND INFORMATION PROFESSIONALS

According to *M.K.R. Naidu* (2002) that the Librarians and Information professionals have an important role in protecting the rights of a copyright holder. The librarians should keep themselves aware with the latest changes in IPR, and to oversee their proper implementation while purchasing the documents, and their use in library. There is an urgent need to understand the Article 27 of 1948 (Universal Declaration of Human Rights) in true sense which reads as 'Every one has the right to the protection of the moral and material interest resulting from any scientific, literary or artistic production of which he is the author, 'Every one has the right to share in scientific advancement and its benefits.

Hence, the major position of the professionals is to balance the interest of the invent or and that of the society optimally.

It is really true that the Librarians and Information Professionals are, in the real sense, to become the Information intermediaries between the generators and receivers of information.

REFERENCES

- Chopra, R N. Dictionary of Library Science. New Delhi: Anmol, 1992.
- Cornish, W R. Intellectual Property. Delhi: Universal, 2003, 5-7.
- Diwan, Parag, Suri, R K and Kaushik, Sanjay. ed. IT Encyclopaedia.Com "Information Technology Laws." 10th vols, New Delhi: Pentagon Press, 2003, 125-144.

- Government of India. The Copyright Act 1957 .Delhi: India Government, 1998.173-181.
- Government of India. A Hand book of Copyright Law. New Delhi: Ministry of HRD,1999. 6-12.
- James, T C. Indian Copyright Law and Digital Technologies." Selective Study Material on IPR from NRDC Depository, IP Consultancy and Management Division. New Delhi: Kailash Colony Extension, 2001. CD ROM. E-mail: cmgaind@nrdc.in.
- Kaula, P N. World Book and Copyright Day." Herald of Library Science". 43. -3-4. Lucknow: 1996, 265.
- Kaula, P N, Copyright law to be made digital- friendly. "Herald of Library Science. 40, 3-4 July-October 2001, 298.
- Kaula, P N. Copyright Agreement. "Herald of Library Science".35, 3-4 July-October,1996, 295.
- Pani, S R, Devi. ed. National Seminar on Copyrights: Emerging Issues In India. "University News". 42, 43, Oct 25-31, 2004, 19.
- Raju, AAN. The Indian Copyright Act and Its Implications to Libraries and Information Centres. "Intellectual Property Rights and Copyright. S P Satarkar" New Delhi: Ess Ess, 8-12.
- Singh, Jnanendra Narayan. Copyright Issues in Digital Era. "Library Herald ed. C P. Vashisth, . 44, 2 June 2006, 141-144.
- Singh, Nishant. Media Law. New Delhi: Naman. 132-148.
- Srivastava, P L. Copyright Act 1957. A Development profile. "National Seminar Paper presented CSIR Dimond Jubilee and NBRI Golden Jubilee Celebrations". Lucknow, 2003.
- Srivastava, P L. Copyright Act 1957and Digital Millennium Act: Role of Librarians in Compliance of the Provisions of Copyright Act. "Granthalaya Vigyan. 36, 1-2, 2005, Jaipur: Kaula Granthalaya Sandan, 2005, 54-62.
- Stenberg, S.H. Cassell's Encylclopaedia of Literature. v1 London: Cassell and Company, 1953, 116-120.
- Suraj, V K. ed. Encyclopaedic Dictionary of Library and Information Science. 3vols. Delhi: Isha Books 2005, 179-181.
- Swain, Nirmal Kumar. Authorship Hegemony, Compulsory License and the Battle for the knowledge Commons. "I L A

Bulletin," XLIII, 3, July-September, 2007,. Delhi: Indian Library Association, 18-22.

- Tripathi, Amrendra N. Emergence of Copyright. New Delhi: Dhir and Dhir Associates.
- Tripathi, R C. The Emerging IPR Regime in Electronics and Information Technology" Selective Study Material on IPR from NRDC Depository "New Delhi: Kailash Colony Extension. CDROM E-mail: *cmgaind @nrdc.in.*
- Thakare, U S. What Is Copyright. " Intellectual Property Rights and Copyright," S.P. Satarkar" New Delhi: Ess Ess, 2003.
- TLA News Letter on Copyright Day 23 April, vol.12, 4, 2005.

3

Copyright : Duration And Infringement

INTRODUCTION

The long term given to authors by copyright law stands in stark contrast to that for patents, industrial designs and other productive subject-matter such as; plant variety rights and semi-conductor layout. It is a provocative choice : Why does the creativity of an authors deserve this distinction? As pointed out, the distinction become possible because of the nature of what is protected and the limited scope of the rights granted.

Duration of Copyright

Under the Copyright Act of 1976, copyright protection of an author work extends throughout the life of the author and to fifty years after the author's death. Thus, It is possible for authors to benefit from royalties on their works until their death, and to pass on copyright and associated royalties to their heirs. In the case of joint works, the termination date of the copyright is fifty years after the death of the last surviving author.

The pseudonymous works, and anonymous works,

the copyright generally expires seventy- five years after publication or one hundred years after creation, whichever occurs first. However, in the case of an anonymous or pseudonymous work, an author or interested party, such as an heir, may reveal to the Copyright Office the true identity of at least one author of the work, and be eligible for the full duration of copyright until fifty years after the author's death.

Duration of the Protection

Copyright is a limited right in the sense it is available for certain duration only. After the expiry of the specified term, the work will deem to be fallen in the public domain then anybody may use the work without fear of infringement actions. Specific and different term of protection is accorded to specific and different works by different instruments on the bases their nature. The term of copyright protection available under TRIPS and Indian law can be seen in this table.

A comparative table of term of protection available under Indian Copyright Act 1057 and the TRIPS Agreement

Works	*Indian Law*	*TRIPS Agreement*
Literary, dramatic, musical, or artistic	For life of the author and 60 years after his death	For life of the author and 50 years after his death
Cinematographic	60 years after the work has been made available to the public.	50 years after the work has been made available to the Public.
Photographic and Applied Art	60 years	A minimum of 25 years.
Sound recording	60 years	50 years
Performers	60 years	50 years
Broadcasting	25 years	20 years
Computer Programmes	60 years	50 years

This tables indicates that there are some differences

between the Indian law and the TRIPS Agreement as regarding the term of protection given to the different works in which copyright subsists. Indian law is more standard and comprehensive than the multilateral agreement on TRIPS.

Copyright Infringement

So far as infringement of copyright is concerned, Copyright in a work is deemed to be infringed when any person, without a license granted by the owner of the copyright does anything, the exclusive right to do which is by the act conferred upon the owner of the copyright. Where a person has copyright in a literary work, and any other person produces or reproduces the work or any substantial part thereof in any material form infringement should be an exact or verbatim copy of the original but its resemblances with the original in a large measure is sufficient to indicate that it is a copy. The piracy in an alleged infringing work may be detected by making a careful examination of it to see whether any of the deviations and mistakes, which license permits,

Infringement involves any violation of the exclusive rights of the copyright.

Infringing means any reproduction, copy or sound recording, as the case may be, made or reported in the contravention of the provision of the Act.

According to the copyright act, infringing copyright means reproduction or import of a copy in contravention of the act or any of the following;

Reproduction of ***literary, dramatic, musical or artistic work*** other than cine-film.

- Copy of cine-film by any means.
- Copy of sound recording by any means.
- Sound recording or video recording of any programme or performance where "broadcast reproduction rights or performer's rights." subsists.

When the exclusive right to do anything to conferred upon the owner of the copyright and any other person does that, without a license either from him or from the Registrar of copyrights or does something in contravention of the express conditions contained in the license granted, the act of the other person amounts to an infringement of the copyright .

The act gives the copyright of every work executed on commission to the person by whom it is commissioned. It makes it compulsory upon every owner of a copy right that he should register it at Stationer's Hall before he can take any action at law to protect it. The copyright does not mistake if unregistered, but so long as it remains unregistered no action at law can be taken on account of any infringement. A copy right can be registered at any time, even after an infringement, but the owner of the copyright cannot recover for any infringement before registration.

The act provides for both penalties and damages in the following cases;

For infringing copyright in the ordinary way by issuing unlawful copies.

For fraudulently dealing with a work so signed.

For fraudulently putting forth a copy of a work of art, whether there be copyright in it or not, as the original work of artist.

For altering, adding to, or taking away from a work during the life time of the author if it is signed, and putting it forth as the unaltered work of the author.

For importing pirates works.

Area's of Infringing Copy-Right

- Infringing of copyright in books.
- Infringing of copyright under section 51 (b).
- Infringing of copyright in pictures, photographs etc.

- Principles for deciding infringement of copyright.
- No Infringement of copyright.
- Absence of copy right.

Copyright law does not prevent any one from making use of copyrighted work and create a new work with additions, deletions or improvements by putting one's own labour, skill and capital, which is sufficient to give the work a quality, which the original work did not have and which make the two works quite different.

Infringement in case of performance also covers persons who permit the use of premises for profit, when such performance amounts to violation of copyright. Only depend upon such a person is lack of knowledge on his part of such an infringement. When a person imports infringing copies of the work or himself makes copies for sale, hire or display converts literary, dramatic, musical or artistic work into cine-film for the purpose of this section the reproduction of a literary, dramatic, musical or artistic work in the form of a cinematograph film shall be deemed to be an "Infringing copy"

Dr. S.P. Satarkar (2002) While specifying the infringement aspects has quoted the various sections and concepts related to the above but a small extract of the same reads as: Copyright is infringing when, a person; makes for sale or hire, or sales for hire by way of trade displays or offers for sale or hire, distributes either for the purpose of trade, or to such as extent as to affect prejudicially the owner of copyright or

- By way of trade exhibits in public or
- Imports to India, any infringing copies of the work.

Even with all the IPR indicators guiding the information professional, it is a closely guarded fact, that management of information in this digital world positively become difficult. Quite a few of us also know, that there are outlets which are freely selling the zerox copies of the various course materials (specially professional) in quite a few meet today, In lieu of the financial crunch, information kiosks have also been relying on these to satisfying their beneficiaries. The user group on the other hand, also prefers such material as the same in cheap and affordable.

What does not stand as Infringement of Copy Right

According to the act :

- When a party submitted along with a tender for contract a plan for the proposed construction, it was held that the plan is an original literary work would not be infringed if the construction is carried out by others according to another plan though the latter plan is a copy of the former in essential features.
- The court will not interfere where the value of the extract taken for the purpose of criticism is very minute .
- Similarity in two dramatic works due to coincidence, both works being derived independently from common stock of dramatic ideas—There is no infringement of the copyright.(1911)28 Tlr69(72).
- Where, both the plaintiff and the defendant have stolen from a foreign books written and published in a foreign country and there was no link between in the work of plaintiff and that of the defendant has not avoided himself in any way of the plain and labour employed by the plaintiff, there is no infringement of copyright. (1951).
- Broken and detached fragments from a literary work consisting of six pages out of forty for criticism—there is no infringement.
- Notes on the books prescribed by the university, published as guides to students amounted to criticism or review of the original book and there was no infringement of copyright under section

51.AIR1965 J&K (101, 102).

- A fair dealing with a literary, dramatic, musical or artistic work for the purposes of research or provide.
- Study, reporting current events in a news- papers, magazine or similar periodical, cinematograph film.

Recently, In India as 50 years passed for publication of Mahatma Gandhi's literature therefore now copyright is not applicable since, 2008. Earlier it was with Navajivan Publishing House, Ahmedabad. Now any one can publish the above said literature.

Certain Acts not to be Infringement of Copyright—— Section 52 [4]

1. The following acts shall not constitute an infringement of copyright, namely;
   (a) A fair dealing with a literary, dramatic, musical or artistic work for the purpose of—
      (i) Private use, including research;
      (ii) Criticism or review, whether of that work or of any other work;
   (b) The making of copies or adaptation of a computer program by lawful possessor of a copy of such computer program, from such copy.
      (i) In order to utilize the computer program for the purpose for which it was supplied; or
      (ii) To make back-up copies purely as a temporary protection against loss, destruction or damage in order only to utilize the computer program for the purpose for which it was supplied.

Criminal Remedies

The infringement of copyright has been made a criminal offence under copyright act, punishable with imprisonment which may be from a minimum period of six month & maximum of 3 years and with a fine ranging from Rs. 50,000 to Rs. 2 lacs.

A Case do Fight On Googles (To The Infringement of Copyright)

Internet company Google, Five great publishers have cased, they have protested on –line searching of several famous books. In the prosecution it is said, that Google has broken the rule of publishers copyright. It makes available all the scanned books on its website without having the permission of authorized persons. (for the comments and summary). The use of some parts of books is proper but it is not proper to make all the books available on internet. The president of Association of Americans publishers Shroader says, that 'It is continues any man will start to prepare the digital copy of any book visiting in the library.'

Knowledge of the Offence

This is an essential in criminal proceedings, In Cheria P Joseph Vs. Prabhakarn AIR 1967 KAR, 234 held that the knowledge is necessary to establish the commission of offence.

Burden of proof is on prosecution, section 65 to 70 of the act deals with the offences, relating to infringement of copyright. The copyright (Amendment) act 1996 enhanced the punishment and provides with imprisonment which may be extended for a minimum period of 6 months to maximum of 3 yrs., and the fine which not be less than Rs.50,ooo/-. The court has discretion to reduce the imprisonment and fine as well, in special cases. The minimum term of imprisonment is enhanced to 1 Yrs., and minimum fine to Rupees 1 lac.

Computer Programme

Any person who knowingly makes use on a computer of an infringing copy of a computer programme will be punishable with imprisonment for a term which will not be less than 7 days, but which may extend to 3 yrs., and with fine which will not be less than Rs. 50,000/-, but which may be extend to 2 lac of Rupees.

Proceeding of Infringement

The act provides not only civil but also criminal remedies, in case of infringement of copyright, against infringe. The two remedies are distinct and independent and can be availed of simultaneously. But in Cheria P. Joseph Vs. K. Prabhakaran Nair AIR 1967 Kar 234. Held that, a criminal court may not give a finding on the question of infringement if the same issue is pending for the decision in a civil suit. However, a criminal proceeding does not enable the owner to get an injunction i.e. condemned criminal repeat the infringement the owner will have to initiate a fresh proceedings. So in such cases it is advisable to initiate criminal as well as civil proceeding simultaneously, if the stakes are very high. In the matters of criminal proceedings the knowledge is essential.

Violation of Law of copyright Vs Theft

If any one stoles some copyrighted work to copy, then he is liable for infringement of copyright and not of theft. The violation of patents and copyright are implant with the tacit approval of the governments. In Thailand, up to 97% of the software in use has been illegally copied and in the U S it was 40%. However, no system of IPR can work unless most of the governments of the world agree to enforce it. With the developments of Information technology (IT), information appears in various forms and formats. These digital information resources can be accessed from networks, particularly over the internet from anywhere in the world. Storing of work in digital medium and digital transmission of copyright material should be protected. Digitized documents, especially the multimedia products are very prone to right violation.

Power of Police to Seize Infringing Copies

Police Officer of the rank of Sub- Inspector and above has been given the power to seize without warrant, if he satisfied that an infringement of copyright in any work has been or likely to be, committed, all infringing copies or plates of the work, whatever found, to be produced before Magistrate (Section 64 (1)), as soon as practicable. Even such copies found at the place of retailer may also be seized. Private individuals who might be possessing infringing copies for their private and domestic use, is not covered by the definition of the infringement U/ Section 51. Further this provision applies only to infringement of copyright and not to broadcasting reproduction rights U/Sec.37 and the performer's right U/Sec. 38. Any person having an interest in any copies of the work or plate so seized may within 15 days of such seizure, make an application to the Magistrate for the return of such copies to him.

"This is a new clause which enables a police officer not below the rank of a sub- inspector to seize all copies of a work which appear to him to be infringing copies after a Magistrate has taken cognizance of an offence relating to infringement of copyright in such work. In the opinion of the committee such a provision is necessary in the interest of authors and publishers particularly in cases of wholesale and deliberate acts of piracy ."—*JCR.*

Knowledge of offences (Jurisdiction Section 70)

According to the act no court inferior to that of (A Metropolitan Magistrate or Judicial Magistrate if the first class) shall try any offence under this act. If the copies are circulated at many places, the offence is committed at every place, where the copies are intended to reach and has in fact reached.

Who can file complaint? Any one can file the complaint. But there is a specific provision U/Sec.4(2) & 190 of CR.PC, a Magistrate will be suitable knowledge of any offence specified in U/Sec.190 upon receiving a complaint of facts which constitutes such offence irrespective of the qualifications of the complainant in any statute.

Filing of FIR Case

Under copyright act procedure after filing of FIR in case of infringement the producer are as under;

A police officer in charge of a police station has reason to suspect the commission to the offence under the copyright act, after registering of FIR I/Sec/ 154 of Crpc.

After the confirm of reasonable cause, the SHO must immediately send a report to the Magistrate having power to take cognizance of such an offence on a police report U/Sec. 157(1).

The SHO shall then proceed to the spot, to investigate the facts and circumstances of the case and to take measures for the discovery and seizer.

The Role of NASSCOM and BSA

The police and Judiciary appointed Commissioners are carrying out the operations against anti- piracy. They are facilitating police raids against this menus, providing information of infringement. The effective remedy complaint/FIR can be made to special cell established for the purpose in various States Viz. Economic offences wing of Delhi police, in Delhi, which conducts raids along with the IPR section of the crime branch of Delhi police.

Copyright Protect

Copyright law is intended to promote and advance art. We all like art, so we would like to see more of it. How do we get artists to create more of it? We can help them get paid for their efforts. Hundreds of years ago, most artists struggled to survive. Even Mozart, a brilliant musician and composer, was reported to be relatively poor.

The first copyright law came from England in 1710 when the "Statute of Ann" was passed to protect booksellers and printers from anyone copying their work without permission. In the United States, the Constitution was first to direct Congress to make laws to promote the arts and sciences. Today, many artists still struggle financially until they produce something that is in high demand.

Eminem says he used to be poor. But now, because he has sold so many CDs, he is a multimillionaire. Stephen King sells many books, so he is paid very well. George Lucas is quite wealthy because he created the Star Wars movies. Because of copyright law, artists, writers, and musicians have a monetary incentive to make as much of their art as they can. It seems to work because we now have artwork everywhere. Radios play music continuously. We have libraries full of books to educate and entertain us. Our clothing has designs created by professional artists. Just about everywhere you look, art in some form can be seen

The Difference Between Copyright, Patent, and Trademarks

Copyrights, patents and trademarks are branch of "Intellectual Property". Patents give inventors the exclusive right to duplicate their inventions design. Patents cover devices, formula, tools and anything that has utility. The recipe for a unique sausage can have a patent. To get a patent, we are apply to the U.S. Patent and Trademark Office and submit the invention's design. We see that the design is unique. A patent examiner will determined if we are entitled to a patent, than a patent is granted that prohibits anyone else from making, using, offering for sale, selling or improving the invention. A patent lasts 20 years.

A trademark is a word, phrase, or logo that identifies a product, a service, or the person or company that offers a product or service to the public. We can apply to the

U.S. Patent and Trademark Office to registered a federal trademark. If our trademark is registered, we can generally prevent anyone else from using a mark that may confuse the public about who offers the product or service. There are also common law trademarks that are automatic in the area where the product or service is being advertised, unless a federal trademark has been previously registered

Copyright apply to art, music, play, movies, literature and scholarly works. They are automatic and require no registration or other formality. They prevent others from copying the work. Copyrights last for the artist's or author's or author's life plus 70 years.

For more information about patents and trademarks, visit: *www.uspto.gov/*

Artist's Exclusive Rights

Copyright law gives artists a monopoly on their work-certain rights that only the artist may exercise. The art work's creators is the only one who can.

- Make copies of the work;
- Make derivatives or revisions;
- Distribute or publish the work;
- Perform the work in public (if the work is a poem, song, play or movie)
- Display the work in public (if the work is a painting, graphic, photo, sculpture or other still-image work); and
- Perform the work in public by digital transmission (if the work is sound recording).

The artist can sell the work or any of the exclusive rights to it. Eminem sold his copyrights to the recording company. Stephen King, for some of his first books, sold his copyrights to the publisher. Artist can sell rights to their work because no one else can entertain the public without the rights or at least permission from the artist.

If someone does anything with an artist's work that falls within any of the exclusive rights without any them or having permission, he "infringes" the artist's copyright. If we made bootleg copies of Eminem's music, his record company can sue us for copyright infringement because they hold the copyrights to the music.

Types of Copyright Protects

There are many types of copyright protected. These are;

Civil liability

If anyone copies a work that is protected by someone else's copyright or does anything else that only the copyright holder may do (exclusive rights), and they do not have the copyright holder's permission, then the copyright holder may enforce the copyright with a lawsuit. In legal terms, the copier has "infringed" the copyright or at least the law suit accuses the copier of infringement. If the copyright holder wins the lawsuit, the court will enter a judgment against the party accused of infringing the copyright and make him/ her pay damages and possibly even the copyright holder's attorney's fees. Three levels of legal liability in copyright infringement cases depend on the activities and knowledge of the people being accused of infringement.

Direct Infringement

The copyright holder must prove that he owns the infringed copyright and that the accused infringe violated one of the copyright's exclusive rights. In other words, the infringes copied, distributed, displayed or performed the work without the copyright holder's permission.

Contributory Infringement

The infringement is liable to the copyright holder if it is proved he/she engaged in personal conduct that encouraged the infringement. In this level of liability, the infringement must have actual knowledge. The infringer must also contribute to the infringement in a material way.

Vicarious Infringement

All the copyright holder has to improve is that the infringer had the right and ability to supervise the activities that infringed the copyright and had a financial interest in the activities. This is the level of the liability that a university incur by hosting an Internet service. If any users or subscribers of the internet service infringe copyrights online, the university is vicariously liable for the copyright holder's damages. In fact, any ISPs is vicariously liable for infringement that subscribers engage in ISPs have conditional and limited immunity from lawsuits for monetary damages under the DMCA. 8

Internet And Copyright : Protect

Internet technology is developing faster than the laws that govern it. New laws that apply to the internet have been established either by legislation. Copyright laws are among them. A common view about the internet is that anything posted online can be copied or downloaded. Anything we see on the internet has the same potential of being protected by copyright as anything we see in the library. Under modern copyright law, the formalities of registration and copyright notice are no longer required.

The copyright statute is triggered by the unauthorized act of copying, publishing, performing (by digital means), displaying in public any copyright protected materials. Our PC automatically makes copies when we search the internet in various ways. Ronald B. Standler explains that copies are made at least four different ways when accessing the internet. One way copies are made is by simply viewing a page on internet. This causes a copy of that page to be made and stored in the Random Access Memory (RAM) of our PC. Browsers also make copies so we can return to a site faster. This means that everyone who use the internet is liable for copyright infringement and take legal action. Legal argue that anyone know, that visitor's PCs will make copies in the process and the web site host grants visitors in implied license or permission to make those copies.

Downloading on the Net

Downloading content from any Web page is the equivalent to making a copy of the content, the same as making copies of a book in the library. It makes sense to presume that by doing so we will infringe the copyright of the author of that content. To comply with copyright law, We must receive permission from the copyright holder before download any content. As in copying printed material such as books in the library, we shall not need permission if we qualify for Fair Use. Some Web Sites give permission to download content.

In education, there are many internet materials that could be used as teaching aids for a class or for the research work. If we qualify for using materials without permission under the TEACH ACT, then we also can use online materials in a face to face classroom setting. If we are concerned about using TEACH procedures- as are many universities- there is always Fair Use. Most of the Fair Use factors that apply to printed media also apply to the internet, with the exception of posting materials on the internet. If disqualify the Fair Use, than we must get permission to post other people's work on the WWW. The best way to qualify the Fair Use when we want to post other people's work online is to use a password- protected web site where only the students enrolled in a class may view the copy, We should also take technological steps to prevent students from copying the materials, such as using a streaming process. 9

Fundamentals of Copy Right Protection Copyright Protected

Copyright ensures certain minimum safeguards of the rights of author over their creations, there by protecting and rewarding creativity. Creativity being the keystone of progress, no civilized society can afford to ignore the basic requirement of encouraging the same. Economic and social development of a society is dependent on creativity. The protection provided by copyright to the efforts of writers, artists, designers, dramatists, musicians, architects and producers of sound recordings, cinematograph film and computer software, creates an atmosphere conductive to creativity. To create more and motivates others to create.

In India any original published or unpublished literary work automatically acquires copyright and is protected by simply recording it in any tangible form. All one needs to do is document or record the work on some tangible medium like ROM, magnetic tape, diskette or paper to get copyright protection. This means that one does not necessarily have to go through the process of registering with the copyright office to get copyright protection.

Copyright Protection

The copyright protection actually means, copyright provides the owner of an original work sweeping rights to do as he wants with his work. Copyright also confers a number of rights, all of which can be granted to others either exclusively or non-exclusively by the owner. He can reproduce his work in any material form including the storing of it in any medium by electronic means. He can release copies of the work to the public if they are not already available, He can translate or any adaptation of the work. He can sell a copy even if such a copy has been sold on earlier occasions.

If copyright protection is applied rigidly, it can to perplex progress of the society . However, copyright laws are enacted with necessary exceptions and limitations to ensure that a balance is maintained between the interests of the creators and of the community.

Scope of protection in the copyright Act 1957

Copyright Act, 1957 protect original works literary, dramatic, musical and artistic work and cinematograph films and sound recordings from unauthorized uses. Unlike the case with patents, copyright protects the expressions and not the ideas. There is no copyright in an Idea. Copyright does not protect the idea by Whitford, J. in LB (Plastics Ltd. V. Swish Products Ltd., (1979) RPC551, 570 stated as under;

"From start to finish, copyright never stops anyone working on the same lines, upon same sort of basic idea, and copyright cannot be effective against anyone who is the produces something independently."

Not protected by copyright

Copyright does not ordinary protect titles by themselves or names, short word combinations, slogans, Short phrases, methods, plots or factual information. Copyright does not protect ideas or concepts. Only original work must be copyright protected.

- Works that have not been fixed in a tangible from of expression (for ex choreographic works that have not been noted or recorded or speeches or performances that have not been written or recorded.)
- Titles, names, short phrases and slogans, familiar symbols or designs, more variations of typographic ornamentation, lettering or coloring, mere listing of ingredients or contents.
- Ideas, procedures, methods, systems, processes, concepts, principles, discoveries or devices, explanation, description and illustration.

- Works consisting entirely of information that is common property and containing no original authorship *such as*; standard calendars, height & weight charts, tape measures and rules and lists or tables taken from public documents or other common sources.

Copyright is secured automatically when the work is created, and a work is" created" when it is fixed in a copy for the first time.

Authorship And Ownership

The author is the first owner of the copyright in a work. Copyright protects the rights of authors, i.e. creators of intellectual property.

Is translation of an original work also protected by Copyright ? Yes, All the rights of the original work apply to a translation work.

Computer Programmes are protected under copyright act, They are treated as literary works. To all the rights applicable to a literary work, owner of the copyright in a computer programme enjoys the rights to sell or give on hire, regardless of whether such a copy has been sold or given on earlier occasion.

Foreign works protected in India

Copyrights of works of the countries mentioned in the International copyright order are protected in India, as if such works are Indian works.

National countries who are members of the Berne convention for the protection of Literary and Artistic works, Universal Copyright Convention and the TRIP Agreement are protected in India through the International copyright order.

Role of Libraries in Protecting the Copyright

Almost all talented, creative, reputed and original works of literature, scientific and art will be made available in the libraries and the museums. Libraries and museums are the storehouses of creative knowledge in the form of books, encyclopedias, dictionaries, text and now in digital form. They are the guardians of this valuable knowledge. They are required to be preserved, observed, and honored the intellectual property rights i.e. copyright of the authors and creators of works otherwise it will be loss to the persons directly connected with these works like authors and to the nation as copyright consists of economics value. Copyright piracy is phenomenon prevalent worldwide. Piracy means "unauthorised reproduction, importing or distribution of whole or of a substantial part of works protected by copyright," The libraries commonly face these problems of copyright infringements. The problems are as under;

1. Copying by library users.
2. Copying for users and inter library loan.
3. Copying for internal use.
4. Copying of sound and images
5. Copying of electronic information
6. Performances to the public of a video or CD.

However, The libraries are permitted to make copies or reproduce the material for specific purpose in which cases the infringement of copyright will not arise. The Indian Copyright Act,1957 also provided certain exceptions to the infringement cases under which libraries and museums can make copies or reproduce the original copyrighted work. It has allowed making maximum of 3 copies for the use of public library and reproduction of unpublished work kept in a museum or library for the purpose of studying or research.

As per old Act 1957, duration of copyright was only 25 years. During the lifetime author can get monetary benefit for his work. In the year 1999 an amendment is made and duration of copyright is increased to 60 years. As per new amendment law copyright continues for a long time even beyond the lifetime of author.

My suggestion is that may be duration should be limited to the lifetime of the author. It is required to be put before the public at any early stage, so that is can be make useful for society. For that licence method can be used.

REFERENCES

- Britannica. Encyclopaedia Britannica. 9th ed. 6 vol., London: Adam and Charles, Black Adinburgh, 1904, 362-366.
- Britannica. The New Volumes of the Encyclopaedia Britannica . 10th ed. xxvii, 239-245.
- Drabble, Margaret. The Oxford Companion to English Literature. Oxford: Oxford University Press, 1989, 1113-1124.
- Government of India. The Copyright Act, Section 51-53 Delhi: India Government, 1998, 214-228.
- Government of India. A Hand Book of Copyright Law. New Delhi: Ministry of HRD, 1 999.
- Harvey, Paul. comp. and ed. The Oxford Companion to English Literature, Oxford: Oxford Press. 904-905.
- The Hindustan times: Google to Test Copyright Laws. NBT News Letter .21. 7 , October ,2005.
- Moorthy, A L. Information Commons: Impact on and Implications for Libraries and Information Centres.. " 52nd All India Library Conference of Indian Library Association." Srinagaar, Uttranchal, 26-27 December 2006., ILA,2006, 450-455.
- Senfransisco. A Case Infringement of Copyright on Google. Amar Ujala News Paper, Bareilly, 21 October, 2005, 2.
- Satarkar, S P. Intellectual Property Rights and Copyright. New Delhi: Ess Ess, 2003, 107-114.
- University News. 42, 43, October, 2004, 19. Association of Indian Universities.

4

Copyright Office and Copyright Board

INTRODUCTION

The Copyright Act, 1957 came into effect from January 1958. This Act has been amended five times since then, i.e., in 1983, 1984, 1992, 1994 and 1999 and 2012 with the amendment of 2012 being the most substantial. The copyright act 1957 as amended in 2012 (updated on 30th January 2015. The copyright (Amendment) Act, 2012 introduced a proviso in section 17 of the Act, clearly providing that clauses (b) and (c). The main reasons for amendments to the copyright act, 1957 include to bring the act in conformity with WCT and WPPT; to protect the music and film industry and address its concerns; to address the concerns of physically disabled and to protect the interests of the author of any work; incidental changes; to remove operational facilities and enforcement of rights. Some of the important amendments to the copyright act in 2012 are extension of copyright protection in the digital environment ssuch as penalties for circumvention of technological protection measures and rights management information and liability of internet service provider and introduction of statutory licences for cover versions and broadcasting organisations; ensuring right to receive royalties for authors, and music composers, exclusive economic and moral rights to performers, equal membership rights in copyright societies for authors and other right owners and exception of copyrights for physically disabled to access any work. Before the Act of 1957, the law of Copyrights in the country was governed by the Copyright Act of 1914. This Act was essentially the extension of the British Copyright Act, 1911 to India. Even the Copyright Act, 1957 borrowed extensively from the new Copyright Act of United Kingdom of 1956. The Copyright Act, 1957 continues with the common law traditions. Developments elsewhere have brought about certain degree of convergence in copyright regimes in the developed world. The Indian Copyright Act today is complaint with most international conventions and treaties in the field of copyrights. India is a member of the Berne Convention of 1886 (as modified at Paris in 1971), the Universal Copyright Convention of 1951 and the Agreement on Trade Related Aspects of Intellectual Property Rights (TRIPS) Agreement of 1995. Though India is not a member of the Rome Convention of 1961, the Copyright Act, 1957 is fully compliant with the Rome Convention provisions. Two new treaties, collectively termed as internet Treaties, were negotiated in 1996 under the auspices of the World Intellectual Property Organization (WIPO). These treaties are called the 'WIPO Copyrights Treaty (WCT)' and the 'WIPO Performances and Phonograms Treaty (WPP)'. These treaties were negotiated essentially to provide for protection of the rights of copyright holders, performers and producers of phonograms in the Internet and digital era. India is not a member of these treaties as yet.

Copyright Office

To administer certain provisions of the Copyright

Act, the Copyright Office has been established under the charge of the Registrar of Copyright. The rules of procedure is contained in the Copyright Rules. Copyright comes into existence as soon as a work is created and no formality is required to be completed for acquiring copyright. However, facilities exist for having the work registered in the Register of Copyrights maintained in the Copyright Office of the Department of Education. The entries made in the Registrar of Copyrights serve as prima–facie evidence in the court of law. The Copyright Office has been set up to provide registration facilities to all type of works and is headed by a Registrar of Copyrights.

The section 9 of the Copyright Act requires for establishment of an office to be called the Copyright office for the purpose of the Act. The Copyright Office is to be under the immediate control of a Registrar of copyrights to be appointed by the Central Government, who would act under the superintendence and directions of the Central Government. The Copyright Office is currently located at the following address: 4th floor, Jeevan Deep Building, Parliament Street New-Delhi- 110001.

The Copyright Office maintains a Register of Copyright containing particulars of the authors of copyright works, particulars of the works and the names and addresses of publishers and owners of copyright. The register has a separate part for each category of work as follows:

Part I: Literary works other than computer programmes, tables and compilations including computer databases, and dramatic works.

Part II: Musical works

Part III: Artistic works

Part IV: Cinematograph films

Part V: Sound recordings

Part VI: Computer programmes, tables and compilations including computer databases.

There is provision for correction and rectification of the entries in the register. The Copyright Office maintains the following indexes: namely, (i) a general Author Index; (ii) a general Title Index; (iii) an Author Index of works in each language; and (iv) a Title Index of works in each language.

Registration of Copyright is not compulsory either for acquiring copyright or for enforcing the copyright by infringement suit. See in details *for further more information in appendix I chapter II & appendix III..*

Evidential value of the register

The register of copyright will be prima facie evidence of the particulars entered therein. Copies of any entries made in the register or extracts there from certified by the Registrar of Copyright and sealed with the seal of Copyright Office will be admissible as evidence in all courts without further proof or production of the original.

Copyright Board

The Copyright Board is a body constituted under the Copyright Act for the discharge of certain judicial functions under the Act. Section 11 of the Copyright Act requires the Central Government to constitute a Copyright Board headed by a Chairman with not less than two and not more than 14 other members. Registrar of Copyrights is to be Secretary of the Copyright Board. Section 12 of the Copyright Act also lays down the powers of the Copyright Board and deems it to be a civil court for the purposes of sections 345 and 346 of the Code of Criminal procedure, 1973 and also that all the proceedings of the Board would be deemed to be judicial proceedings within the meaning of Sections 193 and 228 of the Indian Penal Code.

The Copyright Act, 1957, one of the several legislations in India in the area of Intellectual Property Rights (IPRS), is the responsibility of the Union Ministry of Human Resource Development, Department of Secondary and Higher Education. The Copyright Office was established in January 1958 to register copyright of works under different categories. Section 33 of the Copyright Act, the Central Government also registers copyright societies for doing copyright business. The Indian Copyright Act, 1957 was comprehensively amended in 1994 taking into account the technological developments. The amended act was brought into force on 10 May 1995. The Act further amended in 1999, came into force on 15 January, 2000. Under the provisions of Section 11 of the Copyright Act, 1957, the Government of India has constituted a Board to be called the Copyright Board. The Copyright Board is a quasi-Judicial body consisting of a Chairman and not less than two or more than fourteen other members. The Chairman and other members of the Board are appointed for a term of five years. The Copyright Board was reconstituted for a term of five years with effect from 22 February 2001. The Board hears cases regarding rectification of copyright registration, disputes in respect of assignment of copyright and granting licenses in works withheld from public.

The Chairman must be a person who is or has been a judge of a High Court or is qualified for appointment as a judge of a High Court. The Terms and conditions of service of the Chairman and members are prescribed under the copyright rules. The Registrar of Copyright will perform all secretarial functions of the Copyright Board under the control of the Chairman. *For further information please see the appendix II—*

The main ***functions*** of the Copyright Board are following-

(1) to decide whether a work has been published or as to the date on which the work was published for

the purpose of determining the term of copyright -s 6,

(2) to decide whether the term of copyright for any work is shorter in any other country than under the Act- s.6

(3) to settle disputes arising in respect of assignment of copyright under s. 19A,

(4) to grant compulsory licences to publish unpublished works—s.31A,

(5) to grant compulsory licences in respect of Indian works withheld from public- s. 31,

(6) to grant compulsory licences to produce and publish translation of literary and dramatic works- s.32,

(7) to grant compulsory licences to reproduce and publish certain categories of literary, scientific or artistic works for certain purposes- s. 21A,

(8) to rectify the register on the application of the Registrar of Copyright or of any person aggrieved- s. 50.

The Powers of Copyright Board

The Board has the power to:

(i) hear appeals against the orders of the Registrar of Copyright;

(ii) hear applications for rectification of entries in the Register of Copyrights;

(iii) adjudicate upon disputes on assignment of copyright;

(iv) grant compulsory licences to publish or republish works (in certain circumstances);

(v) grant compulsory licence to produce and publish a translation of a literary or dramatic work in any language after a period of seven years from the first publication of the work;

(vi) hear and decide disputes as to whether a work has been published or about the date of publication or about the term of copyright of a work in another country;

(vii) fix rates of royalties in respect of sound recordings under the conversion provision; and

(viii) fix resale share right in original copies of a painting, a sculpture or a drawing and or original manuscripts of a literary or dramatic or musical work.4

The present composition of the Board is at Appendix –v, vi, vii, viii.

The Registrar of Copyrights has the powers of a civil court Judicial Powers of the Registrar of Copyrights when trying a suit under the Code of Civil Procedure in respect of the following matter, namely,

(a) summoning and enforcing the attendance of any person and examining him on oath;

(b) requiring the discovery and production of any document;

(c) receiving evidence on affidavit;

(d) issuing commissions for the examination of witnesses or documents;

(e) requisitioning any public record or copy thereof from any court or office;

(f) any other matters which may be prescribed.

Guidelines regarding registration of a work under the Copyright Act

Chapter VI of the Copyright Rules, 1956, as amended, sets out the procedure for the registration of a work. Copies of the Act and Rules can be obtained from the Manager of Publications, Publication Branch, Civil Lines, Delhi or his authorized dealers on payment. The procedure for registration is as follows:

(a) Application for registrations to be made on Form IV

(Including Statement of Particulars and statement of Further Particulars) as prescribed in the first schedule to the Rules;

(b) Separate applications should be made for registration of each work;

(c) Each application should be accompanied by the requisite fee prescribed in the second schedule to the Rules; and

(d) The applications should be signed by the applicant or the advocate in whose favour a Vakalatnama or power of Attorney has been executed. The Power of Attorney signed by the party and accepted by the advocate should also be enclosed.

Each and every column of the Statement of Particulars and Statement of Further Particulars should be replied specifically.

Both published and unpublished works can be registered. Copyright in works published before 21st January, 1958, i.e., before the Copyright Act, 1957 came in force, can also be registered, provided the works still enjoy copyright. Three copies of published work may be sent along with the application. If the work to be registered is unpublished, a copy of the manuscript has to be sent along with the application for affixing the stamp of the Copyright Office in proof of the work having been registered. In case two copies of the manuscript are sent, one copy of the same duly stamped will be returned. While the other will be retained, as far as possible, in the Copyright Office for record and will be kept confidential. It would also be open to the applicant to send only extracts from the unpublished work instead of the whole manuscript and ask for the return of the extracts after being stamped with the seal of the Copyright Office.

When a work has been registered as unpublished and subsequently it is published, the applicant may apply for changes in particulars entered in the Register of copyright in Form V with prescribed fee.

Application for registration of copyright along with statement of particulars and instructions for filing up the statement of particulars are at Appendix-v

Enforcement in India

The Indian Copyright Act, 1957, provides penalties for the offences committed under the Copyright Act and empowers the police to take necessary action. The actual enforcement of the law is the concern of the State Governments. However, during the last few years, the Central Government has taken various steps to improve the enforcement of the Copyright Act to curb piracy. These measures include the setting up of a Copyright Enforcement Advisory Council (CEAC), which has as its members from all concerned departments and representatives of industry to regularly review the implementation of the Copyright Act including the provisions regarding anti- piracy. Some other proposal taken by the Central Government include, to convincing the State Government for:

- The setting up of Special Cells in State governments for enforcement of Copyright Laws.
- Appointment of nodal officers in the States for facilitating proper coordination between the industry organizations and enforcement agencies.
- Holding of seminars/ workshops, etc., for sensitizing the public about Copyright Laws.
- Collective Administration by Copyright Societies.

India is a member of the World Intellectual Property Organisation (WIPO), a specialized agency of the United Nations which deals with copyright and other Intellectual Property Rights (IPRS) and plays an important role in all its deliberations. The new amendment in the Government of India Rules, 1961 the work relating to coordination with WIPO has been transferred to Ministry of Commerce and Industry, Department of Industrial Policy and Promotion.

General Agreement on Trade in Services (GAT)

General Agreement on Tariffs and Trade (GATT) in 1994 gave rise to multilateral agreement on Trade under the World Trade Organization (WTO). The WTO came into existence on 1rst January 1995. The next round of negotiations in 1996 led to a comprehensive agreement on International trade in services. The objective of the agreement is the progressive liberalization of trade in services. It is to provide secure and more open market in services in a manner similar as the GATT has done for trade in goods. Education is one of the twelve services, which are to be negotiated under the General Agreement on Trade in services (GATS). Education has been divided into five categories for the purposes of negotiations: Higher Education, Secondary Education, Primary Education, adult Education and Other Education. GATS Education Services are:

- Cross-Border Supply of a service includes any type of course that is provided through distance education or the Internet, any type of testing service and educational materials which can cross national boundaries.
- Consumption abroad mainly involves availing services abroad, i.e., students going abroad and is the most common form of trade in educational services.
- Commercial Presence refers to the actual presence of foreign investors in a host country. This would include foreign universities setting up courses or entire institutions in another country and
- Presence of Natural Persons refers to the ability of people to move between countries to provide educational services.

Under Education Services the Indian revised offer was to open up the Higher Education Sector with the condition that higher Education Institutions can be permitted to charge fees to be fixed by an appropriate authority provided such fees do not lead to charging capitation fees. The provision of the Higher Education Services would also be subject to such regulations, already in place or to be prescribed by the appropriate regulatory authority.

Copyright Office's Reengineering Programe

Copyright Office's Reengineering Programme, which will be completed in FY 2006, requires additional funding authority for FY 2005. The Extensive multiyear Reengineering programme has redesigned the office's business process, developed a new information technology infrastructure, created new work- flows and developed new facilities plan. The programme will allow the Copyright Office to replace outdated information systems with technology that promotes the use of electronically transmitted applications and works.

The library requests $3.66 million, in budget authority and equal offsetting collections authority (Zero net appropriations), in order to implement the facilities portion of the reengineering programme. This funding will support relocation of staff, redesign and construction of current space, and acquisition of furniture and other equipment. In developing the FY 2005 budget request, inflationary factors for mandatory pay and price level increases were applied to both the Copyright Office's net appropriated funds and receipts funds. In reviewing this approach and upon further analysis. The library has determined that the increases needed to cover inflationary growth cannot be met by the initially requested receipt level. As a result, the library is requesting, via a budget amendment, that the FY 2005 level be reduced by the inflationary adjustment, that the $ 810.000, with a corresponding increase in net appropriations. The Register of copyrights will provide in her statement more details about the Reengineering Programme.

CONCLUSION

At the end I say that the processes in the copyright offices need to become more accessible and user friendly and therefore, the ultimate objective of all efforts to modernize. The copyright offices must be facilitate more transparency and procedural ease for the users as well as the common man. The Ministry of Commerce and Industry should aware in this regard, especially those pertaining to modernization of infrastructure, computerization, digitization, e-filing, re-engineering of procedures with information technology integration, human resource development, efficiency, transparency of producers and creation of an operational environment of global standard. The need to be sensitive to the needs of the everyday citizen is crucial; if the copyright offices have to transform themselves in service providers delivering solutions with the greatest efficiency and highest quality standards. Copyright Board must also empowered and trained.

REFERENCES

- Cornish, W R. Intellectual Property. Delhi: Universal, 2003, 293-399.
- Copyright Reenginnering Programme. "Library Herald " ed. C P Vashisth, New Delhi:
- Copyright.gov.in
- Government of India. The Copyright Act 1957. Section 9-12., Delhi: India Government, 1998, 181-183.
- Government of India. A Hand book of Copyright Law. New Delhi: Ministry of HRD, 1999.
- Government of India. Recommendations of the National Knowledge Commission. New Delhi: Academic Foundation, 2009,
- Narayan, P. Intellectual Property Law. 2nd ed. New Delhi: Eastern Law House, 1997, 316-319.
- Singh, Nishant: Media Law. New Delhi: Naman, 2003, 130-150.

5
Universal Copyright Act

INTRODUCTION

The Universal Copyright Convention (UCC), which had as a main purpose the inclusion of the United States (U.S.) in a general system of international copyright, was signed at Geneva in 1952. It was accepted by the U.S. in 1954 and came into effect the following year. The U.S. Copyright law was modified to confirm to the convention, notable by elimination of procedural steps for the establishment of U.S. Copyright in works published in other signatory countries and of the requirement that works in the English language by foreign authors be manufactured in the United States to obtain U.S. Copyright protection. The United Nations Educational, Scientific and Cultural Organization (UNESCO) played a leading part in the negotiations for the UCC, which was revised in 1971. In 1989 the U.S. became a member of the Bern Convention, which was most recently revised in 1971. Most nations subscribe to the convention and most of those who do not are parties to the UCC or member of the World Trade Organization (WTO), whose agreements cover copyright and other intellectual property rights (IPR).

History of Universal Copyright Act

The Bern Convention had been successful as the first and original international copyright convention. From its almost entirely European origin it had spread to the other continents and the Union had at the time of the Brussels Act in 1948, 39 member states. It protected both the moral and the main economic rights of authors and the level of protection had been systematically increased and strengthened with each revision conference. Its weakness, as seen after the 1939-45 war, was two fold. First, the Union had always striven for quality of rights rather than quantity of membership and it therefore lacked university. The two states which has emerged from the war as the 'super powers,' the United States and the Soviet Union, were not members, neither were many Asian and African states who were members of the United Nations. Secondly, the very fact that its level of protection was high prevented countries from joining the Union. The copyright systems not only of the United States but also of many Latin American countries differed from that of the Bern Union and 'by the late 1940s the Bern and the Pan- American systems' were fundamentally incompatible'. The Universal convention which would accepted the states of all five continents, including states of very different stages of economic and cultural development, came from newly founded cultural organization of the United Nations (UNESCO).

Aims of Universal Copyright

The main aim of the Universal Copyright are attracting all countries, particularly by the United States without forcing the Bern union members to lower their standard of protection. it also aimed at bridging the gap between two basic philosophies of copyright, The French Revolution and the concept of the Droit d'auteur' and the other Anglo- Saxon concepts of copyright originating in the statute of Queen Anne of 1709 and the American

Constitution of 1776. The aims of the United Nations and 'one of their articles of faith that if people know each other they will understand each other and that there is no better means of knowing than through reading the books of other peoples, listening to their music, viewing their motion pictures and in general becoming acquainted with what their minds have created.1

Principles of Universal Copyright

The basic principle adopted in the UCC are as under:

- Published works of nationals of any contracting state and works first published in that state shall enjoy in other contracting states, the same protection which that other state accords to works of its nationals first published in its own territory.
- Unpublished works of national of each contracting state shall enjoy in each other contracting state the same protection as that other state accords to unpublished works of its own nationals

Many countries require under their domestic law, compliance with certain formalities (e.g. registration, deposit of copies, notice etc.), for acquisition of copyright within their territory. According to act the UCC dispenses with this requirement and provides that it shall be deemed to have been satisfied if all copies of a work bear at a prominent place merely the symbol © (the letter C in circle) accompanied by name of copyright proprietor and the year of first publication (Article III) ; Indian works have thus not now to comply with, the formalities prescribed in the laws of the non- Bern Universal Copyright Convention countries and will secure copyright protection by reason on the aforesaid symbol.

The UCC also permits translation of publish writing under certain conditions (Article V). The following non-Berne countries have so far ratified the UCC:

Andorra, Argentine Republic, Cambodia, Chile, Costa Rica, Cuba, Ecuador, the German Federal Republic, Gautemala, Haiti, Ireland, Laos, Liberia, Mexico, Nicaragua, Republic of El Salvador, Republic of Honduras, Republic of San Marino, Uruguay, and the United States of America.

Indian law of copyright should enable India to give effect to the terms of Universal Copyright Convention. The Parliament has passed the Copyright Act, 1957 and it is proposed to bring the act into force and make under sections 40 and 41 thereof for the purpose before January 21, 1958. Total articles in Universal Copyrights are I-XXI.

A conference held at Geneva, September 6, 1952 in the English, French and the Spanish languages, the three texts being equally authoritative, put in a single copy which shall be annexed to the original copy of the convention. The Director General shall send certified copies to the signatory States, to the Swiss Federal Council and to the Secretary General of United Nations for registration.

The most important difference between this system adopted by two conventions in 1971 and the system of the rejected Stockholm Protocol of 1967 is that under the protocol it would have been permissible to publisher productions and translations of works in copyright without prior consultation with the right owner and without any waiting period. The waiting period and the consultation with the right owner usually the publisher whenever he can be found open for negotiations.

The members of UCC countries are which have accepted to the 1971 conventions are :

Algeria, Australia, Austria, Bahamas, Bangladesh, Barbados, Bolovia, Bosnia and Herzegovina, Brazil, Bulgaria, Cameron, China, Colombia, Costa Rica, Crotia, Cyprus, Denmark, France, Finland, Germany, Hungry,

Italy, Japan, Kenya, Mexico, USA, Poland, Peru, Russia, UK, Yugoslavia etc.

TEXT OF UNIVERSAL COPYRIGHT CONVENTION
{Geneva, 6 September, 1952.}

The Contracting States, Moved by the desire to assure in all countries copyright protection of literary, scientific and artistic works,

Convinced that a system of copyright protection appropriate to all nations of the world and expressed in a universal convention, additional to and without impairing international systems already in force, will ensure respect for the rights of the individual and encourage the development of literature, the sciences and the arts, persuaded that such a universal copyright system will facilitate a wider dissemination of works of the human mind and increase international understanding, Have agreed as follows;

ARTICLE I

Each contracting State undertakes to provide for the adequate and effective protection of the rights of the authors and other copyright proprietors in literary, scientific and artistic works, including writings, musicals, dramatic and cinematographic works and paintings, engravings and sculpture.

ARTICLE II

1. Published works of nationals of any Contracting State and works first published in that state enjoy in each other Contracting State the same protection as that other State accords to works of its nationals first published in its own territory.
2. Unpublished works of nationals each Contracting State shall enjoy in each other Contracting State the same protection as that other State accords to unpublished works of its own nationals.

3. For the purpose of this Convention any Contracting State may, by domestic legislation, assimilate to its own nationals any person domiciled in that State.

ARTICLE III

1. Any Contracting State which, under its domestic law, requires as a condition of copyright, compliance with formalities such as deposit, registration, notice, notarial certificates, payment of fees or manufacture or publication in that Contracting State, shall regard these requirements as satisfied with respect to all works protected in accordance with this Convention and first published outside its territory and the author of which is not one of its nationals, if from the time of the first publication all the copies of the work published with the authority of the author or other copyright proprietor bear the symbol © accompanied by the name of the copyright proprietor and the year of first publication placed in such manner and location as to give reasonable notice of claim of copyright.
2. The provision of paragraph I of this article shall not preclude any Contracting State from requiring formalities or other conditions for the acquisition and enjoyment of copyright in respect of works first published in its territory or works of its nationals whatever published.
3. The provisions of paragraph I of this article shall not preclude any Contracting State from providing that a person seeking judicial relief must, in bringing the action, comply with procedural requirements, such as that the complainant must appear through domestic counsel or that the complainant must deposit with the Court or an administrative office, or both, a copy of the work involved in the litigation; provided that failure to comply with such requirements shall not affect the validity of the

copyright, nor shall any such requirement be imposed upon a nationals of another Contracting State if such requirement is not imposed on national of the State in which protection is claimed.

4. In each Contracting State there shall be legal means of protecting without formalities the unpublished works of nationals of other Contracting States.

5. If a Contracting State grants protection for more than one term of copyright and the first term is for a period longer than one of the minimum period prescribed in Article IV such State shall not be required to comply with the provisions of paragraph I of this Article III in respect of the second or any subsequent term of copyright.

ARTICLE IV

1. The duration of protection of a work shall be governed, in accordance with the provisions of Article II and this Article, by the law of the Contracting State in which protection is claimed.

2. The term of protection for works protected under this Convention shall not be less than the life of the author and twenty- five years after his death.

However, any Contracting State which, on the effective date of this Convention in that State, has limited this term for certain classes of works to a period computed from the first publication of the work, shall be entitled to maintain these exceptions and to extend them to other classes of works. For all these classes the term of protection shall not be less than twenty- five years from the date of first publication.

Any Contracting State which, upon the effective date of this Convention in that State, does not compute the term of protection upon the basis of the life of the author, shall be entitled to compute the term of protection from the date of first publication of the work or from its registration prior to publication, as the case may be, provided the term of protection shall not be less than twenty- five years from the date of first publication or from its registration prior to publication, as the case may be.

If the legislation of a Contracting State grants two or more successive terms of protection, the duration of the first term shall not be less than one of the minimum period specified above.

3. The provisions of paragraph 2 of this Article shall not apply to photographic works or to works of applied art; provided, however, that the term of protection in those Contracting States which protect photographic works, or works of applied art in so far as they are protected as artistic works, shall not be less than ten years for each of said classes of works.

4. No Contracting State shall be obliged to grant protection to a work for a period longer than that fixed for the class of works to which the work in question belongs, in the case of unpublished works by the law of the Contracting State of which the author is a national, and in the case of published works by the law of Contracting State in which the work has been first published.

   For the purposes of the application of the proceeding provision, if the law of any Contracting State grants two or more successive terms of protection, the period of protection of that State shall be considered to be aggregate of those terms. However, if a specified work is not protected by such State during the second or any subsequent term for any reason, the other Contracting State shall not be obliged to protect it during the second or any subsequent term.

5. For the purposes of the application of paragraph 4 of this Article, the work of a national of a Contracting

State, first published in a non-Contracting State, shall be treated as though first published in the Contracting State of which the author is a national.

6. For the purposes of the application of paragraph 4 of this Article, in case of simultaneous publication in two or more Contracting States, the work shall be treated as though first published in the State which affords the shortest term; any work published in two or more Contracting States within thirty days of its publication shall be considered as having been published simultaneously in said Contracting States.

ARTICLE V

1. Copyright shall include the exclusive right of the author to make, publish and authorize the making and publication of translations of works protected under this convention.
2. However, any Contracting State may, by its domestic legislation,, restrict the right of translation of writings, but only subject to the following provisions:

If, after the expiration of a period of seven years from the date of the first publication of a writing, a translation of such writing has not been published in the national language or languages, as the case may be, of the Contracting State, by the owner of the right of translation or with his authorization, any national of such Contracting State may obtain a non- exclusive licence, from the competent authority thereof to translate the work and publish the work so translated in any of the national languages in which it has not been published; provided that such national, in accordance with the procedure of the State concerned, establishes either that he has requested, and been denied, authorization by the proprietor of the right to make and publish the translation, or that, after due diligence on his part, he was unable to find the owner of the right. A licence may also be granted on the same conditions if all previous editions of a translation in such language are out of print.

If the owner of the right of translation cannot be found, then the applicant for a licence shall send copies of his application to the publisher whose name appears on the work and, if the nationality of the owner of the right of translation is known, to the diplomatic or consular representative of the State of which such owner is a national, or to the organization which may have been designated by the Government of that State. The licence shall not be granted before the expiration of a period of two months from the date of the dispatch of the copies of the application.

Due provision shall be made by domestic legislation to assure to the owner of the right of translation a compensation which is just and conforms to international standards, to assure payment and transfer of fund such compensations, and to assure a correct translation of the work.

The original title and the name of the author of the work shall be printed on all copies of the published translation. The licence shall be valid only for publication of the translation in the territory of the Contracting State where it has been applied for. Copies so published may be imported and sold in another Contracting State if one of the national languages of such other State is the same language as that into which the work has been so translated, and if the domestic law in such other State makes provision for such licences and does not prohibit such importation and sale. Where the foregoing conditions do not exist, the importation and sale of such copies in a Contracting State shall be governed by its domestic law and its agreements. The licence shall not be transferred by the licensee.

The licence shall not be granted when the author has withdrawn from circulation all copies of the work.

ARTICLE VI

"Publication," as used in this Convention, means the reproduction in tangible form and the general distribution to the public of copies of a work from which it can be read or otherwise visually perceived.

ARTICLE VII

This Convention shall not apply to works or rights in works which, at the effective date of the Convention in a Contracting State where protection is claimed, are permanently in the public domain in the said Contracting State.

ARTICLE VIII

1. This Convention, which shall bear the date of September 6, 1952, shall be deposited with the director= General of the United Nations Educational, Scientific and Cultural Organisation and shall remain open for signature by all States for a period of 120 days after that date. It shall be subject to ratification or acceptance by the signatory States.
2. Any State which has not signed this Convention may accede thereto.
3. Ratification, acceptance or accession shall be effected by the deposit of an instrument to that effect with the Director- General of the United Nations Educational, Scientific and Cultural Organization.

ARTICLE IX

1. This Convention shall come into force three months after the deposit of twelve instruments of ratification, acceptance or accession, among which there shall be those of four States which are not members of the International Union for the Protection of Literary and Artistic Works,
2. Subsequently, this Convention shall come into force in respect of each State three months after that State

deposited its instrument of ratification, acceptance or accession.

ARTICLE X

1. Each State party to this Convention undertakes to adopt, in accordance with its Constitution, such measures as are necessary to ensure the application of this Convention.
2. It is understood, however, that at the time an instrument of ratification, acceptance or accession is deposited on behalf of any State, such State must be in a position under its domestic law to give effect to the terms of this Convention.

ARTICLE XI

1. An Inter- government Committee is hereby established with the following duties:
   (a) to study the problems concerning the application and operation of this Convention;
   (b) to make preparation for periodic revisions of this Convention;
   (c) to study any other problems concerning the international protection of copyright, in co-operation with the various interested international organizations, such as the United Nations Educational, Scientific and Cultural organizations, the International Union for the protection of Literary and Artistic Works and the organization of American States;
   (d) to inform the Contracting States as to its activities.
2. The Committee shall consist of the representatives of twelve Contracting States to be selected with due consideration to fair geographical representation and in conformity with the Resolution relating to this article, annexes to this Convention.

The Director– General of the United Nations Educational, Scientific and Cultural organization, the Director of the Bureau of the International Union for the Protection of Literary and artistic Works and the Secretary- General of the organization of American States, or their representatives, may attend meetings of the Committee in an advisory capacity.

ARTICLE XII

The Inter-governmental Committee shall convene a conference for revision of this Convention whenever it deems necessary or at request of at least ten Contracting States, or of a majority of the Contracting States if there are less than twenty Contracting States.

ARTICLE XIII

Any Contracting State may, at the time of deposit of it's instrument of its instrument of ratification acceptance or accession, or at any time thereafter, declare by notification addressed to the Director-General of the United Nations Educational, Scientific and Cultural Organization that this Convention shall apply to all or any of the countries or territories for the international relations of which it is responsible and this Convention shall thereupon apply to the countries and territories named in such notification after the expiration of the term of three months provided for in Article IX. In the absence of such notification, this convention shall not apply to any such country or territory.

ARTICLE XIV

1. Any Contracting State may denounce this convention in its own name or on behalf of all or any of the countries or territories as to which a notification has been given under **Article XIII.** The denunciation shall be made by notification addressed to the Director-General of the United Nations Educational, Scientific and Cultural

Organization.

2. Such denunciation shall operate only in respect of the State or of the country or territory on whose behalf it was made and shall not take effect until twelve months after the date of receipt of the notification.

ARTICLE XV

A dispute between two or more Contracting States concerning the interpretation or application of this Convention, not settled by negotiation, shall, unless the State Concerned agree on some other method of settlement, be brought before the International Court of Justice for determination by it.

ARTICLE XVI

1. This convention shall be established in English, French and Spanish. The three texts shall be signed and shall be equally authoritative.
2. Official texts of this Convention shall be established in German, Italian and Portuguese.

Any Contracting State or group of Contracting States shall be entitled to have established by the Director-General of the United Nations Educational, Scientific and Cultural Organization other texts in the language of its choice by arrangement with the Director-General. All such shall be annexed to the signed texts of this Convention.

ARTICLE XVII

1. This Convention shall not in any way affect the provisions of the Berne Convention for the Protection of Literary and Artistic works or membership in the Union created by that Convention.
2. In application of the forgoing paragraph, a Declaration has been annexed to the present article. This Declaration has been integral part of this Convention for the states Bound by the Berne

Convention on January 1, 1951, or which have or may become bound to it at a later date. The signature of this Convention by such States shall also constitute signature of the said Declaration and ratification, acceptance or accession by such States shall include the Declaration as well as the Convention.

ARTICLE XVIII

This Convention shall not abrogate multilateral or bilateral copyright Conventions or arrangements that or may be in effect exclusively between two or more American Republics. In the event of any difference either between the provisions of such existing Conventions or arrangements and the provisions of this Convention and those of any new Convention or arrangement that may be formulated between two or more American Republics after this Convention comes into force, the Convention or arrangement most recently formulated shall prevail between the parties thereto. Rights in Works acquired in any Contracting State under existing conventions or arrangements before the date this Convention comes into force in such State shall not be affected.

ARTICLE XIX

This Convention shall not abrogate multilateral or bilateral copyright Conventions or arrangements effect between two or more Contracting States. In the event of any difference between the provisions of such existing Conventions or arrangements and the provisions of this Convention shall prevail. Rights in works acquired in any Contracting State under existing Conventions and arrangements before the date on which this Convention comes into force in such State shall not be affected. Nothing in this article shall affect the provisions of Article **XVII** and **XVIII** of this Convention.

ARTICLE XX

Reservations to this Convention shall not be permitted.

ARTICLE XXI

The Director-General of the United Nations Educational, Scientific and Cultural Organization shall send duly certified copies of this Convention to the States interested, to the Swiss Federal Council and to the Secretary-General of the United Nations for registration by him.

He shall also inform all interested States of the ratifications, acceptances and accessions which have been deposited, the date on which this Convention comes into force, the notifications under Article XIII of the Convention and denunciations under Article XIV.

APPENDIX DECLARATION RELATING TO ARTICLE XVII

The States which are the members of the International Union for the Protection of Literary and Artistic Works, and which are signatories to the Universal Copyright Convention.

Desiring to reinforce their mutual relations on the basis of the said Union and to avoid any conflict, which might result from the co-existence of the Convention of Berne and the Universal Convention.

Have by common agreement, accepted the terms of the following declaration:-

(a) Works, which according to the Berne Convention, have as their country of origin a country which has withdrawn from the International Union created by the said Convention after January 1, 1951 shall not be protected by the Universal Copyright Convention in the countries of the Berne Union.

(b) The universal Copyright Convention shall not be

applicable to the relationships among countries of the Berne Union in so far as it relates to the protection of works having as their country of origin, within the meaning of the Berne Convention, a country of the International Union crated by the said Convention.

RESOLUTION CONCERNING ARTICLE XI THE INTER-GOVERNMENTAL COPYRIGHT CONFERENCE

Having considered the problems relating to the Inter-Governmental Committee provided for in Article **XI** of the Universal Copyright Convention, resolves:

1. The first members of the committee shall be representative of the following ten States, each of those States designating one representative and an alternate; Argentina, Brazil, France, Germany, India, Italy, Japan, Mexico, Spain, Switzerland, United Kingdom and United States of America.
2. The committee shall be constituted as soon as the Convention comes into force in accordance with Article **XI** of this convention.
3. The Committee shall elect its Chairman and one Vice-Chairman. It shall establish its rules of procedure having regard to the following principles:-
   (a) The normal duration of the office of the representatives shall be six years; with every one-third retiring every two years;
   (b) Before the expiration of the term of office of any members, the Committee shall decide Which states shall cease to be represented on it and which States shall cease to be represented on it and Which states shall be called upon to designate representatives; the representatives of those States which have not ratified, accepted or acceded shall be the first to retire;

(c) The different parts of the world shall be fairly represented; and expresses the wish that the United Nations Educational, Scientific and Cultural Organization provide its Secretariat.

In faith whereof the undersigned, having deposited their respective full powers, have signed this Convention.

Protocol 1 annexed to the Universal Copyright Convention concerning the application of that Convention to the works of State-Less Persons and Refugees

The States parties hereto, being also parties to the Universal Copyright Convention (hereinafter referred to as the Convention) have accepted the following provisions:-

1. Any State party hereto may, on depositing its instrument or Ratification or acceptance of or accession to the Convention, notify the Director – General of the United Nations Educational, Scientific and cultural Organization (hereinafter referred to as 'Director-General') that instrument shall not take effect for the purposes of Article **IX** of the Convention until any other State named in such notification shall have deposited its instrument.
2. The notification referred to in paragraph 1 above shall accompany to which it relates.
3. The Director-General shall inform all States signatory or which have then acceded to Conversion of any notifications received in accordance with this Protocol
4. This Protocol shall bear the same date and shall remain open for signature for the same period as the Convention
5. It shall be subjected to ratification or acceptance by the Signatory States.Any State, which has not signed this Protocol May accede thereto
6. (a) Ratification or acceptance or accession shall be

effected by deposit of an instrument to that effect with the Director- General.

(b) This Protocol shall enter into force on the date of deposit of not less than four instruments of ratification or acceptance accession. The Director-General shall inform all interested States of this date. Instruments deposited after such date shall take effect on the date of their deposit.

In faith whereof the undersigned, being duly authorized there to, have signed this Protocol.

Done at Geneva, the sixth day of September, 1952 English, French and the Spanish languages, the three texts being equally authoritative, in a single copy of which shall be annexed to the original copy of the Convention. The Director-General shall send certified copies to the Signatory States, to the Swiss Federal Council, and to the Secretary-General of United Nations for registration.

REFERENCES

- Government of India. The Copyright Act 1957. Delhi: India Government, 246-255.
- Khan M A. Principles and Perspectives of Copyrights. New Delhi: Sarup and Sons, 1996, 45-200.

6

Digital Millennium Copyright Act, 1998

INTRODUCTION

In view of the fast developing technology in the modern world the value of information has increases manifold. The exploitation of the labour of others by unlawful means is made by unscrupulous elements.

Copyright and their implementation in letter and spirit have acquired international dimensions specially in view of the expansion and leading role of publishing industry in the economic political and cultural development of the world systems. Copyright develops as the means which 'work' i.e. materials deserving copyright protection reach the public. Academic librarians face the complex issues and challenges in navigating in the maze that is the copyright landscape. Some of the issues are absolute, but others are for more subtle, particularly in a digital environment. Issues that invoke confusion and concern as to the applicability of the copyright law include e–reserves, licensing, document delivery, and fair use. The mission of academic libraries in the most simplistic language is to provide their constituents access to information anywhere and at anytime. However, how a library accomplisher (fulfill finish) the mission within the parameters of the copyright law is usually debatably and is sometimes dependent upon each university's interpretation of the law.

Due to the recent legislation and court cases, the message in some areas of copyright law is ambiguous at best. Also, United -States Copyright law does not exist in a vacuum. It is very much driven by international copyright law. The rapid advancement of technology allows for invisible borders. International partnerships are formed that even ten years ago would have been inconceivable. As the United States becomes a signatory to many international treaties, the U.S. laws must change in order to be in compliance. With the treaties and in copyright harmony with the international community. The international treaties are the world power's attempt to standardize copyright.

Copy- Right : Meaning of Copy - Right In Digital Form

Copyright means the exclusive right to do or authorize others to do certain acts. Copyright is a right given by the law to creators of literary, musical and artistic works and producers of cinematograph films and sound recordings. In fact, it is a "bundle if rights" including; interalia, rights of reproduction, communication to the public, adaptation and translation of the work. There could be slight variations in the composition of the rights depending on the work. The concept of copyright originated with the slogan "*To every cow her calf; therefore to every author his copy,*" *given by Irish King DIArmid in* 6th *century A.D. The nature of the acts varies according to the subject–matter.* Basically copyright is the right to copy or reproduce the work in which copyright subsists.

Exclusive rights in copyrighted works

Under Section 106 the exclusive rights to do and to

authorize any of the following;

- To reproduce the copyrighted work in copies or phono records,
- To prepare derivative works based upon the copyrighted work,
- To distribute copies or phone records of the copyrighted works to the public by sale or other transfer of ownership, or by rental lease or lending,
- In the case of literary, musical, dramatic and choreographic works, pantomimes and motion pictures and other audiovisual works to perform the copyrighted work publicly and
- In the case of literary, musical, dramatic and choreographic works, pantomimes and pictorial graphic, or sculptural works, including the individual images of a motion picture or other audiovisual work, to display the copyrighted work publicly.

According to the Under *section 106,* Exclusive rights in copyrighted works. The general scope of copyright is the five fundamental rights that the bill gives to copyright owners- the exclusive rights of reproduction, adaptation, publication, performance, and display—are stated generally in section 106. These exclusive rights , which comprise the so- called " bundle of rights" that is a copyright, are cumulative and may overlap in some cases. Each of the five enumerated rights may be subdivided indefinitely and as discussed below in connection with section 201, each subdivision of an exclusive right may be owned and enforced separately.

The approach of the bill is to set forth the copyright owner's exclusive rights in broad terms in section 106, and then to provide various limitations, qualifications or exemptions in the 12 sections that follow. Thus, everything in section 106 is made "Subject to sections 107 through 118" and must be read in conjunction with those provisions.

Copyright is a right given by the law to creators of literary, dramatic, musical and artistic works and producers of cinematograph film and sound recordings. In fact it is a bundle of rights including, interalia, rights of reproduction, communication to the public, adaptation and translation of the work. There could be slight variations in the composition of the rights depending on the work.

For the purposes of this act "Copyright" means the exclusive right, by virtue of, and subject to the provision of, this act;

(a) in the case of a **literary, dramatic or musical work**, to do and authorize the doing of any of the following acts, namely;

- (i) to reproduce the work in any form;
- (ii) to publish the work,
- (iii) to perform the work in public,
- (iv) to produce, reproduce, perform or publish any translation of the work,
- (v) to make any cinematograph film or a records in respect of the work,
- (vi) to communicate the work by (broadcast) or to communicate to the public by a loudspeaker or any other similar instrument the broadcast of the work;
- (vii) to makes any adaptation of the work;
- (viii) to do in relation to a translation or an adaptation of the work any of the acts specified in relation to the work in clauses (i) to (vi).

(b) In case of an **Artistic Work**, to do or authorize the doing of any of the following acts namely;

- (i) to reproduce the work in any material form,
- (ii) to publish the work,

(iii) to make any adaptation of the work any of the acts specified in relation to the work in clauses (i) to (iii),

(iv) to include in the work in any cinematograph film,

(c) In case of **cinematograph film**, to do or authorise the doing of any of the following acts namely;

(i) to make a copy of the film;

(ii) to cause the film, in so far as it consists of visual images, to be seen in public and, in so far as it consists of sounds, to be heard in public,

(iii) to make any record embodying the recording in any part of the sound track associated with the film by utilizing such sound track,

(iv) to communicate the film by (broadcast).

(d) In the case of **a record** to do or authorize the doing any of the following acts by utilizing the record, namely;

(i) to make any other record embodying the same recording;

(ii) to cause the recording embodied in the record to be heard in public;

(iii) to communicate the recording embodied in the record by (broadcast).

(2) Any reference in sub- section (1) to the doing of any act in relation to a work for a translation or an adaptation thereof shall include a reference to do the doing of that act in relation to a substantial part thereof.

Digital Millennium Copy – Right Act

The digital Millennium Copyright Act (DMCA) was passed in 1998 to address the use of copyright in a digital world. The DMCA was a direct result of what was happening in the international community. In 1996, the United States became a party to the World Intellectual

Property organization (WIPO) treaties; thus U.S. laws needed to change to reflect international copyright laws.

Digital Millennium Copyright Act (DMCA) is divided into *five Titles*;

- Title 1, the "WIPO Copyright and performances and phonograms Treaties Implementation Act of 1998", implements the WIPO treaties.
- Title II, the " Online Copyright Infringement Liability Limitation Act," creates limitations on the liability of online service providers for copyright infringement when engaging in certain types of activities.
- Title III, the "Computer Maintenance Competition Assurance Act, creates an exemption for making a copy of a computer program by activating a computer for purposes of maintenance or repair.
- Title IV, contains *six* miscellaneous provisions, relating to the functions of the Copyright Office, distance education, the exceptions in the Copyright Act for libraries and for making ephemeral recordings, "web casting" of sound recordings on the Internet , and the applicability of the collective bargaining agreement obligations in the case of transfers of rights in motion pictures.
- Title V, the Vessel Hull Design Protection Act," creates a new form of protection for the design of vessel hulls.

See for further information more details in Appendix ivth Digital Millennium Copyright Act 1998(DMCA).

There are Five major sections to the DMCA, but the most controversial is the anti- circumvention provision. This section prohibits the circumvention of protection technologies to access copyrighted works. It also prohibits the manufacturing of technological devices that would circumvent the protection. Non-profit libraries and educational institutions are exempt from this section if they gain access to the protected material in order to evaluate it for acquisition. Under this new law the Registrar of Copyright is required to conduct proceedings to review and evaluate the effect anti- circumvention provision has and to recommend to the ' Librarian of Congress' classes of works that should be exempted from the anti- circumvention provision of DMCA. The first review is currently being conduct. The anti- circumvention provision of the DMCA did not go into effect until two years after passes of the Act. The first review was structured to take place two years after the provision went into effect, beginning in 2002. Review will take place every three years hereafter.

The anti- circumvention provision has already given rise to *three* note worthy cases. The three cases have a common denominator and that is the restriction of research and academic freedom, which is in essence a direct contradiction of the intent of our forefathers who wanted to encourage creativity, not strife it.

In India the INDIAN COPY RIGHT ACT was amended to include computer programme as 'literary works'. Copyright on electronic documents can be covered by virtue of the act and recognition of electronic documents as equal to written document. In the U.S. and some other countries where a separate law such as the DMCA was enacted, but India has not enacted any special law for copyright protection on electronic documents, since many of the principles that applied to copyright in print are no longer relevant in the cyber world, the extension of copyright law to the internet often leads to complex interpretations that are creating barriers for technological development.

Now a days in India, the internet publishers are ignoring many of these copyright related objections probably lack of legal awareness, such as recently published copyright infringement in *News paper AMAR UJALA Dated 21-10-2005 that* "On Internet company *Googles, Five* world's *great publishers* have cased, they have protested on- line searching of several famous books. In the prosecution it is said that Google has infringement of copyright to the publishers. It makes available all the scanned books on its website without having the permission of authorise persons (for the comments and summary). The use of some parts of books is proper but it is not proper to make all the books available on internet. *Shroeder* the president of Association of Americans Publishers; says "that if it continue. Any man will start to prepare the digital copy of any book by visiting the library."

The web journalism today consists of resenting the print publication in the form of web documents. What a true web-Journal requires is cross linking of article across websites as the same value added service providers would like to offer. This would be possible provided law is not used to prevent such aggregation services as in the case of **www.news booster.com**.

The Copyright Act speaks little about the copyright of the news reporter or the question of news gathering or investigative reporting of reproduction and the issue of the copyright reporting. The issue of the copyright reproduction and the report of lecture delivered in public is determined and the section 52 (m) and (n) of the Act. In certain context the proprietor of the media and in certain circumstance the author becomes the owner of the copyright .

In the case of the literary, dramatic or artistic work made by the author in the course of his employment by the proprietor of a news paper, magazine or similar periodical under a contract of service or apprenticeship for the publication in a news papers, magazine or similar periodical, the said proprietor shall, in the absence of any agreement to the country, be the first owner of the copyright in the work in so far as the copyright relates to the publication of the work in any newspaper, magazine or similar periodical, or to the reproduction of the work for the purpose of its being so published but in all other respects the author shall be the first owner of the copyright in work.

The **owner of a newspapers** must fulfill certain conditions for the acquisition of copyright ;

(i) the author of the work must be employed under the news paper owner, under a contract of service,

(ii) the work must be done in the course of such employment, and

(iii) in the cases unless there is an agreements to the country, the author employee is deprived of his copy right in the work, wholly.

Copy Right / Rights Management

Copy right has been called the single most vexing barrier to digital library development. The current title based concept of copyright break down in the digital environment because the control of copied, and remotely accessible by multiple users simultaneously. The problem for libraries is that they are simply the caretakers of information they don't own the copyright of the material they hold . It is unlikely that libraries will ever be able to freely digitize and provide access to the copyright material in their collections. Instead, that will have to develop mechanisms for managing copyright, mechanisms that allow them to provide information without violating copyright, called rights management.

Intellectual Property Right : Digital Environment

Internet has simultaneously increased the promise of information and communication technologies. By dramatically reducing the cost of limitation and diffusion of illegal copies, it has tremendously increased stakes of intellectual property for entertainment and software companies, as well as for various information providers *such as* ; database producers. The main area of concern has been copyright, with an extension of copyright to software in a large number of countries and the rapidly evolving issue of implementation as new technologies enable better monitoring of diffusion on the web.

IPRS in ECMS (Electronic Copy Right Management Systems)

In the fast Developing Information storage, digital computer and web Technology and widespread use of Internet have become the state of the art libraries. Now CD-ROMs are replacing journals and books. ECMS, which protects digital works, have gained great importance. ECMS build different techniques to fit into various business models;

- The aim of an ECMS is to aid enforcing the copyrights owned by the author, publisher etc, and to protect upon the actions performed by an end user so that the appropriate royalties can be provided to the copyright owner. The design and development of an ideal ECMS should address are as under;
- Technical expression of copyrights i.e. making known the end user that the copyrights are owned by the author etc, by utilizing technological improvements.

Automatic access control, licencing, collection of revenue by way of royalty, enforcing various rights and activities with a view of prevent infringement. Technologies are being developed for protecting electronic or machine-readable copyright works. It is to be clear that the copyright control, Content Registration, Author Registration, Digital watermarking etc. are some of the methods being tried upon to implement ECMS.

- A digital copyright registration and recording system.
- A digital library system with affiliated repositories of copyrighted works.
- A transaction monitoring system to check the illegal uses of works.

Copying and Access : Ways to Infringe Intellectual Property Right

In the digital world, even the most routine access to information invariably involves making a copy. Web pages are viewed by copying them from a remote computer to the local machine. How can the conflict be resolved between the desire to provide access to works and the desire to control copying, if for digital information, access is copying?

Information in digital form has radically changed the economics and ease of reproduction. Reproduction costs are much lower for both rights holders, i.e, content owners and infringers alike. The average computer owner today can easily to do the kind and the extent of copying that would have required a significant investment and perhaps criminal intent only a few years ago.

Today some actions then can be taken casually by the average citizen-down loading, files, forwarding information found on the web has become blatant violation of intellectual property laws without knowing what is acceptable of legal.

Sonny Bono Copy Right Term Extension Act

The Sonny Bono Copyright Term Extension Act (C.T.E.A.) came in force in the year 1998. This new law has extended the term copyright & By this Act protection for corporate authors is extended from the date of its publication. It includes extension in existing works as well as new works. This act is the direct result of powerful Disney lobbyists. The copyright for Mickey Mouse was to expire and was at the stage to enter the public donation. By virtue of this Act protection to Disney is extended and public cannot use Disney's creations without financial gain for Disney. Not only on Disney but to other works also protection is provided by this Act. This Act was challenged by Eric Eldred who was working towards creating a public donation database of famous literary works. He claimed that this new Act has violated the intent of our elders by extending the term copyright beyond reasonable time. In January, 2003 decision has been given by SC confirming the legality of CTEA. It was a major success for corporations like Disney & Others. It was hold on the court that anytime period can be considered limited. Thus, this decision has balanced more in favour of copyright holder. This CTEA permits use for preservation scholarship research if work is not easily available. This Act is named after SONNY BONO who died before the Act became the law Bono was a song writer and film maker. He was having interest in advancement of copyright terms, had favored increasing them before is entry into polities as the mayor of Palm Springs, California.

Both houses of the United States Congress passed the act as public law 105-298 with a voice vote, (2)(3) making it impossible to determine who voted for or against. Present Bill Clinton signed the Sonny Bono Copyright Term Extension Act of 1998 on October 27, 1998.

In addition to Disney (whose extensive efforts inspired the nickname "The Mickey Mouse Protection act"). California congress's woman Mary Bono (Sonny Bone's widow and Congressional Successor) and the estate of composer George Gershwin supported the act. This new Act the term of the life of the author plus 70 years.

Technology, Education and Copyright Harmonization Act (TEACH)

This Act was signed by *President* ***Bush*** in November 2002. This act totally rewrites the distance education section. The purpose of this act was to attempts to equalize distance education with classroom teaching. The TEACH act was applied for classroom teaching and transmission in of digital works. In this law all displays of materials were allowed to be transmitted to distance education students. The TEACH Act allows for complete works of non- dramatic literary and musical works to be transmitted but now also permits limited and reasonable portions of the performances of all other works including audio- visuals and sound recordings. Materials which included course packs, text books and others works that are typically purchased by students for use in one or more class sessions are also prohibited from being transmitted. The purpose of this act restrictions is to protect the educational market for publishers and other content owners. The act applies to only non- profit educational institutions or a government body. Universities are required to institute copy right policies and provide informational material on copy right to faculty, relevant staff and students. There is also a provision in this law that requires a notice to students stating that their course materials may be subject of copyright protection. This act is quite complex and has many ancient areas .

COPY RIGHT LAW EXEMPTIONS

There are two major exemptions generally used by the higher education community; The Education exemption and the Fair use exemption. The exemptions are all independent of each other, so if one is not appropriate for the use of a work then there is no legal reason why the other exemption should not be utilized if applicable, **'FAIR USE'** appears still to be the exemption of choice or may be more by default in most cases. The Fair Use four -factor test is technologically neutral which makes the application of the exemption much easier for many people. This exemption also directly parallels our forefather's intent to strike a balance between the users of the work and the owners of the works.

The library exemption allow copying for various purposes such as; Inter Library Loan, Personal use, and the preservation. There are requirements that must be met in order for libraries to utilize the exemption but academic libraries usually meet the qualifications with little difficulty. Today 50 years old documents (such as Books)are copying by scanner through IIIT (Indian Institute of Information Technology).

Some of the major copyright issues facing libraries have some type of digital component. As a result of the new laws and recent court decisions, copyright compliance for libraries in the digital environment poses constant challenges.

Digital Copy Right Law And Its Revisions

According to university lawyers and scientists who follow Intellectual Property issues says that " among the biggest issues of the coming decade will be long sought revisions to the Digital Millennium Copyright Act. Critics of the law have complained over since it was passed, in 1998. That is favors the financial interests of copyright owners over the needs of librarians, classroom instructor, researchers and just about every one else."

The Association of research libraries and the American Library Association would particularly like to see congress, the U.S. copyright office or the courts loose a provision of the digital copyright law that prevents users from by passing technologies that limit access to digitized copyrighted work. The law should allow consumers to copy and distribute experts from books for research and teaching, just as traditional copyright law allows them to do with print editions of book .

Today state of the art information technologies, should also makes them consent of tomorrow's expectations in information technology sector. This becomes absolutely essential since India has become part and parcel of the global knowledge society.

DMCA & LIBRARIES

The DMCA that relate to libraries in- depth analysis of the DMCA and impact on libraries are;

Title I : New Prohibitions On Circumvention of Protection Technologies:

- Prohibits the "circumvention" of any effective "technological protection measure" (e.g., a password) used by a copyright holder to restrict access to its material,
- Prohibits the manufacture of any device primarily designed to defeat an effective "technological protection measure."
- Defers the effective date of these prohibitions for two years and 18 months, respectively.
- Requires that the Librarian of Congress issue a three year waiver from the anti-circumvention prohibition when there is evidence that the new law adversely affects "fair use" and other non- infringing uses of any class of work.
- Expressly states that many valuable activities based on the "fair use" doctrine (including reverse engineering, security testing, privacy protection and encryption research) will not constitute illegal "anti-circumvention."
- Makes no change to the "fair use" doctrine or to other information user privileges and rights.

Title II. Limitations On Online Service Provider.

- Exempts any OSP or carrier of digital information (including libraries) from copyright liability because of the content of a transmission made by a user of the provider's (e.g.; the user of a library computer system)
- Establishes a mechanism for a provider to avoid copyright infringement liability due to the storage of infringing information of an OSP'S own computer

system or the use of "information location tools" and hyperlinks, if the provider acts " expeditiously to remove or disable access to" infringing material identified in a formal notice by the computer holder.

Title IV: Digital Preservation

This section updates the current preservation provision of the copyright act(Section 108) to;

- Expressly permit authorized institutions to make up to three, digital preservation copies of an eligible copyrighted work.
- Electronically "loan" those copies to other qualifying institutions.
- Permit preservation, including by digital means, when the existing format in which the work has been stored becomes obsolete.

DIGITAL PRESERVATION : AN OVERVIEW

The term digital preservation refers to both preservation of materials that are created originally in digital form and never, exist in print or analog form (also called born-digital and electronic records) and the use of imaging and recording technologies to create digital surrogates of analog materials for access and preservation purposes. The goal of digital preservation is to maintain the ability to display, retrieve and use digital collections in the face of rapidly changing technological and organizational infrastructures and elements. Digital information is not a new one and has been explored at a variety of levels over the last three decades. Digital preservation can therefore be seen as the set of processes and activities that ensure the continued access to information and all kinds of records existing in digital formats. Digital preservation is defined as; long term, error free storage of digital information, with means for retrieval and interpretation, for the entire time span that the information is required for. Preservation involves the use of well –defined techniques to prevent the original artifact from deteriorating further and to perhaps even improve it to the point where it can be used again.

Digital preservation involves quite different methods, skills and outcomes and can complement traditional preservation services, while simultaneously providing unique and dynamic new uses of information.

Definition of digital preservation as proposed by the Research Libraries Group (RLG) as follows: For he long term maintenance of a bye stream (including metadata) sufficient to reproduce a suitable facsimile of the original document and for the continued accessibility of the document contents through time and changing technology.

Short-term preservation –Access to digital materials either for a defined period of time while use is predicted but which does not extend beyond the foreseeable future or until it becomes in accessible because of changes in technology.

Importance of Digital Preservation

The main importance of digital preservation are as under;

- The general outline of digital preservation challenges is well established. Digital materials are especially vulnerable to loss and destruction because they are stored on fragile magnetic and optical media that deteriorate rapidly and can fail suddenly from exposure to heat, humidity, air pollution. If the media are preserved digital material become unreadable, the playback devices necessary to retrieve information from the media become discarded.
- Libraries, archives and other repositories that traditionally have assumed responsibility for preserving information face technical, legal and

organizational challenges in responding to the new demands of digital preservation. Repositories need access to technical resources both information system that support D.P. and the technical expertise to use these technologies effectively.

- Institutions also face legal hindrance in fulfilling their mandates to preserve important information when copyright or licensing agreements prohibit duplication of digital information. Institutions can take action on their own, but there is a strong consensus that coordinated strategies and shared resources are essential for archiving broader solution to D.P. and enhancing the success of local efforts.
- Librarians and archivists must engage in a concerted effort to raise the profile of preservation. The commission on preservation and Access and Research Libraries Group (RLG) in the United States, the Joint Information systems Committee (JISC) in the UK and PADI Working Group and National Library in Australia, among others, have all been active framing the problems of digital preservation within their constituencies. This work needs to be supported, expanded and brought to greater public attention. As a profession, librarians and archivists need to encourage critical thinking and be highly pragmatic about the nature of the new medium and challenges of digital preservation.

The National Digital Preservation Program (NDPP) In USA

The NDPP being led by the Library of Congress is dedicated to ensuring that the digital information that conveys the history and heritage is available. The program's formal name is National Digital Information Infrastructure and preservation Program (DIIPP).The library throughout its history, has committed itself to collecting, preserving, classifying and a vast collection of materials to serve the information seeking needs of the US Congress as well as students, educators and life long readers. The mission of the Library of Congress make it uniquely qualified to lead a national digital preservation.

In December, 2000,Congress appropriated $100 million for a national digital strategy. NDIIPP seeks to convene experts throughout the nation to provide a national focus on policy, standards and technical issues as they relate to digital preservation. This effort falls within the Library's mission, which is " to make its resources available and useful to Congress and the American people and preserve a universal collection of knowledge and creativity for future generations. "The collection of the Library tell the stories of the nation; NDIIPP ensures that the collection of knowledge, regardless of its format, remains accessible for the generations to come.

Copyright Law and Digital Preservation

The information being produced are digital and digital formats are quite fragile. The media on which the information is stored becomes unreadable or the hardware and software needed to read the work becomes obsolete. The magnetic data might not be readable; drives that can read the disk are scarce and few word processing packages can understand WordStar documents.

Digital preservation starts with copying. Every time a digital file is used, it requires to be copied. When digital documents area displayed in a computer, they are copied from the storage medium into the RAM of the computer where it is them displayed. The concept of Digital Preservation and access is all about copying.

In copyright law, copying is understood as "Reproduction" and it is one of the exclusive rights of the copyright owner. The right to publicly display a work is also an exclusive right of the copyright owner as is the right to make an adaptation, known as a "derivative work." Fortunately, while there is no general exemption that can help individuals and especially libraries and archives legally preserve works for the future. In the absence of a specific exemptions, one can always consider fair use as a defense when making a copy.

The concept of "Library" was developed the purpose of preservation of recorded knowledge which ultimately helped to thrive culture and for the betterment of society. The first method is the preservation of knowledge in various forms like; clay tablets, carving on stone or a metal plate, leather was simple and durable. With invention of printing paper of Gutenberg's movable printing press provided another medium to record the knowledge in printing form, which exist longer than nearly hundred years.

Changing forms for preserving the printed media was not a serious problem. Hundred years ago when books started deteriorating efforts to find alternative forms to convert and preserve books. Microfilming was one such technology used to preserve old printed books beyond life of paper. Although, due to atmospheric threat and information retrieving difficulties search for still durable and convenient from continued. With advancement of digital technology "digitization" another technology emerged, which is being looked as an alternative method of converting and preserving the printed books. Preservation material published and displayed in electronic form exclusively also needs conversion as memory tools so into revision or their technologies are changed. Problems in reading of "8 or 5" magnetic discs and maintaining hard disc of PCs we know very well. Converting printed material to digital forms involves copying means reproduction. Converting copyrighted material is against the copyright law.

Digitization of printed books to digital books involves many technical steps including digitizing a printed page or converting it to a digital form. Digitization need to be done with certain digitization standards. It is not the purpose here to discuss the technical steps, but to look into the probable warning signals posed in the light of copyright restrictions while venturing into digitization. These days many vendors visit libraries with proposals of immediately digitization of book collection. One question be come in my mind as the librarian whether it is correct? Should we not see restriction of copyright law before we take up such copying action. If at all one wish to initiate such work should first check that out of book collection on library shelves which could be digitized freely and it will not involve oneself unnecessary in infringement of copyright law. *We can convert books to digital from provided they are in public domain or the copyright on the material has already expired. Currently IIIT, Allahabad converted books in digital form 50 years old books of Allahabad University, Allahabad by dint of scanners.*

Copyright Law poses many challenges for librarians

The mission of academic libraries is to provide their access to information any where any time. The mission of the libraries within the parameters of the copyright law is data table and sometimes.

Copyright is one of the branch intellectual property. Others are patent law and trademark, intellectual property relates to personal. A read copyright can be transferred to another person on entity. It can also become part of an estate. It can be disposed of by a will on trust. It is a valuable commodity. It has become more high in a digital world. All has to do to see the impact as proliferation of pirated works. The value of copyright was recognized during the struggle for independence by United States. Copyright law is nothing but all about balance means rights of the another with the rights of the public to use the information freely. To apply copyright a person is required to understand its concept at micro level.

The importance of copyright was recognized at the time of independent struggle of United States. The major overhaul in copyright occurred in 1976. At that time balance was in favour of copyright holder more. Authors were automatically getting copyright protection. There was no need for them to register their work. In recent years the recent developments are DMCA Sonny Bono CTEA, TEACH Act. By these developments balance is more in favour of copyright owner. Further, courts are also applying copyright in a digital environment which is also giving a significant impact in promoting copyright. Now the concept is developed as E Copyright/ Digital copyright.

DMCA was passed in year 1998. DMCA is the direct result of International happenings such as WIPO treaties. There are Five major sections to the DMCA. One of the controversial section is anti-circumvention provision. It prohibit the manufacturing of technological devices education and libraries sections are exempted from this section.

Another major provision of DMCA is the limited liability clause for on line service providers. Companies who provides on line service and educational institution which provides internet access to their servers required to be protected from infringement on someone's copyright user is responsible for infringement and subsequent liabilities.

The another important promotion in this field is TEACH Act, 2002. Distance education was one of the main object of TEACH Act. It applies to transmission of digital works.

Public Domain

The material is treated as **public domain** situations are as under ;

- The material is created for public access being a government publication.
- Published book where author do not claim its copyright for copying adopting.

- When copyright of book is expired.
- Duration of copyright period is also different from country to country. It general depends on which copyright convention the country has signed or it is defined by the local copyright law of the respective country Example: In USA it is signatory of international copyright convention and therefore the duration of copyright is taken as life of author plus 70 years. Where the Berne convention in the respective signatory countries it is life plus 50 years. In India it is life plus 60 years. In Europe Union it is life plus 70 years.

Process the Books On-Line

The libraries can convert printed book into a digital form provided copyright of the work owned by the library is expired. Library could think of digitization of a printed books if;

- the copyright holder or author has given permission to do so else obtain the permission
- there is special legal exception to libraries or archives.

Legal Exception Given to Libraries

In USA there is a special provision for libraries and archives which was introduced in 1998. As per rule libraries and archives can copy or digitize books during last 20 years of copyright term for preservation or research, reproduce, display or perform in digital form. The following provisions are found out;

- The work is not subject to commercial exploitation.
- Copy or Phone Record of work cannot be obtained at a reasonable price.
- Copyright holder has not filed a notice with copyright office on above conditions.

The provision allows as on 2004 to put certain copyrighted and out of print works published during 1923-28 to be digitizes and put online.

According to provision Carnegie Mellon University has initiated books digitization project entitled Millennium Book project (MBP). In this project includes digitization of book of which copyright has expired. In this work is carried out with the funds provided by Carnegie University at different countries in the world. At the present time one million books are putting online. So for over 50,000 books have been scanned and the work is progressing with the pace of production 5000 scanned pages per day. Internet Address; (*http://www.library/cmu.edu/librarian/MBP-FAQ.html*).

The following institutes in India that are participating in the project;

- Indian Institute of Science, Mangalore.
- Indian Institute of Information Technology.
- Anna University, Chennai.
- Mysore University.
- University of Pune.
- Goa University.
- Tirumalla Tirupati Devasthanam.
- Shanmuga Arts, Science & Technology Research Academy,Tanjore.

Digitization In Publishing and Preservation

Publishing books in multiple copies was possible with the invention of printing press in 15th century. The technology involved in publishing has developed and the modernized with time. The computer technology is the latest technology used for printing and publishing. Acid free paper is used for printing books. The life of paper books could stay on library shelves comfortably for hundred years.

With invention of the films and microfilm technology projects of microfilming of books were to become many libraries. At the same time publishing books in printed as well as in microfilm form has set a new trend of commercial publishing and promotion. Microfilm form was easy and convenient for transporting in addition to its space and cost saving features. Most of the libraries today prefer microfilm publications. Magnetic medium to seemed subsequently was never thoughts as an independent form to publish or preserve the books. There are cases of some journals such as; Current content etc. published in form of diskettes. We find floppies and diskettes to go with books as the reading aids. There are a few examples of journals, Dictionaries, Encyclopedias published in the form of videos, *such as; Wikki Encyclopedia etc.* With advancement of computer and digital technology is transferred to optical technology. Which is also known as digital or electronic form.

CD-ROM Technology was firstly used for publishing especially off line journals and databases. Some of the single and multi volumes reference tools were published and still are being published in print and CD form. CD form was well accepted because of its convenience in retrieving information as compared to handling large volumes and searching pages through indexes. The primary important aspect is that the cost of CD was never cheaper than printed original form. *Example; The cost of DDC 19th ed. in printed form is Rs.5000/= & CD cost is Rs. 19,000/=. Other examples; The Cost of DDC 22nd in printed form is Rs.22,000/ & In CD form is 26950/= ($55o/=).* The CD Technology was hardly accepted as a tool for preserving the printed books. CD forms of entire works where library can own them are not many. Full text journals or bibliographic databases on CDs subscribed in libraries are leased and not owned by them. In the progress of on line resources have almost outdated off line resource or the CD Technology. In Online resources one can get soft copy or on line form of journal along with subscription of printed hard copy. Initially, soft copy was freely provided along with hard copy subscription. Now they are available at paying of additional up to 10% of hard copy cost. There are some commercial vendors who exclusively provide journal archives of back issues independent of online subscription. Library does not create a digital archive of printed journals.

Digital Preservation In D- Space

D-Space plays a great role in preserving digital information. The characteristics are as under :

- D-Space provides long -term physical storage and management of digital items in a secure, professionally managed repository including standard operating procedures such as back up, mirroring, refreshing media.
- D- Space assigns a persistent identifier to each contributed item to ensure its incurable far into the future.
- D- Space provides a mechanism for advising content contributors of the preservation support levels they can expect for the files they submit.
- D- Space submission process allows for the description of each item using a qualified version of the Dublin Core Metadata schema. These descriptions are entered into a relational database, which is used by the search engine to retrieve items.
- D- Space open source platform is freely available through the BSD license. Institute around the world use D-Space to store their digital research materials. Material available on the *Internet* (*http://www.Dspace.org/fedaration-index.html*).

Fair Use Provision In Digital Environment

Since individuals cannot use Section 107 & 108 to

make copies, even for preservation purposes, they must turn to the Fair Use provision in US copyright law. At the heart of the fair use exemption is the assessment of the four factors.

The fair use provision offered to libraries under section 17 USC No.107. According to Section17 (107) Fair Use act should be positive **to PNAM** test. These are as under;

(i) Purpose of use **(P)**

(ii) Nature of work **(N)**

(iii) Amount of substantially **(A)**

(iv) Market impact **(M)**

It is likely that most preservation copying would meet Minow's PNAM test. As Robert Oakley has noted about preservation copying in general.

Preservation copying as socially beneficial. It is consistent with the Constitutional purposed for copyright since the preservation of printed knowledge is necessary for the progress of science and the useful arts.

If preservation is being done for non- commercial, socially beneficial reasons, it seems likely that the **PURPOSE** factor would lean towards fair use.

Generally copying is for preservation and the act therefore successfully passes the **PNAM test.**

The second test **N** (Nature) also gets through there is no restriction to copy for preservation available in different natures.

The Third test **A** (Amount) permits to copy a work entirely as it is necessary for preservations. Since the copy made for preservation will not be used for any commercial benefit.

The fourth test **M** (Market impact) will not have any market impact on the product, the act of copying also passes. Market impact of making of a preservation copy, is likely to be the most important in any fair use assessment, as is always the case with fair use. We can't really know if our use is fair until a court determines if it is fair. When considering the preservation problems of motion pictures, the Senate concluded that given the great danger of loss, "making of duplicate copies for purposes of archival preservation certainly falls within the scope of 'fair use'. It can be hoped that the courts might accept a similar argument for equally fragile digital information. Although, there is an ambiguous situation regarding copying computer programmers protected under provision of act 17 USC No. 117.

Library could create three digital copies of off-line form such as- Database, Journal or reference work subscribed off-line i.e. on CDs and one of them can be a mirror image kept in networked or on-line environment to be used in library premises by the readers if site the license is obtained. Other two copies could be used under conditional situations. *Examples;* Damaged, corrupted, lost or stolen conditions.

The on-line license agreements of journals subscribed on line. It is observed that one cannot create an archival copy of the journals subscribed and accessed on- line through Internet for present or archival purpose even if on- line access received in a package of current plus the archival of back issued of previous 5- 10 years. Library needs to take care to continue adding the archival parts which normally overlaps as the library progresses further while subscribing on-line access in order to preserve the complete archival span till it subscribes. Library could provide browsing access to on-line subscribed journals and databases by associated or affiliated members as per library rules with in the library timing.

Problems & Solutions of On-Line Journals database

There is a critical situation that expiring of copyright not any limit fixed. It is define to have commercial and non- commercial parts which library would be allowed to keep a copy for future preservation purpose for the use of readers. Electronic access to journals is presently looked totally as the commercial activity and the benefits of authors and libraries mostly get secondary treatment. There is no assurance given that readers could get continuous access till it is commercially concerned get traditional access. In the uncertain electronic environment getting continuous access to the electronic resource is doubtful case. It is the matter of concern to the authors and the libraries through which the access is provided. Librarians, publishers and authors do not have difference of opinion that assured long term access to electronic journals must be provided but in the commercial environment nobody shows any concern to it. However, there are evidences where libraries and publishers are trying to takes up mission tasks to provide solution to the problem.

In the current market environment when even owned electronic resource fails to be accessed due to equipment failure or access is affected due to hatching of web pages, through arrangement of creating mirror site.

In the face of changing commercial circumstances likes when commercial rights of some journal or entire group of journals are sold or commercially viable (out of print).

Arrangement of creating traditional archive and provide access through the libraries when commercial impact of source does not remain viz. 100+years.

Preserving the World Wide Web (WWW)

The **World Wide Web** (www) has become a more important information resource; there has been the curiosity in preserving parts of it. The Internet Archive have captured and preserved a sizeable portion of the entire WWW. Other projects have preserved the national web of Sweden, Denmark and the Nordic Countries. Many

Universities and organizations are also working towards capturing and preserving Web pages.

Information available on web pages (free) on Internet has also become important information source not only to browse through but worth to preserve for future use. Many event happen which has historical importance and information about them appearing on web pages becomes necessary for libraries to copy an preserve. Similar other information sources information available on Internet is also automatically copyrighted. Copying and web pages not owned by the library is against the copyright law. The owners put the information on Internet with a purpose of giving it wide publicity. The copyright owner has granted an implies license to allow people to downloaded web page to local machine and display it. Copyright law may not allow such action but under fair use such action it may be qualified. Although, there are no provisions to confirm this. In this context we found the solutions that Internet Archives provided commercially. Under this "Way- Back Machines" allow one to retrieve outdated web pages. Use of such Internet Archive resources like e- Bay of use of robust.txt files is yet to be widely known.

It is not clear how much protection the Internet Archive's policies really provide. In concluding, The Internet Archive largely ignores copyright law in the process of collecting its material, provides only a limited protection for the material once stored and in effect disclaims any responsibilities for what is done with the material by the end user, as well as any liability that the end user may accessing the material. It will be interesting to see if the Internet Archive's success in avoiding the judicial contest over its activities will continue for much longer.

Archiving Computer Programs

In the digital environment prepared the digital file

if we are interested in saving is a computer program, Under the Act 17 USC(117) of the United State Copyright law (USC) can help. This section states " that in spite of copyright owner's exclusive rights, it is permissible for you to make a copy for archival purposes of a copyrighted computer program. A computer program is defined in the law as a 'set of statements or instructions to be used directly or indirectly in a computer in order to bring about a certain result." The law allows to make a copy of the Word Star program and adapt it.

Run on your Windows XP or Linux machine, but not share the file with anyone else. The section only applies to the computer program itself. It does not authorize the reproduction or adaptation of documents created with Word Star when the copyright in those documents is owned by someone other than you.

Special Benefits to Libraries

Libraries making preservation copies under section 17 USC (!17).

Under this provision there are good beneficial privilege given to library and archives by the DMCA. Accordingly libraries are explicitly allowed to make up to three copies of works for preservation purpose. It further allows that the item be in preserved can be in any form such as; text, image or sound. In this case copies could also be in digital form provided they are not publicly shared in digital form out side the library. With such very good provisions libraries needs to take some precautions. These precautions are as under;

- Libraries must be open to public or provides access to non-affiliated researchers through associated library membership as per rules.
- Copying should not be for direct or indirect commercial advantage.
- Unpublished works can be copied for preservation and security.

- Libraries should not make used copies available at fair use.
- Digital copies could be made accessible digitally but within the premises of the libraries and archives.
- Library must own legal copy of original item and copies made must carry a notice copyright.

Good preservation practices have often existed in a legally gray area. Libraries generally made three copies when microfilming long before the law gave explicit permission for the practices and many radio programs have been saved only because individuals systematically taped them from the air, without the permission of the copyright owner.

In addition, there is greater interest in preserving web pages. The lack of legal certainty, although, we should not prevent individuals and libraries from undertaking the socially beneficial task of preserving digital information. The law explicitly authorizes some preservation actions especially if the materials are not made digitally available to others, and a strong fair use defense can be built outside the libraries.

The Role of Police In Compliance of Copyright

The section 64 of the Indian Copyright Act confers the power on the police to catch infringed copies of copyrighted works. The section authorizes any Police Officer, not below the rank of a sub- inspector, to seize without warrant, all copies of the work wherever found if he is satisfied that an offence under section 63 in respect of the infringement of copyright in any work has been, is being and all copies and plates so catch out before a magistrate. According to section 64 (1), the power of seizing infringing copies has been conferred on sub inspector. Many police officers may a phrase from implementing their powers because of the clause ' if he is satisfied.' Based on discussions with some of the owners of copyrighted works. Police in general to accept that infringement of copyright work has not been extended as high priority as in the case of murders, law and order problems. They blamed, that the right holders for not coming forward to either lodge a complaint formally to produce necessary document before the court. The right holders blame the police for not taking quick action and for non-cooperative behavior towards copyright violators.

At the end we found that, it is very difficult for the right holders to be present even after the complaint .Of course police personnel also find it difficult to allocate time to attend such complaints.

In general, the police department accepted that they lacked the orientation towards copyright laws. Such as; Knowledge of distinguishing infringed copies (i.e. duplicate copies from the originals, machines used for making duplicate copies etc. and more particular penalties for violators. The critical problem is in the case of computer software. There is a critical problems that the government and consulted departments are not arranged the training program for the police on the copyright act. Lack of fund is also a problem.

The respective associations should take a lead in this area since ultimately the losses due to piracy affect their members the most. There can also be some sort of revenue sharing whenever raids are conducted between the police personnel and the right holder or copyright societies. The right holders have to fully co-operate with the police departments not only the conducting raids but also appearing before the court as and when required with original documents and necessary materials.

Shortcoming of Copyright in Digital Era

The digital era in which libraries to act originally to change the word copyright. Copyright material has become to unauthorized copying and new technologies have overcome the restrictions upon the diffusion of material that existed in the copyright era. Copyright fails in the digital era because:

- Copying fails because of distributed ownership and rights. The position is often too complicated to fathom out when determining copyright status especially in relation to music where there may be lyrics, music, creator, performer, recorder etc.
- The technology, that allows digital data to be transmitted is the same technology that is used to control access to information such as; article in database.
- Copying something digital is almost without cost. Although there are associated costs such as; having a PC; access to the web; purchasing CD or DVD, there are not viewed by consumers in the same way as purchasing a pre- recorded CD.
- A concept of "fair use" allows copying the general public does not understand the difference between the "infringement" and "fair use."
- Once the term of copyright has expired, a work falls into the public domain.

Challenges contributing to the let- down of copyright in libraries

Short Comings of copyright in libraries are as under;

- Many users with some understanding of copyright laws regard is as being overly protective of publishers and choose to ignore it is a form of conscious or unconscious protest.
- Library's work is to provide very large information in the form of databases. These databases present information in a manner that appears to remove the need for and existence of copyright protection.
- Some libraries will and do circumvent the legislation. For example; the purchasing of high cost of the some DVDs for educational purposes is due to a license fee as a result of copyright. Library may circumvent

this purchasing by faculty who then lend the item to the library. It is a very critical position for a library to be working as upholder of copyright.

- To make back-up of expensive videos or DVDs without permission, so that if he original becomes damages or worm it; the copy can be placed for use in the stack.

Copyright Compliance For Libraries In The Digital Environment

Some of the major copyright issues facing libraries have some type of digital component. As a results of new laws and recent court decisions, copyright compliance for libraries in the digital environment poses constant challenges. E-reservation is a certainly a good examples of copyright. Librarians face in trying to provide the most up to date and best information to their patrons in an effective manner while trying to comply with the many obscure. provisions of the copyright law.

The major mistake to an e- reserves program is initially not the copyright law itself. In many colleges and universities there is no clear cut copyright policy and so many librarians are reluctant to undertake the risk of liability of having their university sued for copyright infringement.

Some librarians play it safe and request permission for any copyrighted work that they put on e- reserve. Others only use works that are in the public domain. The fair use exemption plays a major role in e-reserves .for some institutions. Some libraries have made the decision that all first time use is fair use and any subsequent use requires permission, while others have determined that if they own the material then the use is fair no matter how many times the work is placed on reserve. Links to full-text databases that are licensed by the library are generally considered to provide easy access and worry-free copyright. A conscious decision must be made as to which choice is the best for all parties concerned.

Licensing is an area where librarians can in essence negotiate the terms of copyright. .Licenses are contracts, which can trump copyright. In other words a license agreement can allow a copyright holder to grant to the other party some exclusive rights that the owner has, such as reproduction and distribution rights.

Document delivery issues are many times intertwined with license agreements. Libraries are bound by the terms of the agreement; however, there can be a lack of communication between staff that provide document delivery services and staff that neglected and sign the agreements. It is necessary for all parties to be aware of the content and scope of the agreement to maximized the use of the materials.

The recommendation is for librarian to become as knowledgeable as possible about copyright. The rapid pace of technological innovation constantly challenges the traditional application of the copyright law. Librarians are generally on the cutting edge of such new technology and have the opportunity and responsibility to assist in educating their campuses about the impact of copyright law on libraries, particularly in a digital environment.

REFERENCES

- Copyright Office Summary. Digital Millennium Copyright Act of 1998. United State: Pub. I. No. 105-304,112 Stat. 2860, October, 1998, 1-17.
- Cornish, W R. Intellectual Property. Delhi: Universal, 2003.
- Chandra, Ramesh, Issues of Intellectual Property Rights. Delhi: Isha Book, 2004, 113-250.
- Dave, R K Sharma, K K and OJha, D C. "Copyright Act and author Protection. " Granthalaya Vigyan "39 , 2008, 105-113.
- Donna, L Ferullo. Major Copyright Issues in Academic Libraries: Legal Implication of a Digital Environment. "Journal of Library Administration."40, 1-2, Haworth,

Haworth Press.2004. 23-38.

- Deva, Vasu, e-Crimes and Remedies." Encyclopaedia of Information Technology and e-World." 2 vols. New Delhi: Commonwealth, 2006, 18-110.
- "Executive Summary Digital Millennium Copyright Act Section 104 Report." Online,22,October,2007. *http:// www.copyright.gov/ reports/ studies/ dmca/ _executive.html*
- "Emerging Thrust Areas in Library and Information Science." Alagappa University, Tamilnadu: Karakuri, 2006.
- Government of India. A Hand Book of Copyright Law. New Delhi: Ministry of HRD, 1999. 5-20.
- Government of India. Recommendations of National Knowledge Commission. New Delhi: Academic Foundation, 2009.
- Gupta, Neha. Copyright: Infringement, Remedies and Enforcement, "National Seminar on Changing Dimensions of Copyright and Other Neighbouring Rights, October, 9-10, 2004." Bareilly.: M J P Roohilkhand University, 2004.
- Gupta, Pallavi, Management of Copyright in Digital Environment. "National Seminar on Changing Dimensions of Copyright And Other Neighbouring Rights, October, 9-10 October, 2004." Bareilly: M J P Roohilkhand University, 2004.
- Gupta, Sangita. Digital Preservation: Changes and Strategies."I L A Bulletin. XLIII-1, January- March 2007 Delhi: Indian Library Association, 2007.
- Kuffalikar, C R. Managing Information: Some IPR Indicators for Library Professionals, "B B Shukla, Indian Journal of Information, Library and Society." 18 vol, 3-4, Oridssa.
- Khan, M H and Makhdumi, Gayas. Copyright Fails in Libraries in Digital Era. "From Automation to Transformation. 6th International Caliber 2008" Feburary, 28029 and 1 March, 2008. Allahabad: Inflibnet Centre, 2008.
- Khan P A. Copyright and Judicial Attitude. "National Seminar on Changing Dimensions of Copyright and Neighbouring Rights. October, 9-10, 2004." Bareilly: M J P Roohilkhand University, 2004.
- Litman, Jessica. The Art if Making Copyright Laws: Digital Copyright. http:// www.msen.com/- litman/ digital-copyright/ch2. html.

- Lohani, Minoo, Mathpal, Neelu and Malik, S K. Impact of Information Management and Services on CSIR Research Community and Its Libraries." Convention Paper-"National Convention of CSIR Libraries and Information Centre, August, 25-27,2003." Lucknow: NBRI, 2003.
- Lutzker, p. Arnold. Primer on the Digital Millennium. Washinggton Office: ALA Pennsylvania Avenue. *arnie@lutzker.com.*
- Moorthy, AL. ed. Information Commons: Impact and Implications for Libraries and Information Centres. "52 All India Library Conference Papers. Srinagar, Uttranchal, December 26-29, 2006" Delhi: Indian Library Association, 2006.
- Phadke, D N. Digital Preservation and Digitization and Copyright. Article.
- Pane, S R Devi. University News. Association of Indian Universities. 42 vols, 27-28, 43, 2004.
- Rajendra, L and Rajendran, P selvi. Preservation Methods For Digital Library. "Indian Journal of Information, library and Society." 18, 1-2, January- June, 2005, ed: B B Shukla. Cuttack: Bharti Shukla, Nua Sahi.
- Samuel. T M and Samuel Maria. Encyclopaedia of Information Technology. 8 vols, New Delhi: Commonwealth, 2008.
- Satarkar, S P. Intellectual Property Rights and Copyright. Delhi: Ess Ess, 2003, 1-146.1-146.
- Satpathy, S K, Swain Chandrakant and Rautaray. Modernisation of Libraries: A Challenge in Digital Era. New Delhi: Mahamaya, 2008, 46-79.
- Sharma, R K. New Choices for Bibliographic Services in Wired Planet: Reflections on the National Library of India. 'Rethinking Copyright.' "Library Herald."44, 2 June 2006. Delhi: DLA.169.
- Shastri, Siddharth. Intellectual Property Rights: The Emerging Issues for Industry. Rajasthan: WISDOM, Navjeewan, 2004.
- Singh, Jnanendra Narayan. Copyright Issues in Digital Era. "Library Herald." 44 Vol. 2 June, 2006, Delhi: Delhi Library Association, 2006. 141-145.
- Suri, R K. IT Encyclopaedia . Com. "Information Technology

Laws." 4th ed.10th vols. New Delhi: Pentagon 2003, 112-348.

- Suri, R K. IT Encyclopaedia . Com "Cyber Crime" 4th Reprin.ed.,11th vol.. New Delhi: Pentagon, 2003, 219-247.
- Tiwari, Ashwani. Intellectual Property Protection in Digital Age. "Granthalaya Vigyan 36, 1-2 , 2005" Kaula, P.N. Jaipur: Jawaharnagar, 2005, 69-75.
- V, Jalaja, MCK, Veeran and Koovakkai, Dineshan. ed. Organisation, Processing and Use of Informaion in the Digital Era. New Delhi: Ess Ess, 2004. 90-150.
- Vinitha, K,. Kanthimathi, S. and Tharani, K. Digital Information Management: Preservation Issues and Strategies. "Libraries in Digital Environment: Problems and Prospects" 'Satpathy, Swain and Rauraray', New Delhi: Mahamaya, 2008, 240—248.
- Wikipedia. Encyclopaedia. Copyright Term Extension Act. 2-2-2008.*http://en.wikipedia.org/wiki/Sonny_Bono_Copyright_Term Extension_ Act*

7

International Copyright Act : Its Impact in the Field of Library and Information Science

INTRODUCTION

Almost every nation has some form of copyright protection for the authors and artists. Several important international treaties also deal with copyright law among nations. The first and perhaps the most important international treaty concerning copyright law is called the Berne Convention, first adopted in Bern (Berne), Switzerland, in 1886 and revised several times since. Most countries of the worlds are members of the Berne Convention, including the United States and Canada. Members of the Berne Convention grant copyright protection to works of authors who area citizens of any member country. The treaty also forbids members from placing conditions on copyright protection based on the observance of formalities, such as registration of the copyright or placement of the copyright notice on copies of the work. Thus although no such thing as an international copyright exists, the Berne Convention makes it easy for an author to obtain copyright protection in many nations.

In 1994 most countries of the world signed another important treaty dealing with copyright law, this agreement, called the Agreement on Trade Aspects of Intellectual Property Rights (TRIPS), clarified several aspects of copyright law and strengthened copyright protections internationally.

Some nations of the world have weak copyright laws or few resources devoted to enforce those laws. These countries often have a large market for counterfeit goods made in violation of the copyright protections of authors. Unauthorized recordings of music on compact discs, computer software, and video cassettes or DVDs of movies are often available at very low prices in these countries. This activity costs American copyright owners billions of dollars each year in lost sales and royalties. To protect these copyright owners, the United States attempts to persuade other countries to enforce copyright laws vigorously. This issue has been a source of particular tension between the United States and China. Although the Chinese government has signed agreements promising to combat copyright piracy, copyright violation continues to be a serious problem there. Certain provisions of the TRIPS agreement may help the United States persuade foreign governments to fight piracy more vigorously.

The International Copyright Acts were passed in order to give foreign authors the same sort of privilege as is accorded to English authors, on the basis of reciprocity. The principal Act is the 7 and 8 Vict.c.12, repealing an earlier Act, 1 and 2 Vict. c. 59, and amended by Vict. c 12. *See for further information in Copyright Act 1957 Chapter IXth International Copyright Act in Appendix Irst.*

The International Copyright Act is the first U.S. Congressional act that extended limited protection to foreign copyright holders from select nations. Formally known as the "International Copyright Act of 1891", but more commonly referred to as the "Chace Act" after Sen. Jonathan Chace of Rhode Island. The act (26 Stat.1106) was passed on March 3, 1891, by the 51st Congress.

The Act went into effect on July1, 1891. On July 3, 1891, the first foreign work, a play called Saints and Sinners by British author Henry Arthur Jones, was registered under the act.

The International Copyright Act of 1891 was created because many people avoid the ideas of literary piracy. In the United States of America, the only authors protected were American, the great authors such as Mark Twain, Louisa May Alcott, Edward Eggleston, and Bill Nye wrote letter to the Century requesting international copyright. These letters were written in the mid 1880s.

The American Copyright League was organized in 1883. The league was a great supporter for an International Copyright Act, and on April 28 and 29, 1885 at the Madison Square Theater the league sponsored readings by American authors in aid of the Leagues cause. Act of 1709.To protect their works they had to either gain residency, for example; Mark Twain did this so he could protect any of his other works. To protect foreign literature in the United States, British authors would have an American citizen serve as a collaborator in the publishing process and then have the book registered in Washington, D.C. under the collaborator's name.

When the International Copyright Act of 1891 was finally passed, foreign authors had to have their works in Washington, D.C." on or before the day of publication in this or any foreign country," This too would create a problem, but by the early 1900s British authors were granted American Copyright since it was published abroad thirty days from its deposit in Washington, D.C. This would then allow American publishers time to release an authorized edition. 1

International Copyright Act 1886 and Berne Convention

In 1875 a Royal Commission suggested that the present Acts should be improved and codified and strongly advised the Government to enter into a bilateral copyright agreement with America to provide reciprocal protection of British and United States authors.

After preparatory work had been carried out for the forthcoming Conference of powers (resulting in the framing of the Berne Convention for the Protection of literary and Artistic Works), the International Copyright Act of 1886 was passed.

The 1886 Act abolished the requirement to register foreign works and introduced an exclusive right to import or produce translations.

Berne Convention

According to the Encyclopeadia of Britanica, "As the result of conferences at Bern in 1885 and 1887, this system was simplified and made more general by the treaty known as "The Bern Convention," signed at Bern on 5th September 1887. The contracting parties were the British Empire, Beljium, France, Germany, Italy, Spain, Switzerland, Monaco, Norway and Japan have since joined. Austria and Hungary have a separate convention with Great Britain concluded on 24th April 1893. The notable absentees among European powers are Holland and Russia. The basis of the Bern Convention was that authors of any of the countries of the Union or the publishers of works first published in one of them, should enjoy in each of the other countries of the Union the same rights as the law of that country granted to native authors. The only conditions were that the work should comply with the necessary formalities, such as registration, in the country where it was first published, in which case it was exempt from all such formalities elsewhere; and that the protection required from any country should not exceed that given in the country of origin. The rights conferred included the sole right of making a translation of the work for Ten years from its first publication. The Convention was retrospective; that is to say, it applied to copyright works published before its coming into existence, each country being allowed to protect vested interests or copies already made by others, as it should think best.

The rights of foreign authors in Great Britain rest on legislation giving effect to the Bern Convention, namely, the International Copyright Act of 1886 (49 and 50 Vict.c.33), and an order in council made under that Act, dated 28th November 1887. These confer on the author or publisher of work of literature or art first published in one of the countries which are parties to the Convention, after compliance with the formalities necessary there, the same rights as if the work had been first published in the United Kingdom, provided that those rights are not greater than those enjoyed in the foreign country.

The rights of British authors in foreign countries rest in each country on the domestic legislation by which the particular country has given effect to its promise contained in the Bern Convention and are enforced by the courts of that country. The Bern Convention was revised in minor details not affecting its broad principles by a conference meeting in Paris and Great Britain adopted the results of their labours by an order in council dated 7th March 1898."

British copyright law was extended to works produced in British Possessions. The United Kingdom (UK) ratified the Berne Convention with effect from 5 December 1887. Britain and all European countries maintain a single copyright system. Under the Bern convention, to which virtually all European countries belong, the members accord protection to the unpublished works of the members nationals and to works first published in one of the convention countries, even though the author is not a national of a convention country. No other formality need be observed as a condition of obtaining such copyrights. Practical problems frequently have arisen because first or simultaneous publication in a convention country is not always feasible.2

History of International Copyright Act

According to **Encyclopeadia of Britanica,** "International copyright has been remodeled since 1877, by the Berne Convention; the United States, has conferred a species of international copyright on foreign authors; and considerable changes have been made in the English law of copyright."

The International Copyright Act,1886, contains provisions designed to extend the benefit of the British Copyright Acts to works first produced in the colonies, while allowing each colony to legislate separately for works first produced within its own limit. The latter permission has been adopted by several of the colonies. The desire of the Canadian printers to allow or require copyright works to be printed/ reprinted in Canada has given rise to a very difficult controversy. The colonies at present are all included in the system of International Copyright established by the Berne Convention.

In 1886, International copyright in Great Britain rested on a series of orders in council, made under the authority of the International Copyright Acts, 1844, conferring on the authors of a particular foreign country the same rights in Great Britain as British authors, on condition of their registering their work in Great Britain within a year of first publication abroad. A condition of the granting of each order was that the Sovereign should be satisfied that reciprocal protection was given in the country. As the result of conferences at Berne in 1885 and 1887, this system was simplified and made more general be the treaty known as "The Berne Convention", signed at Berne on 5th September 1887. The contracting parties were the British Empire, Belgium, France, Germany, Italy, Spain, Switzerland, Tunish and Haiti, Luxemburg, Monaco, Norway and Japan have since joined. Austria and Hungry have a separate convention with Great- Britain, concluded on 24th April, 1893. The notable among European powers are Holland and Russia. The basis of the Berne convention was that authors of any of the countries of the union, or publishers of works published in one of them, should enjoy in each of the other countries of the union the same rights as the law of that country granted to native authors.3

Commonwealth Copyright Convention

The Commonwealth owns the copyright in a diverse range materials produced under its direction and control. Generally, the commonwealth is the owner of copyright where material has been produced by its employees or has been commissioned or first published by the Commonwealth. There may be some material where copyright appears to be owned by the Commonwealth, but where ownership is shared under the terms of a contract.

1. Commonwealth copyright materials.
2. Commonwealth copyright and who is responsible for it?
3. Advice on Copyright notices for Commonwealth agencies.

Permission to use Commonwealth copyright must be obtained in all instances except for those allowed in the Copyright Act 1968. Substantial free usage is provided for under the Act, including reproduction for criticism or review, news reporting, research and private study.

The Commonwealth Copyright Administration (CCA) is responsible for the administration and protection of copyright in Commonwealth publications. Requests for reproduction of unpublished Commonwealth copyright material should be directed to the relevant author body.

Generally, an exclusive permission to use Commonwealth will not be issued because of the public's right to access government information. However, consideration is given to all requests for more extensive copyright licence arrangements, including subsidiary rights, if the request has substantial commercial benefits for the Commonwealth.

As a general principle, no fees are charged where the reproduced material is being provided free of charge to the public. Where permission is sought to use Commonwealth copyright material for advertising or commercial purposes to generate a financial return, the Commonwealth may set an appropriate payment or requires an equitable share of the revenue. Additional service fees are applicable for the commercial use of the Commonwealth added value, for example: the type setting, graphic design or electronic formatting, which provides savings in cost and time. All permissions granted are subject to full acknowledgment of the Commonwealth of Australia copyright and the source.

Requests seeking permission to reproduce Commonwealth of Australia copyright material should be on the copyright request form or a letter containing the same information.

Commonwealth Copyright and Responsibility

Commonwealth claims copyright on all material written by its employees in the course of their employment whether published or unpublished. Responsibility for copyright administration is currently divided as follow:

- The responsible author body administers copyright for print material that is not published.

- Requests to reproduce copyrights administered by the High Court of Australia should be directed to the Registrar, High Court of Australia.
- Parliamentary documents, other than legislation, are the responsibility of the Parliamentary Departments.

The Commonwealth of Australia asserts its copyright in all publications and all published material produced by Commonwealth author organizations.

Australia is a signatory of two international copyright conventions that concern published works—the Berne Convention for the protection or Literary and Artistic works and the Universal Copyright Convention.

The Berne Convention provides that a work, created by an author in a country which is party to the convention is accorded the same protection in member countries. There is no requirement for authors to complete any formalities to receive such protection. If rights are to be pursued in member state under the Universal Copyright Convention, all copies of a work published with the authority of the copyright owner are required to include the symbol © accompanied by the name of the copyright owner and year of publication. It should be in a manner and location that enables reasonable notice of the claim of copyright. The Commonwealth of Australia conforms to this requirement.

Advice on Commonwealth Copyright notices

Two standard copyright notices have been developed for use by Commonwealth agencies. Variations to these may be appropriate. *For example*, an agency may wish to encourage free copying of certain materials by educational institutions.

Power of copyright to foreign works: The Act shall apply—

(a) to works first published in any territory outside India

to which the order relates in like manner as if they were first published within India;

(b) to unpublished works, or any class thereof, the authors where the time of the making of the works, subjects, or citizens of a foreign country to which the order relates, in like manner as if the authors were citizens of India always, " that the protection has been secured by the foreign power, so named in such order in council, for the benefit of the parties interested in works first published in domains of Her Majesty similar to those comprised in such order"

International understanding and protection of neighboring rights, which are considered auxiliary to the copyright regime has developed since Rome Convention of 1961. The International Convention for protection of performers, producers of phonograms and broadcasting organization, 1961, conferred related rights are International level. This convention was adopted in 1961 under the Joint administration of UNESCO and WIPO. Copyright and neighboring rights as part of TRIPS Agreement, 1994 came into force on 1-1-1995. Indian copyright holders get rights in those countries which are members of these convention agreement treaties.

Power to restrict rights in works of foreign authors first published in India

If it is appears to the government of India that a foreign country does not give or has not undertaken to give adequate. Protection to the works of Indian authors, the government may by order published in the official gazette, direct that such of the provisions of this Act as confer copyright on works first published in India shall not apply to works, published after the date specified in the order, the authors where are subjects of such foreign country and are not domicile in India and there upon those provisions shall not apply to such works.

Copyright as provided by the Indian Copyright Act is valid only within the boarders of the country. To secure protection to Indian works in foreign countries. India has become a member of the following International convention on copyright and neighbouring rights:

1. Berne Convention for the protection of literary and artistic works;
2. Universal Copyright Convention;
3. Convention for the protection of producers of phonograms against Unauthorized Duplication of their phonograms;
4. Multilateral Convention for the Avoidance of Double Taxation of copyright royalties;
5. Trade Related Aspects of Intellectual Property Rights (TRIP) Agreement.

Copyright: Its Impact in the field of Libraries

Copyright law is an integral part of working in a library. The Copyright Act 1968 has shaped the services provided by libraries in the print environment for so many years that the conditions have become second nature to the majority of library staff. The advent of CD-ROMs and on-line services in the 1980s introduced library staff to licenses and contracts, which had the capacity to apply more limited conditions than the Copyright Act. However it has been in the 1990s, with the development of the Internet and multi-media, that the most revolutionary changes have occurred, and the "shape of copyright has changed dramatically.

The importance of these changes for libraries is illustrated by the fact that at the ALIA conference in Albury in 1992 there was one session on copyright, presented by Derek Fielding, the University Librarian at the University of Queensland. At this conference there is an entire stream with eighteen speakers drawn from various sectors, all presenting aspects of copyright and

Intellectual property and its impact on libraries. The impact on libraries in various sectors such as; Print Environment, Changes in Environment, License agreements, Digital Environment, WIPO, IP and Competition Review Committee, Copyright Amendment (Digital Agenda Bill) and Information Technology.

The most highly visibly influence on the 'shape' of copyright for libraries is the Copyright Amendment (Digital Agenda) Bill 1999.While the majority of material in digital form which libraries provide access to will be governed by license agreement the Bill will have a major impact on copyright when it comes into effect in 2001.

REFERENCES

- Britannica, Encyclopaedia of Britannica. Xth ed. xxvii vol., London: Adam and Charles Black Adinburgh, 1904, 240-245.
- Britannica, Encyclopaedia of Britannica. Ixth ed. 6 vol.. London: Adam and Charles Black Adinburgh., 1904. 363-366.
- Cornish, W R. Intellectual Property. Delhi: Universal, 2003.
- Davis Bainbridge. Intellectual Property. 5th ed. Delhi: Pearson, 2003, 253-255.
- Encyclopaedia of Americana. 7 vol, Danbury: Grolier Incorporated International, 1988.
- Government of India. The Copyright Act 1957. Section 40-43.
- Narayan, P. Intellectual Property law. Delhi: Eastern Law House, 1997, 310.
- University News. 42, 43, October, 2004, 19. Association of Indian Universities.

8

Intellectual Property Right : (Its impact in the fields of library and Information Science)

Na Chouraharyama, Na Cha Rajaharyam,
Na Bhratrabhajyam, Na Cha Bharakari,
Vyaye Krite Vardhata Eva Nityam,
Vidya Dhanam, Sarva Dhanam Pradhanam.

— **"Bhartruhari"**

"Education, Knowledge and Wisdom are invaluable for a complete intellectual and spiritual development of man The invaluable wealth or treasure of knowledge can neither be stolen by a thief nor can it be usurped by a king, nor can it be divided among brothers as a common inherited property, nor it is ever tiresome or burdensome; rather, the more it is spent or utilized, the more it increases in amount and size. Hence, Knowledge or learning is the supreme and the best of all wealth and treasures available is world."

INTRODUCTION

The 21st century is the knowledge based society and India is one of the leaders of such a society. The foundation of the knowledge based economy is intellectual property. Inaugurating India's first state of the art integrated intellectual property rights office building at Dwarka in New-Delhi, then the Union Minister of Commerce and Industry, Mr. Kamal Nath said, intellectual property, in the form of patents, design, trademarks copyright or geographical indications is becoming increasingly important not only for wealth creation but also for providing employment and improved living standard.

Intellectual property rights (IPR) are becoming more and more important as the emphasis is shifting away from a "brick and mortar" to the click economy. This is evident from the fact that while in 1982 some 62% of the corporate assets in the United States were physical assets the figure shrunk to mere 30 in 2000.

A report issued by Price Waterhouse Coopers in 1999 found that the global intellectual property licensing marked added up to more than $100 billion up from $ 50 billion in 1990. The valuation of intellectual property rights of microsoft was put at $211 billion. A Website of IP offices namely, *www.ipindia.nic.in* has been launched. This is being made dynamic to ensure availability of information about the status of an application pending with the office.

In a global market if a nation intend to stand it has to generate new ideas and to innovate in science technology China, Japan, Korea have improved I P R systems with a view to achieve innovation. Now it has become necessity for India to make efforts to improve IPR for the benefit of society.

Intellectual Property Right

Properties are of *two* types, that is *Tangible and Intangible, or Touchable and Non- touchable.* land, house, jewellery, cash etc. are some examples of the tangible property that can be seen and touched. But there is a kind of property that cannot be touched. This can be counted as Intellectual Property, which is more valuable than the tangible ones. Intellectual Property although a hidden property, is an important means of accumulating tangible wealth. IP and tangible assets are joint from the most important driving force of the world economy. New generation international corporations have invested huge amount for the wealthy of their intellectual properties.

With every property, The question of its protection and security comes. The intellectual properties have different kind of dangers. A tangible property can be stolen, while an intellectual property has the fear of being pirated. Piracy or illegal copying is the most serious concern of the IP protection because it gives to shake with a sudden jerk to the originally and reality of an intellectual product and its creators. But protection of these invisible properties is not easy as that of the tangible one. It is a delicate yet complex issue because it is directly linked with the intellectual works of a person (Individual/ Company/Group of individuals) and also because of the market value of these hidden assets. That is why there is need of a proper policy framework and on efficient mechanism for the protection of the intellectual properties and the interests of their owners. This mechanism is Intellectual Property Rights popularly known as IPR.

IPR mainly statutory rights once granted and allows the creator or owner of the product/ work to prevent others from exploiting the same commercially for a certain period of time.

These rights make the creators as the owner of the product work. IPR is not a modern concept but its root can be traced back in 15th century when invention of the printing press enabled copying of literary works in an unprecedented manner. This unlawful copying to the emergence of certain statutes to protect individual creations and inventions. That was the beginning of IPR which has now taken a global shape in the form of world Intellectual properties (WIPO) And TRIPS (Trade Related Intellectual Property Rights Agreement).

As there are several ways and means of protecting the tangible assets, similarly there are several tools to safeguard the intangible properties i.e. a book, a poem, a scientific or technological invention, industrial or agricultural creation, a broadcast, a film or anything that is created originally by human resources.

COPY RIGHT IPR LAW IN ON-LINE

The Information Technology Act, 2000 does not contain provisions relating to ECMS (Electronic Copyright Management System). Electronic Copyrights and protection of Phonogram- producers against unauthorized duplication of their Phonograms etc. The question of copyrights for software programmes have not been dealt with in the IT Act. Once the concept of 'On-Line-Copyright' is included in India IPR Legislation's, performers and makers of phonograms and software producers would be benefited from the following namely;

(i) Legal remedy against misuse of copyright, both direct and indirect in any manner.

(ii) Right of the owner of copyrights to make available to the public programmes' performance stores in electronic media, by interactive, on demand, on-line delivery methods.

There are some of the following important *IPRS laws* of India:

- Trade Marks Acts (1958 original).
- Patent Act (1970).

- Copyright Act (1957)
- Geographical indication of goods (Registration & Protection) Act (1999).
- The Design Act (2000).
- Plant variety and Farmers Rights protection Act (2001).

Trade Mark Acts (1958)

Trademark is a symbol of goodwill and an instrument of publicity and a new link between manufacturer and customer to enable the customers to distinguish products of one manufacturer from the products of other manufactures including fake manufacturers. It is a visual symbol in the form of word, a device or a label applied to the articles of manufacturer or commerce with a view to indicate to the purchasing member of public about the origin of the manufacturer of the good affixed with that mark.

In AIR 1986 Bombay 149 is referred by the plaintiff in which it has been observed that Trade Mark includes mark and mark includes name, thus Trade Mark includes "trade name" as also mark "business name" and also name under which articles goods are sold. The necessary is nexus between the mark used in relation to the goods and person claiming right to use the same.

In AIR 2002 SC page 275 is referred by the plaintiff in which it has been observed that person may sell goods or deliver his services *such as* in case of a profession under a trading name or style. With the lapse of time, such business or services associated with a person acquired a reputation or goodwill which becomes a property which is protected by the courts. A competitor initiating sale of goods or services in the same name or by initiating that name results in injury to the business of one who has the property in that name. The law does not permit anyone to carry on his business in such a way as would persuade the customer or clients in believing that the goods or services belonging to someone else are his or her associate there with. It does not matter whether the latter person does so fraudulently or otherwise.

In AIR 1986 345. Delhi It is observed that the question whether there is an infringement of a registered trademark within the meaning of S.29depends on whether the defendant's act comes within the scope of S.29 and whether the act comes within the exception mentioned in S.30. Three types of cases may arise where the defendant's use of his mark is alleged to constitute, the infringement of the plaintiff's registered trade mark under S.29 namely;

1. whether the defendant's trademark is identical with the plaintiff's trademark,
2. whether the defendant's trademark contains or consists of the whole or any essential or leading features of the plaintiff's mark combined with other matter,
3. whether the defendant's mark is deceptively similar to and is a colourable imitation of the plaintiff's mark notwithstanding hat none of the integers appearing in the defendant's mark is identical with any of them in the plaintiff's mark. Under S.29(2) if the defendant establish that the use of his mark is not likely to deceive or cause confusion, an injunction or other relief cannot be granted to the plaintiff. The only persons who can defeat the exclusive user of the plaintiff of his trademark are the persons covered by S33. In short, if there is a user prior to the date of registration then the user may continue. For the purpose of defense under S. 33 there must be substantial continues use by the defendant before the date of registration or the date or commencement of use by the registered proprietor whichever is earlier.

The trademark law in our country came in to November 25, 1959. The act now superseded by Trademark Act,1999, was governed by the Trademarks and Merchandise Marks Act, 1958 and Trade and Merchandise marks rules 1959. It is administered by Controller of Patents, Designs and Trademarks. Who is the Registrar of the Trademarks. It has head office at Bombay and branch offices at Delhi, Kolkata, Chennai and Ahmedabad.

Patent Act 1970

Patent, is a legal document granted by the government giving an inventor the exclusive right to make, use and sell an invention for a specified number of years. Patents are also available for significant improvements on previously invented items. The goal of the patent system is to encourage inventors to advance the state of technology by awarding them special rights to benefit from their inventions. Books, Movies and works of art cannot be patented, but protection is available for such items under the law of copyright. Patent law is one branch of the larger legal field known as intellectual property, which also includes trademark and copyright law.

Under the law of the European Patent Convention (EPC), patents, are only granted for inventions which are capable of industrial application, which are new and which involve an inventive step. An invention may be defined as a proposal or the practical implementation of an idea for solving a technical problem. The term of the patent is prescribed renewal fee within the prescribed period. An invention claiming process or method of manufacture of a substance intended for use such as a medicine or drug 5 years from the date of sealing of the patent or 7 years from the date of the patent whichever period is shorter; this has been amended to a uniform period 20 years. Any other invention, 14 years from the date of the patent; subsequently amended to 20 years.

In India as per the Patent Act of 1970, an application for a patent may be made by the actual inventor of the invention. It is the person who first applies for a patent who is entitled to the grant. A prior inventor of the invention who applies subsequently will not get the patent as against the first applicant. A person who has merely communicated the idea to another, who actually gave practical shape to the idea and developed the invention, cannot claim to be the first and true inventor

Patent Offices- Head Office : Kolkata and Other branches are — New –Delhi, Mumbai and Chennai.

For further information in details patent see Appendix III.

Copyright Act 1957

The Indian Copyright Act was first passed in 1957. A few amendments were made in 1983 & in 1984 with the latest developments in the field of technology, especially in the field of computers and digital environment. The new amendment Act is called The Copyright (Amendment) act, 1994. *A detail study is in Copyright Act, 1957 see Appendix I Chapter II.*

The Geographical Indications Act 2000 has also been passed by Parliament. The Second Amendment (2001) Bill to the Patent Act 1970 under consideration of the parliament.

IT Act 2000 [1] has also been passed by Parliament. It enables to enforce certain IPRs on global level and also poses certain new challenges.

Designs Act 1911

The earlier Indian Patents And Design Act, 1911, after introduction of patent Act 1970, remained confined to designs only. Accordingly, IPD Act, 1911 Act came to be known as the Designs Act, 1911 w.e.f. 20th April, 1972 and is currently in force with Designs Rules 1973 as amended. New Designs Act 1999 has been passed by

Parliament and has come in force. The law for protection of designs in our country basically started with the objective of protecting designs of textiles, linen, cotton, muslin, patterns and prints made by modeling, casting or embossment of any impression on any ornament or any impression of any ornament or any article of manufacture. A design is basically a conception or idea like two- dimensional pattern or a three dimension article (s) related to the feature of the shape, configuration, pattern, and ornament applied to an article. For being registered, it must be new or original. It should not have been published prior to the date of filing the application for registration. Design of the certain items cannot be registered. These include items *like*; stamps, labels, cards and similar other things as well as any mode of principle of construction. Similarly any trademark, brand name or logo forming part of an article or a very generic conception of an article providing several different specific appearances made within it cannot be registered under the Design Act. A combination of colors can be registered under Designs Act, 1999.

There are many different classes of goods under whom a design registration is made in India. Their details are available under the aforesaid Designs Act [3]. The design is simply for a computer software product or package, office of Registrar of Copyrights is the sole authority for its registration. Copy of a design was to be obtained from the Controller after the said period of two years when it is open to the public inspection. The new Act, however, has done away with these limitation.

In the present time different courses are available on IPR mainly geared towards latest technology trends, Strategies, IP laws, types of IPS, industrial, agricultural, literary and IT related, management of IPRS, national & international IPR issues and such other aspects.

Types of Courses

- P.G. Diploma in IPRS.
- P.G. Diploma in Patents litigation.
- P.G. Diploma in Cyber laws and IPRS.
- P.G. Diploma in Patents basics and introduction to IPR.
- Diploma in IP law.
- Diploma in IPRS (full time).
- Diploma in IPRS (Distance Learning)
- Certificate courses in IPR.

Duration of Different Courses

As per type of the courses (Ranging from One year to *two* years.

Course Fee : Ranging from Rs.5630/- to 18,000/-

Institutions : offering courses in IPR and related issues;

- Bio-Informatics Institute of India, Noida *e-mail:info@bioinformatics.org.*
- Symbiosis society's law college, Senapati Bapat Road, Pune, India.

  e- mail: info@ symlaw.ac.in
- Express Pharma Pulse, Business Publications Divisions, Indian Express News-papers,(Mumbai Ltd) Mumbai.
- Indira Gandhi National Open University.

  www.ignou.ac.in

Electronic Intellectual Property

Electronic commerce systems demands greater vigilance to ensure that parties do not violate upon existing copyrights, trademarks, patents, or other intellectual property rights. In addition to copyright and trademark litigation regarding the content of certain communications, there has been significant legal activity in the trademark area with respect to the use of Internet Domain names. Some companies have registered domain names using the trademarks or trade name of their competitors.

Electronic commerce participants should be apprised of developments in the area of computer crimes. Even inexperience users have the ability to gain access to use, destroy information records, or communications, including sensitive payment information or trade secrets. There are many issues relevant to electronic commerce which remain unsolved by formal legal systems. Because the most efficient solutions are often best implemented on a global scale, these uncertainties, if left untreated at a high level, will prevent electronic commerce from fully capitalizing on its technological efficiencies.

On a global scale, the efforts to address legal issues relevant to electronic commerce has been U.N. Model Law on electronic commerce. The model law is intended to advance the legal standing of EC by removing barriers to computer based trade. Because no jurisdiction to date has adopted the Model Law as its own law. The model law is not binding upon any party to EC. The Model Law has greatly impacted the law of EC and the actions of participants in electronic transactions.

Intellectual Property Theft In Web Services

Illegal copying and distribution of software. These copies work often as well as the originals, but may sell for little more than the cost of recording media. With illegal reproducing copyright material on the web being as easy as a matter of a few clicks, it's hardly surprising that IP theft is being threat. According to a US task force report, losses to the information industry due to IP theft each year range from US $ 15-17 billion in that country alone.

Copyright Protected In IPR Software

In India any original published or unpublished literary work automatically acquires copyright and is protected by simply recording it in any tangible form. All one needs to do is document or record the work on some tangible medium like ROM, Magnetic tap, diskette or paper to get Copyright Protection. This means that one does not necessarily have to go through the process of registering with the copyright office to get the Copyright Protection. Although it is advisable to register programmes with the authorities.

Meaning of Copyright Protection

Copyright provides the owner an original work comprehensive rights to do as he wants with his work. Copyright also confers a number of rights, all of which can be granted to others either exclusively or non-exclusively by the owner. He can reproduce his work in any material form including the storing of it in any medium by electronic means. He can release copies of the work to the public if they are not already available. He can translate or make any adaptation of the work. The owner can Hire out or hire a copy even if such a copy has been given on hire on earlier occasions

Protecting Needs of Copy – Right And Effective Implementation

The purpose of protection of copy right would be well served by a programme of education explaining why respect for copyright is beneficial for society as a whole making aware about both the privileges and limitations of copyright protection. Copyright is the focus here because it is the form of intellectual property law must routinely encountered by the general public. A better understanding of the basic principles of copyright law would lead the greater respect for this law and greater willingness to abide by it, as well as produce a more informed public better able to engage in discussion about Intellectual property.

According to **Dr. R.A. Mashelkar, Director-General, CSIR** "Emergence of India as global destination for R&D, this emergence should be consolidated with strong IPR regime to show our commitment to global economy."

India should effectively implement IPR law to become dominant to harness intellectual capital providing proper protection, the U.S. experts opined that Indian IPR laws are good but implementation is bad.

Doris Estelle Long of the John Marshal Law School in United States commented ," Indian IPR and copyright are good but their implementation is slow because there is no central agency as in U.S." We need to have special prosecutors for IPR law violations and more significantly IPR laws must be implemented strictly and effectively.

Protecting Intellectual Property Right In Digital Environment

Intellectual Property trademark and copyright protection has become hornet's nest since the commercialization of WWW. Here the issue of privacy in the digital environment is an important subject where unauthorized date sharing, data integration, unethical data utilization, and unauthorized public disclosure are the major areas of concern. The Issue is more of concern because;

- Since it is easy to capture, store, process and redistribute digital information.
- It is impossible to observe or keep a track of trademarks and copyright infractions in the digital environment.
- It is a simple to download any information value to the original creator if one has a multimedia computer and Internet account.

- Internet is a public information superhighway.

In the digital environment all over the world the owners of the copyright of the intellectual works are confronted and exploited by a variety of technological innovations. Computer programmes and data bases are also considered literary works and hence are protected by copyright even in India. The emergence of information super high way in the recent years has wider implications in the protection and dissemination of intellectual works. The main issues concern today are, security of data, fair use, appropriate long term preservation measures availability of digital publication.

Digital revolution has made the problems more acute and hence, consideration of IPR has become more crucial and timely. Internet has posed many questions and hence it has become mandatory to protect commercial interests of creators works. As the information available on internet is in public domain it is extremely important to make the digital resources as reliable as possible. Sever efforts are being made to improve the authenticity of digital data, to make the global digital environment more reliable.

The National Humanities Alliance (NHA) first released basic principles for managing intellectual property in the digital environment in 1997. The principles were developed by the NHA Committee on Libraries and intellectual property in an effort to build consensus within the educational community on uses of copyrighted works in the rapidly evolving digital and legal environments.

International Federation of Library Association (IFLA) is an international organization which exists to undertake, support and co-ordinate research and studies, and disseminate information about all aspect of library and information work world wide and to organize meeting and training in this field. A library's ability to provide access to its users will we severely restricted in order to maintain a balance between the interests of rights holders and users. IFLA has developed some principles.

Mr. Harish Suryavanshi says in the Articles University News, "That the recent years have seen the exploration of many technical mechanisms intended to protect IP in digital form. Along with attempts to develop commercial products and services based on mechanisms. In digital way E- Security involves any and all areas of protecting computers, information systems and online transaction."

In digital security considerations include protection against attack from Internet and Intranet enabling trust and privacy protection for e- transactions, controlling access to systems and performing security management. Host and Network – based intrusion detection systems to enhance the protection offered by anti-virus software, firewalls and VPNS by warning administrators of real and attempted intrusions both inside and outside the organization.

It is obvious that information is increasingly being produced in digital format. New communication technologies bring unprecedented opportunities for mass publication in less time, improves access to information. The technology has the potential to improve communication and access for all irrespective of their location and other character. If reasonable access to copy right works is not maintained in the digital environment, a further barrier will be erected which will deny access to those who cannot afford to pay.

Libraries will continue to play a critical role in ensuring access for all in the information society. Various national and International networks of library and information services are critical to the provision of access to information. Traditionally, libraries have been able to provide reasonable access to the purchased copies of copy right works held in their collections. However, if in future all access and use of information in digital format becomes subject to payment , a library's ability to provide access to its users will be severely restricted .

Information is vulnerable to copying and imitation. It is particularly more the case in the digital environment, where for the example a multimedia document production needs the work of more manpower and considerable investment but copies can be easily made and distributed.

Digital information is much more than a legal issue alone. The basic concept of publication is changed in the digital world, because the information infrastructure such as- computer networks and the world wide web (www) these factors have change the concept of ' publishing'. In the physical world, publication has three important characteristic: It is public, irrevocable and provides a fixed copy of the work. In the digital worlds, these are not applicable. For instance, powerful programmes can be written to restrict public access to digital information and old information is routinely overwritten with new. A perfect illustration is the access to database is controlled by the IP address of a work station. This distinction matter as a basic element of intellectual property policy, and knowing whether a work is published has significant legal consequences for those who distribute it.

Information and database producers float licensing provisions and technical protection services to manage access to information. Licensing is commonly used to provide access to some types of digital information such as databases and research journals, reports and more recently to even e- books. Licenses are in strict sense contracts and we would not expect the inclusion of the common element, "fair use." If these types of licenses come into widespread use for content distribution, there is the potential for contract law to become a widespread substitute for copy right law. That would imply a change in the balance of private ownership and public access associated with copy right.

Digital information becomes a common means to users and hence the concession Copyright Laws may not hold true which necessitate to understand the basic principles of modern Copy Right Laws. "Fair Use" is an established content in many Copy Right Laws that have come under question with the proliferation of digital information. Particular concern is the extent to which copying for private use can be justified without violating the law. Legal, economic and public – policy research are being undertaken to help determine the extent to which fair use and other exceptions and limitations to copy right should apply in the digital environment.

IPR's Criminal Jurisprudence : Changing Scenario

The different crimes adopted by the criminals in any branch of criminal law have not left the field of IPRs untouched. Cracking of websites, hacking of Internet, demolishing of security, use of common trade names as domain names without permission from the owners of the same is done regularly and unscrupulously by highly trained professionals in order to make wrongful economic gains at the expense of IPR of the others. *For further information in details ' The role of judiciary in the effective Protection of Intellectual Property Right See Appendix ixth.*

Cyber Crimes and IPR

The problem of infringement of IPR was not very acute because there was no photocopiers, no computers, no internet. Now the canvas has changed; the milieu is different.

WIPO in digital environment

The Berne Convention permits members of the Berne Union to grant exceptions in certain special cases that do not conflict with a normal exploitation of the work and do not unreasonably prejudice the proper interests of the author.

In 1996, the members of the World Intellectual Property Organisation adopted two treaties to update copyright law for digital environment. In confirming that exceptions and limitations can be carried forward and extended in the digital environment, WIPO countries rejected the claim that " digital is different," contracting parties are allowed to carry forward and extend such limitations in the digital environment.

In national copy right legislation, exceptions to copyright and related rights, allowed in the Berne Convention and endorsed by the WIPO treatise should be revised if necessary to ensure that permitted uses apply equally to information In electronic form and to information in print.

For copying over and above in these provisions there should be administratively simple payment scheme. IFLA has advocated many presentations, but they are not considered while framing IPR laws.

In brief the Intellectual Property Act exists between two sets of rights: The right of those who produce intellectual property to profit from their work and the right of the public to a free flow of information. In the print worlds, the balance has been established and adjusted again over hundreds of years. However, the digital world faces unexpected issue from different spectrum and there is an uncertainty what constitutes and what comes under the purview of IPR. There are quite few cases in the digital environment in the last few years. For example, 2001 was the year that copyright law got exciting. One of the major sources of the excitement was Digital Millennium Copyright Act and in particular, section 1201 of the US copyright act, the "anti-circumvention" provision of the act.

The IPR act provisions and components are undergoing radical changes and no one can able to predict what improvements we would have in the near_future.

WORLD INTELLECTUAL PROPERTY ORGANIZATION) (WIPO) IN THE TERM OF 'IT'

World Intellectual Property Organization (WIPO), Specialized agency of the United Nations (UN) dealing with the protection of Intellectual property. WIPO was founded in 1967 to take over the work of the united International Bureaux for the protection of Intellectual property, an independent body set up in 1893 to administer international agreements in the field, and began operation in 1970. In 1974 WIPO was incorporated within the UN: by 2001 it had 175 member states. The organization acts to protect intellectual; property and copyright in all fields: artistic, commercial, and scientific attempts to harmonize global protection in such areas; it deals with patents, trademarks and other means of legal regulation and registration. WIPO administers the Paris convention of 1883, the Berne Convention of 1886 and other conventions on intellectual property including 2 drawn up under its own observation for 1996, making a total of 21 treaties and agreements. WIPO organized a conference in December , 1996, inviting around 160 member countries, the agenda being modification of the existing norms and creation of new norms on Intellectual Property Rights, so as to coupe with the new developments.

WIPO is governed by a General Assembly of all its members, a conference and a co-ordination committee. The Director - general of WIPO is elected by the General

Assembly. There are also governing bodies to administer each treaty and convention controlled by WIPO, as well as permanent committees dealing with particular areas of responsibility, Finances for WIPO are chiefly derived from registration and publication activities. WIPO'S headquarters are in Geneva, Switzerland.

WIPO's Activities

WIPO's Activities are;

In promoting the protection of IP is the progressive development and application of in international norms and standards.

The Organization currently administers Eleven treaties that set out internationally agreed rights and common standards for their protection, that the States which sign them agree to apply within their own territories. There are two examples of treaties; WIPO Copyright Treaty (WCT) 1996, and the WIPO Performance and Phonograms Treaty (WPPT). These treaties contain basic rules updating the international protection of copyright and related rights to the internet age.

Today WIPO also initiated a new policy to adapt to rapid changes in the field of industrial property, in the fast growing Technological information and development of internationally harmonized principles and rules. The adoption of international recommendations on the protection of well- known marks in 1999 and on trademark licenses in the year 2000 complements the traditional and lengthier treaty- based approach to international legal standard setting.

WIPO's Services

Some of the major services provided by WIPO are;

- Patent Cooperation Treaty.
- Impact Project.
- Madrid and Huge Systems.
- Classification of Industrial Property.
- Training and Education.
- WIPONET

WIPONET

WIPONET is the World Intellectual Property Right Organization Network. It is Worldwide network. This network will help in the process of generation, valuation and protection of intellectual property. WIPO has taken a decision to create a world wide network. The decision was taken in its budget meeting on 21 January, 1998.

The WIPONET is a global information network. It is the first step enhancing communication between WIPO and the IP community. It will interconnect 332 IP offices in 171 countries.

WIPONET Provide Services are;

Email, List services, Web hosting, File transfer services (FTS), Virus scanning and the provision of updated signatures and use administration. It also provides portal like Intellectual property digital libraries (IPDL) and on line filing under the patent cooperation treaty.

The WIPONET project will be completed in two phases. First phase will be centered on setting up the project's infrastructure at the WIPO International Bureau in GENEVA, establishing basic connectivity for those member states with no internet facility and providing basic services to the whole IP community. 64 countries will be connected in this phase and others countries will be covered under second phase. A Web site is established on Internet, which provides all information on WIPO. Website Address is *www.WIPO.org*

It provides world wide academic information distance education through Internet. WIPONET will provide help desk in SIX language which will be for 24 hours without any break.

INTELLECTUAL PROPERTY RIGHTS IN "E" ENVIRONMENT

According to National Knowledge Commission's Report, 1996: (NKC) "For India to become a global knowledge leader, we would need to be at the forefront of creating knowledge. This requires a favourable eco-system that not only protects the ingenuity of the creator but also rewards knowledge creation through commercial applications. In order to facilitate the creation of knowledge NKC has recommended scaling up efforts to build a world class IPR infrastructure. Including steps to modernize the patent offices with computerization, e-filing, process re-engineering, human resource development, transparency, documentation, accessibility and building global standard s. IPR training in IP Offices as well as in educational institutions needs to be intensified, and IPR Cells should be developed. In addition NKC has recommended establishing new structures such as a separate IPR Tribunal, a national institution for cutting edge IPR policy and Global Technology Acquisition Fund. NKC recommendations also highlight the need to protect traditional knowledge, create incentives for it and also explore mechanisms for identification of key IPR issues in new technology areas."

National Knowledge Commission's Recommend in his Reports , 1997 that, "A nation's future and its ability to compete in the global market depend greatly on how it generates new ideas and innovates in science and technology. I P creation and protection are critical issues in global knowledge bases competition. Countries like China, Japan and Korea have improved their respective IPR systems through intense capacity building efforts, with a view to achieving greater innovation. It has become imperative for India to scale up efforts to build a world class IPR infrastructure and ensure that IPR is used in the best national interest or more extensive innovative research, technology transfer, wealth creation and overall benefit of society. NKC's consultations with various stakeholders have help IPR to identify some key areas that will facilitate such system reform. Some of these areas involve the granting of product and process patents, in which both the configuration and the systematization of a substantive perspective of patent examination keeping both treaty obligations and national interests in mind are crucial issues. Other critical areas involve alternative non-patent modalities for the creation and sharing of knowledge and inventions. Below, one area, namely, the configuration of the patent examination mechanisms, is discussed, with some reference to allied issues in patent utilization."

1. Modernization of IP Offices

1.1. The process in the IP offices need to become more accessible and user friendly and therefore, the ultimate objective of all efforts to modernize the patent offices must be to facilitate more transparency and procedural case for the inventor as well as the common man. NKC is aware of the initiatives proposed be the Ministry of Commerce and Industry in this regard, especially those pertaining to modernization of infrastructure, computerization, digitization, e-filing, re-engineering of procedures with information technology integration, human resource development, efficiency, transparency of procedures and recreation of an operational environment of global standards. The need to be sensitive to the needs of the everyday citizen is crucial if the IP offices have to transform themselves into service providers delivering solutions with the greatest efficiency and highest quality standards. In this respect, some suggestions are as follows:

a. The patents offices must be adequately e-enabled in real time with adequate search facilities so that all its transactions are transparent and publicly accessible.

b. The examination procedures, practices and decisions in the IP offices should be streamlined and consistent.

c. A new detailed and clear manual of the examination procedure and practice, accompanied by full text versions of all the relevant IP laws of the country, should be created, periodically updated and made available to the public, in soft and hard copy. Interested stakeholders, particularly including a civil society as the major stakeholder, must be involved in its preparation. This is particularly important since new Indian Patent examination procedures will need to be devised keeping both treaty obligations and national interests in mind, and creation of an adversarial process of patent examination will be crucial in these procedures

d. There must be an educational section for public awareness on IP (including the current status of IP law on various topics) made available in the public domain in all official languages; of the country

e. The patent granting procedure must involve adequate web based notification of an application with complete details to give sufficient opportunity for any pre- grant objections to be filed. It is particularly essential to provide e- access in real time to all steps of a patent application, from the detailed patent description, examination reports at each stage and all amendments introduced at various points, in order to maintain complete transparency.

f. There is urgent need to develop a comprehensive patent database that provides the latest information on patents, including patent applications and decisions of patent offices. At the same time, the patent offices must have access to relevant international databases and search engines, including databases with prior art literature.

g. To achieve the best global standards in quality and access, the IP offices should aim to become International Search Authority (ISA) and International Preliminary Examination Authority (IPEA) under the PCT and to this end, aim to conform to the PCT standards in respect of possession or access to minimum documentation, number of administrative and technically qualified staff and IT support systems.

h. Efforts should also be made to develop quantifiable indices for measuring, monitoring and managing quality and efficiency.

i. To ensure that the services of the IP offices reach the common people engaged in rural technologies, artisanry, crafts and traditional knowledge, there should be special schemes and establishments in the patent offices to deal with claims involving the creation and protection of traditional knowledge in its various forms. Since ensuring effective and competent legal representation is a critical problem for such groups, mechanisms should be evolved that incentive such representation by the best patent lawyers in the country.

j. For each sector of highly technical patents, it may be necessary to constitute specific empowered committees of experts as part of the patent evaluation process in the patent office to decide on the suitability of granting a patent, in accordance with the provisions of the law. These committees must adhere to strict time bound procedures of examination and sufficient safeguards must also be maintained to ensure confidentiality and prevent any subversion of the process.

Internet: and Intellectual Property Rights

The Intellectual Property regime fails when it comes to deal computer software on the Internet. There is a very regime that protects computer software -line but this existing regime fails when faced with the problems that the Internet throws up. A New system of law that would govern Intellectual Property on the Internet. The Information Technology Act, 2000 has made significant amendments such as the Indian Penal Code, the Indian Evidence Act and the Code of Criminal Procedure. However, the existing principles of Copyright may be applied to the Internet through an analogy could be made to the Indian Copyright Act, 1957.

Under Section 2(ff) defines what is meant by communication to the public, to be amended to include an explanation to take account of the Internet.

Under section 2(ffc) defines what is meant by computer software to include web pages also.

Under Section 2(hh) define the term duplicating equipment to include floppy drives, electronic copying on the Internet to increase the fine and enforcement mechanism to take into account the Internet.

Internet Crime

We never will be a hundred percent safe on the Internet. That is more to do with what human being than the technology of the Internet. That is possibly why the lines between e- crimes and real world crimes are blurring very rapidly. Any person who uses the Internet is attacking their computer network. Most people want to damage computer's Hard drive and destroy our data, Steal our ID (Identity), use other people's credit card etc. Computer network break-Such as using software tools installed on a computer in a remote location, hackers can break into computer systems to modify or steal data, plant viruses, and change & use the password.

Illegal copying and distribution of software. These copies work often as well as the originals, but may sell for little more than the cost of recording media.

Infringement of IP in Electronic Commerce

Electronic commerce systems demands greater vigilance to ensure that parties do not violate or infringe upon existing copyrights or other intellectual property rights. In addition to copyright and trademarks litigation regarding the content of certain communications, there has been significant legal activity in the copyright/ trademark area with respect to the use of Internet domain names. Some companies have registered domain names using the trade name of their competitors.

In the digital technology the *Keefe* (2002) has rightly opined that, many contemporary right holders view Internet as their enemy. He further quotes 'After copyrighted music and movies move to the internet, it is almost impossible to stop the material from being used over and over again despite copyright laws. Scanners which are largely being used to store and transmit information cannot determine whether a particular sheet of paper contains copyright protected works. The same holds good for sound and video recordings, as analog sources provide no unambiguous clues about possible infringement. One can easily argue, that once the information is available on the net, it is meant for free access, and digital copy suffice for world wide distribution.

Michael Seadle (2004) clearly said, that 'No government agency has a responsibility to check for potential copy right infringements, and taken legal action against them.'

Foster 2003 has quoted the example of the Recording Industry Association of America which files 261 law suits alleging copyright violation. This is turn and, those under taken by universities have brought awareness among university students and faculty which in turn has reduce the illegal downloads. Pew Internet and American Life Project come Score Media Metrix have also revealed that, the illegal downloading have reduced to a considerable extent.

Although, such kinds of reports are not readily accessible. In the Indian context stray cases have been positively reported by ' *Pravin Kumar Chaudhary* et. Al.' (2004).

Case I : deals with the Indian Performing Rights Society vs. Eastern India Motion Pictures Association, (AIR 1977 SC 1443')

Case II : Najma Heptulla vs. MLS Orient Longman Ltd.AIR 1989 DEL. 63;

Case III : Associated Electronic and Electrical Industries MLS Sharp Tools (AIR 1991 KANT 406). Apart from the above, case of 'plagiarism' has also been reported time and again in the news papers and news tracks, prominent being, the involvement of a former VC of a renowned university along with his students.

IPR Issues For Librarians and Libraries

Internet as one of the biggest copying machine and demand the measurement of each drop of knowledge being put in 'Cyberspace.' The issues are of extreme concern to all the libraries specially the professional Information Centres They are mainly because;

Digital data is easy to capture, store, process download.

It is just impossible to keep a track of the copyright infringement in the digital environment, because of the facilities like Structuring, restructuring, mixing and remixing of information with the sound wave etc.

In the present Internet environment where, more and more universities and colleges are computerizing their operations and services, It is time to ponder over questions as:

Is the website copyrightable in terms of content, the source code, layout etc.

Is linking and downloading from website legal/ illegal?

Viability of new invention, ID and password etc.

Librarians and Informational professionals have their responsibility the serving of the information places in their custody as true to its original intellectual content as they can Librarians have the responsibility to see that author's works are preserved. And organized for use, not only by our generation but also be succeeding generations of scholars and students.

Librarians have been trying to find out the solutions to protect the intellectual property rights (IPR) and the solutions to protect the IPR and the fix a text or documents in some way so that user can be sure of the original text when it is needed. This solution is called "authentication" which is used in verifying the resources. There are various important techniques proposed for authentication, *such as;* digital signature, digital certificates, digital watermarking etc.

CONCLUSION

To improve intellectual property rights, creators incentives are required to be recognized so that creators can feel that their works can be disseminated without fear of copyright or piracy. There is need of study of laws and management relating to printing and other at different levels. Intellectual Property Rights in digital environment has very important role. We have to look- after practically it to gain more benefits.

REFERENCES

- Balkwill, Richard.con. Intellectual Property. Microsoft ® Encarta ® 2006 © 1993-2005.
- Chandra, Ramesh. ed. Issues of Intellectual Property Rights. Delhi: Isha Book, 2004, 1-250.
- Cornish, W R. Intellectual Property. Delhi: Universal, 2003, 293-399.
- David, Bainbridge. Intellectual Property. 3rd ed. London: Pitman, 1996, 1-22.
- David, Bainbridge, Intellectual Property, 5th ed. Singapore: Pearson, 2003, 3-23, 309-640.
- Deva, Vasu. Encyclopaedia of Information Technology and e-world. 'e-Crimes and Remedies' 2 vol. New Delhi" Commonwealth, 2006, 80- 173.
- Goel, Ghanshyam. ed. Employment News. Weekly. "Intellectual Property Rights " xxx-28, 8-14, October, 2005, New Delhi: Government of India, 2005, 1 and 48.

- Goel, Ghanshyam. ed. Employment News. Weekly, Career In Intellectual Property Rights. Xxxi vols.33,11-17 November, 2006, New Delhi: Government of India, 1 and 48.
- Government of India, Recommendations of the National Knowledge Commission, Report to the Nation 2006 & 2007, New- Delhi.
- Government of India. Recommendations of the National Knowledge Commission. New Delhi: Academic Foundation, 2009, 161-165.
- Jacob, Q C. Robin and Alexander, Daniel. A Guide Book of Intellectual Property. 4th ed. London: Sweet and Maxwell, 1993, 14-15, 186-187, 197-199.
- Moorthy, A L. ed. Information Commons: impact and Implications for Libraries and Information Centre. "52 All India Library Conference Papers, Srinagar, Uttranchal. December 26-29, 2006" Delhi: Indian Library Association, 2006.
- Narayan, P. Intellectual Property Law. 2nd ed. Calcutta: Eastern Law, 1997, 1-180.
- Samuel, T M and Samuel Maria. Encyclopeadia of Information Technology. 8th vols. New Delhi: Commonwealth, 2008,
- Satarkar, S P. Intellectual Property Rights and Copyright. Delhi: Ess Ess, 2003, 1- 146.
- Satpathy, S R., Swain, Chandrakant and Rautaray Bijaylaxmi. Modernisation of Libraries: A Challenge in Digital Era. New Delhi: Mahamaya, 2008, 259-268.
- Satpathy, S R. Swain, Chandrakant and Rautaray Bijayalaxmi. Libraries: In Digital Environment, Problems and Prospects. New Delhi: Mahamaya, 2008, 217-230.
- Shastri, Siddharth. Intellectual Property Rights: The Emerging Issues fir Industry. Rajasthan: WISDOM, Navjeewan, 2004, 1-75.
- Suri, R K Chhabra, T N. IT Encyclopadia. Com. "Cyber Crime" 4th Rep. 11 vols. New Delhi: Pentagon, 2003, 155-315.
- Suri, R K. IT Encyclopaedia. Com 'Information Technology Laws" 4th Rep. 10th vols. New Delhi: Pentagon, 2003, 121-420.

- Verma, S K. and Mittal Raman. ed. Intellectual Property Rights: A global Vision. New Delhi: Indian Law Institute, 2008, 104-106.
- V, Jalaja, MCK, Veeran and Koovakkai, Dineshan. ed. Organisation, Processing and Use of Information in the Digital Era. New Delhi: Ess Ess, 2004, 121

9

Conclusion And Suggestions

Recommendations are necessary for libraries to have upto date knowledge with Copyright Act, 1957 along with latest amendments. Librarians are required to have knowledge regarding the challenges of new technology which applies in the copyright law on libraries specially in a digital environment. The copyright law changes from time to time. There are controversial areas of internet site where this law is being neglected. Internet and websites are violating the DMCA because there is no unique legislation of copyright in digital environment. Authors as well as librarians must have also generate awareness in themselves regarding the Copyright Act in relation to the digital environment that has been exceedingly popular.

Due to the changes in production, distribution and consumption of the copyright work need of management of copyright has arisen in digital arena. Today mostly PC owners are looking more and more product online and use of internet is increasing day by day.

In digital arena management of copyright is a new issue. Several actions have been taken by different countries to manage the copyright but no uniform standard has been set till yet. Therefore a uniform formula for proper management of the copyright in digital environment has to set up.

The issues arena thus is becoming more complicated with pricing of information in electronic media and thus the whole issue of copyright is being reviewed all over the world, as regards to the use of books and issues pertaining to libraries. The existing norms, convention and regulation in kept in mind.

In conclusion, it can be said that the object of the universal declaration of the human rights is to provide every kind of right to the human family, every person has a creative ideas and desires to convert it in creative act. By virtues of this quality Intellectual Property comes in picture and those are required to be protected. There must be some law to protect such as Intellectual Property.

Many rights are conferred to the copyright holder by virtue of its owner. Sometimes copyright holder does not share their work for public good. In that circumstance advancement of the society are stopped. For this purpose compulsory licensing system is being used which brings balance between monopoly of owner and advancement of the knowledge of society. Copyright is one of the key elements in development as creativity and newness is inherent in it. The object behind copyright law is to advance the progress of society and to benefit the people at large as they can read and use the materials for the advancement of society. The benefit of the society lies in encouraging new knowledge and it should be spread over in the society.

Copyright is in alarming position. A film is produced by a producer by investing a huge amount while pirates prepare video copy immediately just after release of film. Not only they copy the film but distribute it in public at large. Thus it causes loss to distributors.

Production of duplicate audio cassettes without

license is also one of the alarming position in the world of copyright. It also loss to music industry and government.

Invention of copying technology is a hammer on copyright. Internet has allowed the free flow of information and has made it easy to copy. Development of information technology has helped dissemination of information and on the other hand, it is a hammer on creator's interest.

Considering the issues related to the librarianship, reprography and copyrights, it can be concluded that the library authorities should permit a minimum photocopying works. This is to be done only after judicious thinking on the demand from the user. Further it should be borne in mind that the circulars issued by the association/ u.g.c. /government etc. will not overdue the provision in the copyright act.

The following *suggestions* may be considered to become copyright law more useful in India:

- Awareness the concept of copyright is one of the important factor. Necessary steps to promote awareness in this respect in public are required to be taken.
- Duration should be limited to the life time of the author. It is required to be put before the public at an early stage. So that it can be make useful for society. For that license method can be used. Ruling body can impose a compulsory licensing system.
- Copyright and its origins must be set in a larger context.
- Copyright system is required to be governed by some guidelines of author- user system of copyright.
- To encourage authorship economic incentive are required to be provided to the creators.
- Some rules are required to be set for the use of copyright by the users.
- An environment to produce more creativity and

newness is required to be created.

- In this digital world, copyright is an important issue. Many countries have taken several steps on this issue, but there is no uniform policy. A uniform policy can only solve this issue properly.
- As per TRIP agreement, amendment in copyright act is required to be made to the extent that at primary stage also the information which is not disclosed should be protected.
- Provisions of article 2 (1) & (2) of U.D.H.R.,1948 are required to be adopted just to take action against violation of copyright as copyright and human right are two in one.
- Copyright Board is required to be established at all level like; District, State and a national level. Para judicial remedy other than board is to be established & recognized to resolve the dispute regarding infringement of copyright. Copyright office should be modernized. There is also a need to constitute expert committees on copyright. Copyright should be in special area, to resolve the disputes speedily and sufficiently, a separate tribunal is also required to be established and there is a need of trained judges to deal with copyright disputes. To avoid undue delays and legal uncertainties, there should be arbitration provision to resolve such disputes and for that special rules and regulations are required to be framed.
- Help of pare judicial system will also be helpful in resolving the disputes regarding infringement/ violation of copyrights and those decisions should be given legal force and those should be recognized legally.
- Government should adopt policies for educational, research and literary uses in nationwide copyright law.

- There should be fair use of rights for educational and research purposes by interest users.
- Making of copies may be legalized on payment of fees which should be paid through libraries/ societies/organizations etc. which in turn will go to owner.
- Onus is on the people at large to safeguard our creative interest and adopt copyright culture.

LIBRARIANS AND ON-LINE USERS

In our present education system there is no direct close touch of the librarian with the users. Users obtain their required information from the internet. For this purpose students are bound to pay a fix payment. In case librarian sees this act he is unable to assess how much text from the original literature has been copied out and how much infringement of copyright act has been done by the users. First of all a librarian and users cannot meet face to face on the internet.

In case, at any internet, librarian and users are meet face to face, the librarian having a desire to see the original literature cannot see it and in case librarian wants to give advice about it to user, first user will not like to hear advice of the librarian but he can disgrace to the librarian. In these critical situations, how the librarians can prevent disobedience of copyright act online users and can achieve their object, is a most important problem, In my opinion, following suggestions will be helpful to infringement of copyright act:

- A daily news are delivered by the news channels, the librarians be also invited with regard by the news channels to give important information regarding copyright act and how much part of the original literature can be copied out, in which way Government, Institutions and Organizations as well as news channels should necessary steps on this point. Permanent and retired experienced librarians can be appointed for this purpose.

- There should be advertisement in the news- papers, radio news, T.V. channels and by other resources about it and how much penalty/ punishment may be awarded on the delinquent person by the authority / court concerned.
- A subject/ chapter should be included in the curriculum of the students/users about copyright act at every stage so that users may get knowledge and born about copyright act, its uses, its infringement and punishment etc.
- More seminars/ workshops are required to be organized so that people can have better knowledge about the copyright act.
- Implementation authorities should be trained so that they can take proper steps for infringement of copyright.
- Strict views/ steps should be taken against the violators.

The copyright act and its knowledge should be given a shape of subject in the education by the government such as; Environmental Science and Physical Education are compulsory in the graduate level. We should protest to make this subject compulsory by the state government and central government. In my opinion this subject should be from the stage of secondary and higher education. Attention of the government should be drawn towards it as early as possible.

The user should know how and when he can copy from the original literature/copy. Further in my opinion that knowledge of the copyright act should be given to users and public in general in such a way so that they may easily pick up it without any difficulty as advertisements are distributed in the TV Channels, Radio, Newspapers, Magazine, Posters etc.

Bibliography

- Britannica Encyclopaedia. 9th ed. 6th vols, London: Adam and Charles. Black Adinburgh,1904
- Britannica Encyclopaedia. 10th ed. xxvii vols, London: Adam and Charles. Black Adinburgh,1904.
- Britannica, Micropaedia Ready Reference, Encyclopaedia of Britannica. 15th ed. Chicago: Britannica, 3 Vol , 2003.
- Encyclopaedia Americana. 7Vols, Danbury: Grolier Incorporated International, 1988.
- Chamber's. Encyclopaedia, A Dictionary of Universal Knowledge for the People. Rev. ed. 10 Vols, London: W and R, Edinburg, 1880.
- Copyright Office Summary. Digital Millennium Copyright Act of 1998. United State: Pub. L. No. 105- 304, 112 Stat. 2860, October , 1998.
- Cornish, W R . Intellectual Property. Delhi : Universal, 2003.
- Chandra, Ramesh. Issues of Intellectual Property Rights. Delhi : Isha book, 2004.
- Chopra, R N. Dictionary of Library Science. New-Delhi : Anmol, 1992.
- David, Bainbridge . Intellectual Property. 3rd ed. London : Pitman, 1996.
- David, Bainbridge . Intellectual Property. 5th ed.

Singapore : Pearson, 2003.

- Dave, R K, Sharma, K K and Ojha, D C. "Copyright Act and Author Protection." *Granthalaya Vigyan* 39 (2008) : 105-113.
- Deva, Vasu . *e-crimes and Remedies Encyclopaedia of Information Technology and e- World.* 2 vol. New Delhi: Commonwealth, 2006.
- Diwan, Parag, Suri, R K and Kaushik, Sanjay. IT Encyclopaedia.com. Rev. 3rd ed. 12 vols. New-Delhi: Pentagon, 2ooo.
- Donna, L. Ferullo. Major Copyright Issues in Academic Libraries: Legal Implications of a Digital Environment. *"Journal of Library Administration."* 40, 1-2. Haworth, 2004.
- Drabble, Margaret. The Oxford Companion to English Literarute. Oxford : Oxford University Press, 1989.
- "Executive Summary Digital Millennium Copyright Act Section 104 Report" *Online*22,October2007. *http://www.copyright.gov/reports/studies/dmca/dmca_executive.html.*
- "Emerging Thrust Areas in Library and Information Science." Alagapa, Tamilnadu: Karakuri, 2006.
- Goel, Ghanshyam. ed. Employment News. weekly. Intellectual Property Rights.vols xxx-28, 8-14 October 2005, New Delhi : Government of India, p. 1 and 48.
- Goel, Ghanshyam. Ed. Employment News. Weekly. Career In Intellectual Property Rights. Vols. xxxi-33, 11-17 November 2006 , New Delhi : Government of India, p.1 and 48.
- Government of India. A Hand Book of Copyright Law. New Delhi: Ministry of HRD, 1999.
- Government of India. The Copyright Act 1957. Delhi: India Government, 1998.

- Government of India. Recommendations of the National Knowledge Commission, Report to the Nation, 2006 & 2007.
- Government of India. Recommendations of the National Knowledge Commission. New Delhi : Academic Foundation, 2009.
- Gupta, Neha. Copyright: Infringement, Remedies and Enforcement. *"National Seminar on Changing Dimensions of Copyright and Other Neighbouring Rights. October, 9-10, 2004."* Bareilly : MJP Roohilkhand University, 2004.
- Gupta, Pallavi. Management of Copyright in Digital Environment.: *National Seminar on Changing Dimensions of Copyright and Other Neighbouring Rights, October, 9-10, 2004."* Bareilly : MJP Roohilkhand University, 2004.
- Gupta, Sangita. Digital Preservation: Changes and Strategies. *" ILA Bulletin. XLIII -1 , January- March 2007.* Delhi : Indian Library Association.
- Harvey, Sir Paul. The Oxford Companion To English Literature. London; Oxford Press, 1970.
- Jacob, Q C Robin, and Alexander, Daniel . A Guide Book of Intellectual Property. 4th ed. London: Sweet and Maxwell, 1993.
- Kaula, P N. Copyright Law to be made Digital-friendly. *"Herald of Library Science."* 40, 3-4 July-October,2001, Lucknow: 2001.
- Kaula, P N. Copyright Agreement." *Herald of Library Science."* 35, 3-4 July- October 1996. Lucknow: 1996.
- Kaula, P N. World Book and Copyright Day . *" Herald of Library Science."* 43, 3-4, Lucknow: 2004.
- Kuffalikar, C R. Managing Information: Some IPR Indicators for Library Professionals. *"B B Shukla, Indian Journal of Information, Library Society."* 18

vol 3-4, Oridssa.

- Khan, M A. Principles and Perspective of Copyrights. New Delhi: Sarup and Sons, 1996.
- Khan, M H and Makhdumi, Gayas. Copyright Fails in Libraries in Digital Era. *"From Automation to Transformation. 6th International Caliber 2008" February, 28- 29 and March 1, 2008.* Ahmedabad and Allahabad : Inflibnet Centre,2008.
- Khan, P A. Copyright and Judicial Attitude. *"National Seminar on Changing Dimensions of Copyright and Neighbouring Rights. October, 9-10, 2004."* Bareilly : MJP Roohilkhand University, 2004.
- Lessing, Doris. The Cambridge Guide to Literature in English. ed. New York: University Cambridge. 1993.
- Litman, Jessica. The Art if Making Copyright Laws: Digital Copyright. http:// www.msen.com/-litman/ digital-copyright/ch2.html.
- Lohani, Minoo, Mathpal. Neelu and Malik, S K. Impact of Information Management and Services on CSIR Research Community and Its Libraries. *"Convention Paper-National Convention of CSIR Libraries and Information Centre August, 25-27, 2003."* Lucknow : NBRI, 2003.
- Lutzker, P. Arnold. Primer On The Digital Millennium, 8 March, 1999 .Washington Office: ALA Pennsylvania Avenue . *arnie@lutzker.com.*
- Moorthy, A L. ed. Information Commons: Impact and Implications for Libraries and Information Centres. *"52 All India Library Conference Papers Srinagar, Uttranchal, December 26-29, 2006"* Delhi: Indian Library Association, 2006.
- Narayana, P . Intellectual Property Law. 2 ed. Calcutta : Eastern Law, 1997.
- Narayana's, P.S (Justice) Intellectual Property Law

in India. 4th ed. Hyderabad : Gogia Law Agency, 2008.

- Phadke, D N. Digital Preservation and Digitization and Copyright. Article.
- Pandey, Alok. Rights Conferred by Copyright Act 1957. *"National Seminar on Changing Dimensions of Copyright and Neighbouring Rights. October, 9-10, 2004."* Bareilly, MJP Roohilkhand University, 2004.
- Pane, Sista Rama Devi. University News. Association of Indian Universities. Vols, 42, 27-28 and 43 ,2004.
- R R and T D. ed. India 2004. New Delhi : Government of India. 2004.
- Rajendran, L. and Rajendran, P. Selvi. Preservation Methods For Digital Library."Indian Journal of Information, Library and Society.18,1-2, January-June, 2005: ed. B.B. Shukla. Cuttack : Bharti Shukla, Nua Sahi.
- Sainy, O M Prakash. Library and Society. Agra, Y.K., 1998.
- Samuel, T M and Samuel Maria. Encyclopaedia of Information Technology. 8vols, New Delhi : Commonwealth, 2008.
- Satarkar, S P. Intellectual Property Rights and Copyright. Delhi : Ess Ess, 2003.
- Satpathy, S K, Swain, Chandrakant and Rautaray, Bijayalaxmi. ed. Modernisation of Libraries: A Challenge in Digital Era. New Delhi : Mahamaya. 2008.
- Satpathy, S K, Swain, Chandrakant and Rautaray, Bijayalaxmi. ed. Libraries in Digital Environment Problems and Prospects. New Delhi : Mahamaya, 2008.
- Saxena, Priti. Private Creations Entitling Public Protection with Special Reference for Protection of Neighbouring Rights in India. *"National Seminar on*

Changing Dimensions of Copyright and Other Neighbouring Rights 9-10 October 2004." Bareilly : MJP Roohilkhand University, 2004.

- Sharma, R K. New Choices for Bibliographic Services in a Wired Planet : Reflections on the National Library of India. 'Rethinking Copyright.' *"Library Herald. 44, 2 June 2006."* Delhi : DLA.
- Shastri, Siddharth. Intellectual Property Rights: The Emerging Issues For Industry. Rajasthan : WISDOM, Navjeewan,2004.
- Shukla, B B. ed. Celebration of the World Book and Copyright day and Padmashree Prof. Kaula's effort in establishing National Book Museum at Delhi: *"Indian Journal of information, Library and Society 18, 1-2, January- June, 2005*, Cuttack: Bharti Shukla, Nua Sahi.
- Singh, C. Praveen. Documentation and Information Science in Libraries. New Delhi: ALFA,2008.
- Singh, S K. Copyright Protection with Special Reference to Music and Film Industrial. *"National Seminar on Changing Dimensions of Copyrights and other Neighbouring Rights in India 9-10 October 2004."* Bareilly : MJP Roohilkhand University, 2004.
- Singh, Jnanendra Narayan. Copyright Issus in Digital Era. *"Library Herald."* Vol. 44,2. Delhi : Delhi Library Association, June 2006.
- Singh, Nishant. Media Law. New Delhi : Naman, 2003.
- Siwatch, Ajit. Approaches to Modern Librarianship. Delhi : Sanjay, 2006.
- Srivastava, P L. Copyright Act 1957: A Development Profile. Paper presented at *"National Seminar CSIR Dimond Jubilee and NBRI Golden Jubilee Celebrations."* Lucknow: 2003.
- Steinberg, S H. Cassell's Encyclopaedia of

Literature. vols.1 London : Cassell and Company, 1953.

- Suraj, V K . ed. Encyclopaedic Dictionary of Library and Information Science. 3 vols. Delhi : Isha Books, 2005.
- Swain, Nirmal Kumar. Authorship Hegemony, Compulsory License and the Battle for the Knowledge Commons. "*Library Herald 43, 3 2007.*" Delhi : DLA.
- S, S K. Copyright Law, Print Media and Technology: New Challenge. " *National Seminar on Changing Dimensions of Copyright and other neighbouring Rights 9-10 October, 2004.* Bareilly : MJP Roohilkhanad.
- Senfransisco. A Case Infringement of Copyright On Google. News paper Amar Ujala . Bareilly 21, October, 2005, p.2.
- The Hindustan Times. Google to Test Copyright Laws. NBT News Letter. Vols. 21-7 October 2005.
- Times of India: Times News Networks : Ahmedabad,21-1-2007.
- TLA News Letter On Copyright Day 23 April, 2005 vols 12-4.
- Tiwari, Ashwani. Intellectual Property Protection in Digital Age. "*Granthalaya Vigyan 36, 1-2,2005.*" Kaula. Jaipaur : Jawaharnagar, 2005.
- Tripathi, S M. Documentation and Information Services and Network. 2vols. Agra : Y. K., 1998.
- Verma, S K, and Mittal, Raman. ed. Intellectual Property Rights A Global Vision. Rep. 2nd, New Delhi: Indian Law Institute, 2008.
- V, Jalaja, MCK, Veeran and Koovakkai, Dineshan. ed. Organisation, Processing and Use of Information in the Digital Era. New Delhi : Ess Ess, 2004.

- Wikipedia, the free encyclopedia. History of Copyright. 2007.
- *www.mhrdiprchairs.org.*

Abbreviations

ALA	American Library association
A C	Anti-Circumvention
AULA	Actual User License Agreement
BC	Berne Convention
BLOG	Binary Large Objects
CCA	Commonwealth Copyright Administration
CITED	Copyright in Transmitted Electronic Documents
CMI	Copyright Management Information
CMCA	Computer Maintenance Competition Assurance Act
CRM	Copyright Right Management
CTEA	Copt Right Term Extension Act
CSIR	Council of Scientific And Industrial Research.
CLA	Copy Right Licensing Agency
CEAC	Copy Right Enforcement Advisory Council
CDs	Compact Disks
DAB	Digital Agenda Bill
DDC	Dewey Decimal Classification
DDE	Digital Distance Education
DMCA	Digital Millennium Copy Right Act
DPRA	Digital Performance Right in Sounding

	Recording Act
DPSP	Directive Principles of State Police
E-Security	Electronic Security
E-C	Electronic Commerce
ECMS	Electronic Copyright Management System
EIP	Electronic Intellectual Property
EPC	European Patent Convention
EU	European Union
EUCD	European Union Copyright Directive
F-U	Fair Use
FTS	File Transfer Services
FR	Fundamental Right
GATT	General Agreement On Tariff and Trade.
GATS	General Agreement on Trade and Services
GIA	Geographical Indications Act
GIIC	Global Information Infrastructure Commission
HRD	Human Resource Development
HTML	Hyper Text Marketed up Language
IP	Intellectual Property
IPD	Indian Patents and Design Act
IPDL	Intellectual Property digital Libraries
IPR	Intellectual Property Rights
ICRA	Indian Copy Right Act
ICRA	International Copy right Acts
IP	Internet Protocol
IFLA	International Federation of Library Association
IMPA	India Motion Pictures Association
IPEA	International preliminary Examination Authority
IT	Information Technology
IIIT	Indian Institute of Information Technology

IIM	Indian Institution of Management
ICESCIR	International covenant on Economics, Social and Cultural Rights.
IEG	Internet Entertainment Group
IPDLS	Intellectual Property Digital Libraries
ISA	International Search Authority
JISC	Joint Information System Committee
OSPS	On-Line Service Providers
MBP	Millennium Book Project
MIT	Ministry of Information Technology
MMPA	Mickey Mouse Protection Act
NCST	National Centre for Software Technology
NBRI	National Botanical Research Institute
NDIIPP	National Digital Information Infrastructure and Preservation Programme
NPC	National Productivity Council
NTIA	National Telecommunication Information Administration
NTIS	National Technical Information Services
NKC	National Knowledge Commission
NHA	National Humanities Alliance
NRDC	National Research Development Corporation
PNAM	Purpose of use, Nature of work, Amount, Substantially, Market
PII	Publisher Item Identifier
PCs	Personal Computers
PCT	Patent Corporation Treaty
PTO	Patent & Trademark Office
RC	Rome Convention
RAM	Random access memory
RASS	Ranganathan Society For Book Culture

RLG	Research Library Group
R & D	Research & Development
SNO	State Nodal Officers
SICI	Serial Item and Contribution Identifier
SWDC	Steamboat Willie And Plane Crazy
TEACH	Technology, Education and Copy Right Harmonize
TRIPS	Trade Related Intellectual Property Rights
TMA	Trade Mark Act
TPM	Technological Protection Measures
UCC	Universal Copy Right Convention
UK	United Kingdom
USA	United State of America
USC	United States Code
USSR	Union Soviet Socialism Republic
UNESCO	United Nation Educational Scientific Cultural Organization
UDHR	Universal Declaration of Human Rights
UGC	University Grants Commission
VCD	Video Cassettes
VHDPA	Vessel Hull Design Protection Act
WIPO	World Intellectual Property Organisation
WTO	World Trade Organisation
WIPO	NET World Intellectual Property Organisation Network
WCT	WIPO Copy Right Treaty
WWW	World Wide Web
WDC	Walt Disney Company

Appendices

COPYRIGHT RULES

Copyright is the exclusive statutory right of authors, composers, playwrights, artists, publishers of distributors to publish of their works for a limited time. "Copyright is usually described as ' literary and artistic work' i.e. original creations in the field of 'literature and arts'; the works may be expressed in words, symbols, music and picture. Indian law protects original literary, dramatic, musical and artistic work; cinematograph film and sound recordings, broadcasting, cable relay and telecasting rights are some of the new branches of copyrights."

Copyright Rules are following;

- Copyright law is the legal foundation protecting the work of many major industries, including book publishing, motion picture production, music recording and computer software development.
- Copyright owner can reproduce his work in any material form including storing of it in any medium by electronic means. He can release copies of the work to the public if they are not already available. He can translate or make any adaptation of the work. He can sell a copy even if such a copy has been sold on earlier occasions. If copyright protection is rigid, it can perplex the progress of the society. However, copyright laws are enacted

with necessary exceptions and limitations to ensure that a balance is maintained between the interests of the creators and of the community.

- There is no copyright in an ideas or concepts. From start to finish, copyright never stops anyone working on the same lines, upon same sort of basics idea and copyright cannot be effective against anyone who is the produces something independently.
- Copyright does not protect title, names, short words combinations, slogans, short phrases, methods. Familiar symbols, designs, more variations of typographic ornamentation, lettering or coloring, mere listing of ingredients or contents, discoveries or devices, explanation, description, illustration, and factual information.
- The work of cine artist his performance as an actor in a cinema is not protected; it is the film that enjoys protection along with its sound track.
- There is no copyright in Technology, Education and Copyright Harmonization Act (TEACH Act). TEACH Act totally rewrites the distance education section with classroom teaching.
- Copyright does not protect titles, names, short word combinations, slogans, short phrases, methods, plots, familiar symbols, designs, more variations of typographic ornamentation, lettering or coloring, mere listing of ingredients or contents, discoveries or devices, explanations, descriptions, illustrations and factual information.
- Copyright is infringing when a person; makes for sale or hire, or sales for hire by way of trade displays or offers for sale or hire, distributes either for the purpose of trade, or to such an extent as to affect prejudicially the owner of copyright or; by way of trade exhibits in public or import to India, any infringing copies of the work.

- The duration of copyright is life of the author and fifty years after the author's death. In the case of joint author, the termination date of copyright is fifty years after the death of the surviving author. In the case of Pseudonymous and anonymous works, the copyright generally expires *seventy- five* years after publication or one hundred years after creation, whichever occurs first.
- The authors association with writers guild and publishers association has stated certain norms for the extent of copying, including books and periodical materials. The norms are as under;
    1. A maximum of a chapter or 5% (whichever is less) can be copied from a literary work.
    2. Up to 10% (Not more than 20 pages or 2 pages in brief) can be copied from short books, reports, standards, pamphlets etc.
    3. One copy of a short story, poem etc. or 5% (which ever is less). The details of the norms regarding the copying of books, periodicals, and other non- book material is explained in various sections of the copyright act,
- The violation of copyright has been made a criminal offence under copyright act, punishable with imprisonment which may be from a minimum period of six month and maximum 3 years and with a fine ranging from Rs. 50,000/= to Rs. 2 lacks.
- Non- profit libraries, institutions and organizations are exempted from the copyright law. 'Fair Use' also exempted from the copyright laws.
- The library exemption allows copying for various purposes Such as; Inter library loan, Personal use, research work and the preservation.

The copyright rules, 2013 was notified on 14 March, 2013 replacing the old copyright rules ,1958. The rules inter alia, provide for procedure for relinquishment of copyright; grant of compulsory licences in the matter of work withheld from public; to publish or republish works (in certain circumstances) to produce and publish a translation of a literary or dramatic work in any language; licence for benefit of disabled; grant statutory licence for cover versions; grant of statutory licence for broadcasting literary and musical works and sound recordings, registration of copyright societies and copyright registration.

APPENDIX I

THE COPYRIGHT ACT, 1957

(Act No. 14 of 1957)

{4th June, 1957}

(An Act to amend and consolidate the law relating to copyright.)

Be it enacted by Parliament in the Eight Year of the Republic of India as follows:-

CHAPTER I : PRELIMINARY

1. Short title, extent and commencement

(1) This Act may be called the Copyright Act,1957.

(2) It extends to the whole of India.

(3) It shall come into force on such date2 as the Central Government may, by notification in the Official Gazette, appoint.

2. Interpretation

In this Act, unless the context otherwise requires,-

(a) "adaptation" means,

(i) in relation to a dramatic work, the conversion of the work into a non- dramatic work;

(ii) in relation to a literary work or an artistic work, the conversion of the work into a dramatic work by way of performance in public or otherwise;

(iii) in relation to a literary or dramatic work, any abridgement of the work or any version of the work in which the story or action is conveyed wholly or mainly by means of pictures in a form suitable for reproduction in a book, or in a newspaper, magazine or similar periodical;

(iv) in relation to a musical work, any arrangement of transcription of the work; 4 {and}

(v) in relation to any work, any use of such work

involving its re-arrangement or { alteration;}

(b) "1{work of architecture}" means any building or structure having an artistic character or design, or any model for such building or structure;

(a) "artistic work" means—

(i) a painting, a sculpture, a drawing (including a diagram, map, chart or plan) an engraving or a photograph, whether or not any such work possess artistic quality;

(ii) An 1 {work of architecture }; and

(iii) any other work of artistic craftsmanship;

(b) "author" means

(i) in relation to a literary or dramatic work, the author of the work;

(ii) in relation to a musical work, the composer;

(iii) in relation to an artistic work other than a photograph, the artist;

(iv) in relation to a photograph the person taking the photograph;

(v) in relation to a cinematograph film or sound recording, the producer; and

(vi) in relation to any literary, dramatic, musical or artistic work which is computer generated, the person who causes the work to be created;}

3(dd) "broadcast" means communication to the public –

(i) by any means of wireless diffusion, whether in any one or more of the forms of signs, sounds or visual images; or

(ii) by wire,

(iii) and includes a re-broadcast;}

(c) "calendar year" means the year commencing on the 1st day of January;

4{f) "cinematograph film" means any work of visual recording on any medium produced through a process from which a moving image may be produced by any means and includes a sound recording accompanying such visual recording and "cinematograph" shall be construed as including any work produced by any process analogous to cinematography including video films;}

1{ff) "communication of public" means making any work available for being seen or heard of otherwise enjoyed by the public directly or by any means of display or diffusion other than by issuing copies of such work regardless of whether any member of the public actually sees, hears or otherwise enjoys the work so made available.

Explanation : For the purposes of this clause, communication through satellite or cable or any other means of simultaneous communication to more than one house hold or place of residence including residential rooms of any hotel or hostel shall be deemed to be communication to the public;

(ffa) "composer", in relation to a musical work, means the person who composes the music regardless of whether he records it in any form of graphical notation;

(ffb) "computer" includes any electronic or similar device having information processing capabilities;

(ffc) "computer programme" means a set of instruction expressed in words, codes, schemes or in any other form, including a machine readable medium, capable of causing a computer to perform a particular task or achieve a particular result;

(ffd) "copyright society" means a society registered under sub- section (3) of section33;}

(g) "delivery", in relation to a lecture, includes delivery by means of any mechanical instrument or by 2{broadcast};

(h) "dramatic work" includes any piece for recitation, choreographic work or entertainment in dumb show, the scenic arrangement or acting form of which is fixed in writing or otherwise but does not include a cinematograph film;

3(hh) "duplicating equipment" means any mechanical contrivance or device used or intended to be used for making copies of any work;}

(i) "engravings" include etchings, lithographs, wood-cuts, prints and other similar works, not being photographs;

(j) "exclusive licence" means a licence which confers on the license or on the licensee and persons authorised by him, to the exclusion of all other persons (including the owner of the copyright), any right comprised in the copyright is a work and " exclusive licensee" shall be construed accordingly;

(k) "Government work" means a work which is made or published by or under the direction or control of –

(i) the Government or any department of the Government;

(ii) legislature in India;

(iii) any court, tribunal or other judicial authority in India;

1(l) "Indian work" means a literary, dramatic or musical work.

(i) the author which is a citizen of India; or

(ii) which is first published in India; or

(iii) the author of which, in the case of an unpublished work, is at the time of the making of the work, a citizen of India;}

2(m) "infringing copy " means,—

(i) in relation to literary, dramatic, musical or artistic work, a reproduction thereof otherwise than in the form of a cinematographic film;

(ii) in relation to a cinematographic film, a copy of the film made on any medium by any means;

(iii) in relation to a sound recording, any other recording embodying the same sound recording, made by any means;

(iv) in relation to a programme or performance in which such a broadcast reproduction right or a performer's right subsists under provisions of this Act, the sound recording or a cinematographic film of such programme or performance, if such reproduction, copy or sound recording is made or imported in contravention of the provisions of this Act;}

(n) "lecture" includes address, speech and sermon;

3(o) "literary work" includes computer programmes, tables and compilations including computer data bases;}

4{(p)"musical work" means a work consisting of music and includes any graphical notation of such work but does not include any words of any action intended to be sung, spoken or performed with the music;}

5{(q) "performance," in relation to performer's right, means any visual or acoustic presentation made live by one or more performers;}

6({qq) "performer" includes an actor, singer, musician, dancer, acrobat, juggler, conjurer, snake charmer, a person delivering a lecture or any other person who makes a performance;}

(s) "photograph" includes photo- lithograph and any other work produced by any process analogous to photography, but does not include any part of a cinematograph film;

(t) "plate" includes any stereotype or other plate, stone, block, mould, matrix, transfer, negative 1{ duplicating equipment} or other device used or intended to be used for printing or reproducing copies of any work, and any matrix or other appliance by which 2{sound recording} for the acoustic of the work are or are intended to be made;

(u) "prescribed" means prescribed by rules made under this Act:

3(uu) "producer," in relation to a cinematograph film or sound recording, means a person who takes the initiative and responsibility for making the work;}

6{(x) "reprography" means the making of copies of a work, by photocopying or similar means;

(xx) "sound recording" means a recording of sounds from which such sounds may be produced regardless of the medium on which such recording is made or the method by which the sounds are produced;}

(y) "work" means any of the following works, namely:—

(i) a literary, dramatic, musical or artistic work;

(ii) a cinematograph film;

(iii) a 2{ sound recording};

(z) "work of joint authorship" means a work produced by the collaboration of two or more authors in which the contribution of one author is not distinct from the contribution of the other author or authors;

(za) "work of sculpture" includes casts and models.

3. Meaning of publication

For the purposes of this Act, "publication" means making a work available to the public by issue of copies or by communicating the work to the public.}

4. When work not deemed to be published or performed in public

Except in relation to infringement of copyright, a work shall not be deemed to be published or performed in public, if published, or performed in public, without the licence of the owner of the copyright.

5. When work deemed to be first published in India

For the purposes of this Act, a work published in India shall be deemed to be first published in India, not with standing that it has been published simultaneously if some other country, unless such other country provides a shorter term of copyright for such work; and a work shall be deemed to be published simultaneously in India and in another country if the time between the publication in India and the publication in such other country does not exceed thirty days or such other period and the Central Government may, in relation to any specified country, determine.

6. Certain dispute to be decided by Copyright Board

If any question arises,—

(a) whether a work has been published or as to the date on which a work was published for the purposes of Chapter V, or

(b) whether the term of copyright for any work is shorter in any other country than that provided in respect of that work under this act,

It shall be referred to the Copyright Board constituted under section 11 whose decision thereon shall be final:

Provided that if in the opinion of the Copyright Board, the issue of copies or communication to the public referred to in section 3 was of an insignificant nature it shall not be deemed to be publication for the purposes of that section.}

7. Nationality of author where the making of unpublished work is extended over considerable period

Where, in the case of an unpublished work, the making of the work is extended over a considerable period, the author of the work shall, for the purposes of this Act, be deemed to be a citizen of, or domiciled in, that country of which he was a citizen or wherein he domiciled during any substantial part of that period.

8. Domicile of corporations

For the purposes of this Act, a body corporate shall be deemed to be domiciled in India if it is incorporated under any law in force in India.

CHAPTER II : COPYRIGHT OFFICE AND COPYRIGHT BOARD

9. Copyright Office

(1) There shall be established for the purposes of this Act an Office to be called the Copyright Office.

(2) The Copyright Office shall be under the immediate control of the Registrar of Copyrights who shall act under the superintendence and direction of the Central Government.

(3) There shall be a seal for the Copyright Office.

10. Registrar and Deputy Registrars of Copyrights

(1) The Central Government shall appoint a Registrar

of Copyrights and may appoint one or more Deputy Registrar of Copyrights.

(2) A Deputy Registrar of Copyrights shall discharge under the superintendence and direction of the Registrar of Copyrights such functions of the Registrar under this Act as the Registrar may, from time to time, assign to him; and any reference in this act to the Registrar of Copyrights shall include a reference to a Deputy Registrar of Copyrights when so discharging any such functions.

11. Copyright Board

(1) As soon as may be after the commencement of this Act, the Central Government shall constitute a Board to be called the Copyright Board which shall consist of Chairman and not less than two or more than 2{fourteen} other members.

(2) The Chairman and other members of the Copyright Board shall hold office for such period and on such terms and conditions as may be prescribed.

(3) The Chairman of the Copyright Board shall be a person who is, or has been, a Judge of 1*** a High Court or is qualified for appointment as a Judge of a High Court.

(4) The Registrar of Copyrights shall be the Secretary of the Copyright Board and shall perform such functions as may be prescribed.

12. powers and procedure of Copyright Board

(1) The Copyright Board shall, subject to any rules that may be made under this Act, have power to regulate its own procedure, including the fixing of places and times of its sittings:

Provided that the Copyright Board shall ordinarily hear any proceeding instituted before it under this Act within the Zone in which, at the time of the institution of the proceeding, the person instituting the proceeding actually and voluntarily resides or carries on business or personally works for gain.

Explanation : In this sub- section" Zone" means a zone specified in section 15 of the States Reorganisation Act, 1956 (37 of 1956).

(2) The Copyright Board may exercise and discharge its powers and functions through Benches constituted by the Chairman of the Copyright Board from amongst its member, each Bench consisting of not less than three members:

2{Provided that, if the Chairman is of opinion they any matter of importance is required to be heard by a large bench, he may refer the matter to a special bench consisting of five members.}

(3) If there is a difference of opinion among the members of the Copyright Board or any Bench thereof in respect of any matter coming before it for decision under this, Act, the opinion of majority shall prevail:

(4) 4{The Chairman) may authorise any of its members to exercise of the powers conferred on it by section 74 and any order made or act done in exercise of those powers by the member so authorised shall be deemed to be the order or act, as the case may be, of the Board.

(5) No member of the Copyright Board shall take part in any proceedings before the board in respect of any matter in which he has a personal interest.

(6) No act done or proceeding taken by the Copyright Board under this Act shall be questioned on the ground merely of the existence of any vacancy in, or defect in the constitution of, the Board.}

(7) The Copyright Board shall be deemed to be a civil court for the purposes of 5{sections 345 and 346 of the Code of Criminal Procedure, 1973 (2 of 1974)}, and all proceedings before the Board shall be deemed to be Judicial proceedings within the

meaning of sections 193 and 228 of the Indian Penal Code. (45 lf 1860).

CHAPTER III : COPYRIGHT

13. Works is which copyright subsists

(1) Subject to the provisions of the section and the other provisions of this Act, copyright shall subsist through out India in the following classes of works, that is to say,—

(a) original literary, dramatic, musical and artistic works;

(b) cinematograph films; and

(c) 1{sound recording}.

(2) **Copyright shall not subsist in any work specified in sub-section** (i), other than a work to which the provisions of section 40 or section 41 apply, unless,—

(i) in the case of published work, the work is first published in India, or where the work is first published outside India, the author is at the date of such publication, or in a case where the author was dead at that date , was at the time of his death, a citizen of India;

(ii) in the case of an unpublished work other than an 2 {work of architecture}, the author is at the date of the making of the work a citizen of India or domiciled in India; and

(iii) in the case of an 2{work of architecture}, the work is located in India.

(iv) **Explanation :** In the case of a work of joint authorship, the conditions conferring copyright specified in this sub-section shall be satisfied by all the authors of the work.

(3) **Copyright shall not subsist,**

(a) in any cinematograph film if a substantial part of the film is an infringement of the copyright in any other work;

(b) in any 1{ sound recording} made in respect of a literary, dramatic or musical work, if in making the 1{sound recording}, copyright in such work has been infringed.

(4) **The copyright in a cinematograph film** or a 1{sound recording} shall not affect the separate copyright in any work in respect of which or a substantial part of which, the film, or as the case may be, the 1{sound recording} is made.

(5) **In the case of an 2{work of architecture}, copyright** shall subsist only in the artistic character and design and shall not extend to process or methods of construction.

3{14. Meaning of copyright.—For the purpose of this Act, "Copyright" means the exclusive right subject to the provisions of this Act, to do or authorise the doing of any of the following acts in respect of a work or any substantial part thereof, namely:—

(a) in the case of literary, dramatic or musical work, not being a computer programme.—

(i) to reproduce the work in any material form including the storing of it in any medium by electronic means;

(ii) to issue copies of the work to the public not being copies already in circulation;

(iii) to perform the work in public, or communicate it to the public;

(iv) to make any cinematograph film or sound recording in respect of the work;

(v) to make any translation of the work;

(vi) to make any adaptation of the work;

(vii) to do, in relation to a translation or an adaptation of the work, any of the acts specified in relation to the work in sub-clauses (i) to (vi);

(b) In the case of a computer programme.—

(i) to do any of the acts specified in clauses (a);

(ii) to sell or give on hire, or offer for sale or hire, any copy of the computer programme, regardless of whether such copy has been sold or given on hire on earlier occasions;

(c) In the case of an artistic work,—

(i) to reproduce the work in any material form including depiction in three dimensions of a two dimensional work or in two dimensions of a three dimensional work;

(ii) to communicate the work to the public;

(iii) to issue copies of the work to the public to the public not being copies already in circulation;

(iv) to include the work in any cinematograph film;

(v) to make any adaptation of the work;

(vi) to do in relation to an adaptation of the work any of the acts specified in relation to the work in sub-clauses (i) to (iv);

(d) In the case of a cinematograph film,—

(i) to make a copy of the film, including a photograph of any image forming part thereof;

(ii) to sell or give on hire, or offer for sale or hire, any copy of the film, regardless of whether such copy has been sold or given on hire on earlier occasions;

(iii) to communicate the film to the public;

(e) In the case of a sound recording ,—

(i) to make any other sound recording embodying it;

(ii) to sell or give on hire, or offer for sale or hire, any copy of the sound recording regardless of whether such copy has been sold or given on hire on earlier occasions;

(iii) to communicate **the sound recording** to the public.

Explanation : For the purposes of this section, a copy which has been sold once shall be deemed to be a copy already in circulation.}

15. Special provision regarding copyright in designs registered

Special provision regarding copyright in designs registered or capable of being registered under the Design act, 1911.—(1) Copyright shall not subsist under this Act in any design which is registered under the 1* * * * Design Act, 1911 (2) of 1911).

(2) **Copyright in any design**, which is capable of being registered under the 1* * * * Design Act, 1911 (2 of 1911), but which has not been so registered, shall cease as soon as any article to which the design has been applied has been reproduces more than fifty times by an industrial process by the owner of the copyright or, with his licence, by any other person.

16. No copyright except as provided in this Act

No person shall be entitled to copyright or any similar right in any work, whether published or unpublished, otherwise than under and in accordance with the provisions of this Act or of any other law for the time being in force, but nothing in this section shall be construed as abrogating any right or jurisdiction to restrain a breach of trust or confidence.

CHAPTER IV : OWNERSHIP OF COPYRIGHT AND THE RIGHTS OF THE OWNER

17. First owner of Copyright

Subject to the provisions of this Act, the author of a work shall be the first owner of the copyright therein:

Provided that—

(a) **in the case of a literary, dramatic or artistic work** made by the author in the course of his employment by proprietor of a newspaper, magazine or similar periodical under a contract of service or apprenticeship, for the purpose of publication in a newspaper, magazine or similar periodical, the said proprietor shall, in the absence of any agreement to the contrary, be the first owner of the copyright in the work in so far as the copyright relates to the publication of the work in any newspaper, magazine or similar periodical, or to the reproduction of the work for the purpose of its being so published, but in all other respects the author shall be the first owner of the copyright in the work;

(b) **subject to the provisions of clause (a), in the case** of a photograph taken, or a painting or portrait drawn, or an engraving or a cinematograph film made, for valuable consideration at the instance of any person, such person shall, in the absence of any agreement to the contrary, be the first owner of the copyright therein;

(c) in the case of a work made in the course of the author's employment under a contract of service or apprenticeship, to which clause (a) or clause (b) does not apply, the employer shall, in the absence of any agreement to the contrary, be the first owner of the copyright therein;

2(cc) in the case of any address or speech delivered in public, the person who has delivered such address or speech or if such person has delivered such address or speech on behalf of any other person., such other person shall be the first owner of the copyright therein not with- standing that the person who deliver such address or speech, or as the case may be, the person on whose behalf such address or speech is delivered, is employed by any other person who arranges such address or speech or on whose behalf or premises such address or speech is delivered;}

(d) in the case of a Government work, Government shall, in the absence of any agreement to the contrary, be the first owner of the copyright therein;

1(dd) in the case of a work made or first published by or under the direction or control of any public undertaking, such public undertaking shall, in the absence of any agreement to the contrary, be the first owner of the copyright therein.

Explanation : For the purposes of this clause and section 28 A, "public undertaking" means,—

(i) an understanding owned or controlled by Government; or

(ii) a Government company as defined in section 617 of the Companies Act,1956 (1 of (1 of 1956); or

(iii) in the cases of a work to which the provisions of section 41 apply, the international organisation concerned shall be the first owner of the copyright therein.

18. Assignment of copyright

(1) the owner of the copyright in an existing work or the prospective owner of the copyright in a future

work may assign to any person the copyright either wholly or partially and either generally or subject to limitations and either for the whole term of the copyright or any part thereof:

Provided that in the case of the assignment of copyright in any future work, the assignment shall take effect only when the work comes into existence.

(2) Where the assignee of a copyright becomes entitled to any right comprised in the copyright, the assignee as respects the rights so assigned, and the assignor as respects the rights not assigned, shall be treated for the purposes of this Act as the owner of copyright and the provisions of this Act shall have effect accordingly.

(3) In this section, the expression "assignee" as respects the assignment of the copyright in any future work includes the legal representative of the assignee, if the assignee dies before the work comes into existence.

19. Mode of assignment

2{1)} No assignment of the copyright in any work shall be valid unless it is in writing signed by the assignor or by his duly authorised agent.

3{(2) The assignment of copyright in any work shall identify such work, and shall specify the rights assigned and the duration and territorial extent of such assignment.

(3) The assignment of copyright in any work shall also specify the amount of royalty payable, if any, to the author or his legal heirs during the currency of the assignment and the assignment shall be subject to revision, extension or termination on terms mutually agreed upon by the parties.

(4) Where the assignee does not exercise the rights assigned to him under any of the other sub- sections

of this section within a period of one year from the date of assignment, the assignment in respect of such rights shall be deemed to have lapsed after the expiry of the said period unless otherwise specified in the assignment.

(5) If the period of assignment is not stated, it shall be deemed to be five years from the date of assignment.

(6) If the territorial extent of assignment of the rights isnot specified, it shall be presumed to extend within India.

(7) Nothing in sub- section (2) or sub –section (3) or sub-section(4) or sub-ssection (5) or sub- section(6) shall be applicable to assignments made before the coming into force of the Copyright (Amendment) Act,1994.}

1{19A. Dispute with respect to assignment of copyright.- (1) If an assignee falls to make sufficient exercise of the rights assigned to him, and such failure is not attributable to any act or omission of the assignor, then, the Copyright Board may, on receipt of a complaint from the assignor and after holding such inquiry as it may deem necessary revoke such assignment.

(2) If any dispute arises with respect to the assignment of any copyright the Copyright Board may, on receipt of a complaint from the aggrieved party and after holding such inquiry as it considers necessary, pass such order as it may deem fit including an order for the recovery of any royalty payable:

Provided that the Copyright Board shall not pass any order this sub-section to revoke the assignment unless it is satisfied that the terms of assignment are harsh to the assignor in case the assignor is also the author:

Provided further that no order of revocation of assignment under this sub-section, shall be made within a period of five years from the date of such assignment.}

(20) Transmission of copyright in manuscript by testamentary disposition

Where under a be quest a person is entitled to the manuscript of a literary, dramatic or musical work, or to an artistic work, and the work was not published before the death of the testator, the bequest shall, unless the contrary intention is indicated in the testator's will or any codicil thereto, be construed as including the copyright in the work in so far as the testator was the owner of the copyright immediately before his death.

Explanation.—In this section, the expression "manuscript" means the original document embodying the work, whether by hand or not.

20. Right of author to relinquish copyright

(1) The author of a work may relinquish all or any of the rights comprised in the copyright in the work by giving notice in the prescribed form to the Registrar of Copyright s and there upon such rights shall, subject to the provisions of sub-section (3), cease to exist from the date of the notice.

(2) On receipt of a notice under sub- section (1), the Registrar of Copyrights shall cause it to be published in the Official Gazette and in such other manner as he may deem fit.

(3) The relinquishment of all or any of the rights comprised in the copyright in a work shall not affect any rights subsisting in favour of any person on the notice referred to in sub-section(1).

CHAPTER V : TERM OF COPYRIGHT

22. Term of copyright in published literary, dramatic, musical and artistic works

Except as otherwise here in after provided, copyright shall subsist in any literaary, dramatic, musical or artistic work (other than a photograph) published within the lifetime of the author until 2{Sixty years} from the begining of the calendar year next following the year in which the author dies.

Explanation : In this section the reference to the author shall, in the case of a work of joint authorship, be construed as a reference to the author who dies last.

23. Term of copyright in anonymous and pseudonymous works

(1) In the case of a literary, dramatic, musical or artistic work (other than a photograph), which is published anonymously or pseudonymously, copyright shall subsist until 1(sixty years} from the begining of the calendar year next following the year in which the work is first published;

Provided that where the identity of the author is disclosed before the expiry of the said period, copyright shall subsist until 1(sixty years) from the beginning of the calendar year next following the year in which the author dies.

(2) In sub-section (1), reference to the author shall, in the case of an anonymous work of joint authorship, be construed,-

(a) where the identity of one of the authors is disclosed, as references to that author;

(b) where the identity of more authors than one is disclosed, as references to the author who dies last from amongst such authors.

(3) In sub-section (1), references to the authors shall,

in the case of a pseudonyms work of joint authorship, be construed,—

(a) where the names of one or more (but not all) of the authors are pseudonyms and his or their identity is not disclosed, as references to the author whose name is not a pseudonyms or, if the name of two or more of the authors are not pseudonyms, as references to such of those authors who dies last;

(b) where the names of one or more (but not all) of the authors are pseudonyms and the identity of one or more of them is disclosed, as references to the author who dies last from amongst the authors whose names are not pseudonyms and the authors whose names are pseudonyms and are disclosed; and

(c) Where the names of all the authors are pseudonyms and the identity of one of them is disclosed, as references to the author whose identity is disclosed or if the identity of two or more of such authors is disclosed, as references to such of those authors who dies last.

Explanation : For the purposes of this section, the identity of an author shall be deemed to have been disclosed, if either the identity of the author is disclosed publicly by both the author and the publisher or is otherwise established to the satisfaction of the Copyright Board by the author.

24. Term of copyright in posthumous work

(1) In the case of a literary, dramatic or musical work or an engraving, in which copyright subsists at the date of the death of the author or, in the case of any such work of joint authorship, at or immediately before the date of the death of the author who dies

last, but which, or any adaptation of which, has not been published before that date, copyright shall subsist until(sixty years) from the beginning of the calendar year next following the year in which the work is first published or, where an adaptation of the work is published in any earlier year, from the beginning of the calendar year next following that year.

(2) For the purposes of this section a literary, dramatic, or musical work or an adaptation of any such work shall be deemed to have been published , if it has been performed in public or if any1{sound recording} made in respect of the work have been sold to the public or have been offered for sale to the public.

25. Term of copyright in photographs

In the case of a photograph, copyright shall subsist until 2(sixty years) from the beginning of the calendar year next following the year in which the photograph is published.

26. Term of copyright in cinematograph films

In the case of a cinematograph film, copyright shall subsist until 2(sixty years), from the beginning of the calendar year next following the year in which the film is published.

27. Term of copyright in records

In the case of a 1(sound recording), copyright shall subsist until 2(sixty years) from the beginning of the calendar year next following the year in which the 1(sound recording is published.

28. Term of copyright in Government work

In the case of Government work, where Government is the first owner of the copyright therein, copyright shall subsist until 2(sixty years) from the beginning of the calendar year next following the year in which the work is first published.

3{28 A. Term of copyright in works of public undertakings : In the case of a work, where a public undertaking is the first owner of the copyright therein, copyright shall subsist until 2(sixty years) from the beginning of the calendar year next following the year in which the work is first published.

29. Term of Copyright in works of International Organisations

In the case of a work of an international organisation to which the provisions of section 41 apply, copyright shall subsist until 2(sixty years) from the beginning of the calendar year next following the year in which the work is first published.

CHAPTER VI : LICENCES

30. Liences by owners of copyright

The owner of the copyright in any existing work the prospective owner of the copyright in any future work may grant any interest in the right by licence in writing signed by him or by his duly authorised agent;

Provided that in the case of a licence relating to copyright in any future work, the licence shall take effect only when the work comes into existence.

Explanation : Where a person to whom a licence relating to copyright in any future work is granted under this section dies before the work comes into existence, his legal representatives shall, in the absence of any provision to the contrary in the licence, be entitled to the benefit of the licence.

4{30 A. Application of sections 19 and 19A.— The provisions of sections 19 and 19 A shall, with any necessary adaptations and modifications, apply in relation to a licemce under section 30 as they apply in relation to assignment of copyright in a work.}

31. Compulsory licence in works withheld from public

(1) If at any time during the term of copyright in any Indian work which has been published pr performed in public, a complaint is made to the Copyright Board that the owner of copyright in the work.-

(a) has refused to republish or allow the republication of the work or has refused to allow the performance in public of the work, and by reason of such refusal the work is withheld from the public; or

(b) has refused to allow communication to the public by 1{ broadcast},of such work or in the case of a 2{sound recording) the work recorded in such 2{sound recording} on term which the complaint considers reasonable;

the Copyright Board, after giving to the owner of the copyright in the work a reasonable opportunity the being heard and after holding such inquiry as it may deem necessary, may if it is satisfied that the grounds for such refusal are not reasonable, direct the Registrar of copyrights to grant to the complainant a licence to republish the work, perform the work in public or communicate the work to the public by 1{broadcast}, as the case may be, subject to payment to the owner of the copyright of such compensation and subject to such or the terms and conditions as the Copyright Board may determine; and thereupon the Registrar of Copyrights shall grant the licence to the complainant in accordance with the directions of the Copyright Board, on payment of such fee as may be prescribed.

Explanation : In this sub- section, the expression "Indian work" includes-

(i) an artistic work, the author of which is a citizen of India; and

(ii) a cinematograph film or a 2{sound recording} made or manufactured in India.

(2) Where two or more persons have made a complaint under sub- section (1), the licence shall be granted to the complainant who in the opinion of the Copyright Board would best serve the interests of the general public.

3{31A. Compulsory licence in unpublished Indian works.—

(1) Where, in the case of an Indian work referred to in sub- clause (iii) of clause (1) of section 2, the author is dead or unknown or cannot be traced, or the owner of the copyright in such work cannot found, any person may apply to the Copyright Board for a licence to publish such work or a translation thereof in any language.

(2) Before making an application under sub-section (1), the applicant shall publish his proposal in one issue of a daily newspaper in the English language having circulation in the major part of the country and where the application is for the publication of a translation in any language, also in one issue of any daily newspaper in that language.

(3) Every such application shall be made in such form as may be prescribed and shall be accompanied with a copy of the advertisement issued under sub-section (2) and such fee as may be prescribed.

(4) Where an application is made to the Copyright Board under this section, it may, after holding such inquiry as may be prescribed, direct the Registrar of Copyright to grant to the applicant a licence to publish the work or a translation thereof in the language mentioned in the application subject to the payment of such royalty and subject to such

other terms and conditions as the Copyright Board may determine, and thereupon the Registrar of copyright shall grant the licence to the applicant in accordance with the direction of the Copyright Board.

(5) Where a licences is granted under this section, the Registrar of Copyrights may, by order, direct the applicant to deposit the amount of the royalty determined by the Copyright Board in the public account of India or in any other account specified by the Copyright Board so as to enable the owner of the copyright or, as the case may be, his heirs, executors or the legal representatives to claim such royalty an any time.

(6) Without prejudice to the forgoing provisions of this section, in the case of a work referred to in sub-section (1), is the original author is dead, the Central Government may, if it considers, that the publication of the work is desirable is the national interest, require the heirs, executors or legal representatives of the author to publish such work within such period as may be specified by it,

(7) Where any work is not published within the period specified by the Central Government under sub-section (6), the copyright Board may, on an application made by any person for permission to publish the work and after hearing the parties concerned, permit such publication on payment of such royalty as the Copyright Board may, in the circumstances of such case, determine in the prescribed manner,}

32. Licence to produce and publish translations

(i) Any person may apply to the Copyright Board for a licence to produce and publish a translation of a literary or dramatic work in any language 1{ after a period of seven years from the first publication of the work}.

1{(1A) Notwithstanding anything contained in sub-section (1(, any person may apply to the Copyright Board for a licences to produce and publish a translation, in printed or analogous forms of reproduction, of a literary or dramatic work, other than an Indian work, in any language in general use in India after a period of these years from the first publication *of such work, if such translation is required for the purposed of teaching scholarship or research*:

Provided that where such translation is in a language not in general use in any developed country, such application may be made after a period of one year from such publication.}

(2) Every 2{application under this section} shall be made in such form as may be prescribed and shall state the proposed retail price of a copy of the translation of the work.

(3) Every applicant for a licence under this section shall, along with his application, deposit with the Registrar of Copyrights such fee as may be prescribed.

(4) Where an application is made to the Copyright Board under this section, it may, after holding such inquiry as may be prescribed, grant to the applicant a licences, not being an exclusive licence, to produce and publish a translation of the work in the language mentioned in 3(the application-

(i) subject to the condition that the applicant shall pay to the owner of Copyright in the work royalties in respect of copies of the translation of the work sold to the public, calculated at such rate as the Copyright Board may, in the circumstances of each case, determine in the prescribed manner: and

(ii) where such licence is granted on an application under sub- section (1A), subject also to the condition that the licence shall not extend to the export of copies of the translation of the work outside India and every copy of such translation shall contain a notice in the language of such translation that the copy is available for distribution only in India.

Provided that nothing in clause (ii) shall apply to the export by Government or any authority under the Government of copies of such translation in a language other than English, French or Spanish to any country if— such copies are sent to citizens of India residing outside India or to any association of such citizens outside India ; or

(1) such copies are meant to be used for purposes of teaching, scholarship or research and not for any commercial purpose; and

(2) in either case, the permission for such export has been given by the Government of that country:}

(3) Provided further that no licence under this section} shall be granted, unless—

(a) a translation of the work in the language mentioned in the application has not been published by the owner of the copyright in the work or any person authorised by him, 2{within seven years or three years or one year, as the case may be, of the first publication of the work}, or if a translation has been so published, it has been out of print;

(b) the applicant has proved to the satisfaction of the Copyright Board that he has requested and had been denied authorisation by the owner of the copyright to produce and publish such translation, or that 2{ he was, after due diligence on his part, unable to find} the owner of the copyright;

(c) where the applicant was unable to find the owner of the copyright, he had sent a copy of his request for 2{such authorisation by registered air mail post to the publisher whose name appears from the work, and in the case of an application for aliens under sub- section (1)}, not less than two months before 2{such application};

3{(cc) a period of six months in the case of an application under sub- section (1A)(not being an application under the proviso thereto), or nine months in the case of an application under the proviso to that sub-section, has elapsed from the date of making the request under clause (b) of this proviso, or where a copy of the request has been sent under clause (c) of this proviso, from the date of sending of such copy, and the translation of the work in the language mentioned in the application has not been published by the owner of the copyright in the work or any person authorised bi him within the said period of six months or nine months, as the case may be;

(ccc) in the case of any application made under sub- section (1A),—

(i) the name of the author and the title of the particular edition of the work proposed to be translated are printed on all the copies of the translation:

(ii) if the work is composed mainly of illustrations, the provisions of section32A are also complied with;}

(d) the copyright board is satisfied that the applicant is competent to produce and publish a correct translation of the work and possesses the means to pay to the owner of the copyright the royalties payable to him under this section;

(e) the author has not withdrawn from circulation copies of the work; and

(f) an opportunity of being heard is given, wherever practicable, to the owner of the copyright in the work.

1{(5) Any Broadcasting authority may apply to the Copyright Board for a licence to produce and publish the translation of—

(a) a work referred to in sub- section (1A) and published in printed or analog us forms of reproduction: or

(b) any text incorporated in audio- visual fixations prepared and published solely for the purpose of systematic instructional activities, for broadcasting such translation for the purposes of teaching or for the dissemination of the results of specialised, technical or scientific research to the experts in any particular field.

(6) The provisions of sub- sections (2) to (4) in so far as they are relatable to an application under sub-section (1A), shall, with the necessary modification, apply to the grant of a liccence under sub-section (5) and such licence shall not also be granted unless—

(a) the translation is made from a work lawfully required;

(b) the broadcast is made through the medium of sound and visual recordings;

(c) such recording has been lawfully and exclusively made for the purpose of broadcasting in India by the applicant or by any other broadcasting agency; and

(d) the translation and the broadcasting of such translation are not used for any commercial purposes.

Explanation : For the purposes of this section,—

(a) "developed country" means a country which is not a developing country;

(b) "developing country" means a country which is for the time being regarded as such in conformity with the practice of the General Assembly of the United Nations;

(c) "purposes of research" does not include purposes of industrial research, or purposes of research by bodies corporate (not being bodies corporate owned or controlled be Government) or other associations or body of persons for commercial purposes;

(d) "purposes of teaching, research or scholarship" includes—

(i) purposes of instructional activity at all levels in educational institutions, including Schools, Colleges, Universities and tutorial institutions; and

(ii) purposes of all other types of organised educational activity.}

2{32A. Licence to reproduce and publish works for certain purposes

(1) Where, after the expiration of the relevant period from the date of the first publication of an edition of a literary, scientific or artistic work,—

(a) the copies of such edition are not made available in India; or

(b) such copies have not been put on sale in India for a period of six months, to the general public, or in connection with systematic instructional activities at a price reasonably related to that normally charged in India for comparable works by the owner of the right to reproduction or by any person authorises by him in this behalf, any person may apply the Copyright Board for a licence to reproduce and publish such work in printed or analogous forms of reproduction at the price at which such edition is sold or at a lower price for the purposes of systematic instructional activities.

(2) Every such application shall be made in such form as may be prescribed and shall state the proposed retail price of a copy of the work to be reproduced.

(3) Every applicant for a licence under this section shall, along with his application, deposit with the Registrar of Copyrights such fee as may be prescribed.

(4) Where an application is made to the Copyright Board under this section, it may, after holding such inquiry as may be prescribed . grant to the application a licence, not being an exclusive licence, to produce and publish a reproduction of the work mentioned in the application subject to the conditions that,—

(i) the applicant shall pay to the owner of the copyright in the work royalties in respect of copies of the reproduction of the work sold to the public, calculated at such rate as the Copyright Board may. in the circumstances of each case, determine in the prescribed manner;

(ii) a licence granted under this section shall not extend to the export of copies of the reproduction of the work outside India and every copy of such reproduction shall contain a notice that the copy is available for distribution only in India;

Provided that no such licence shall be granted unless—

(a) the applicant has proved to the satisfaction of the Copyright Board that he had requested and has been denied authorisation by the owner of the copyright in the work to reproduce and publish such work or that he was, after due diligence on his part, unable to find such owner;

(b) where the applicant was unable to find the owner of the copyright, he had sent a copy of his request for such authorisation by registered airmail post to the publisher whose name appears from the work not less than three months before the application for the licence;

(c) the copyright Board is satisfied that the applicant is competent to reproduce and publish an accurate reproduction of the work and possesses the means to pay to owner of the copyright the royalties payable to him under this section;

(d) the applicant under takes to reproduce and publish the work aat such price as may be fixed by the copyright Board, being a price reasonably related to the price normally charged in India for works of the same standard on the same or similar subjects;

(e) a period of six months in the case of an application for the reproduction and publication of any work of natural science, physical science, mathematics or technology, or a period of three months in the case of an application for the reproduction and publication of any other work, has elapsed from the date of making the request under clause (a), or where a copy of the request has been sent under clause (b), from the date of sending of a copy, and a reproduction of the work, has not been published by the owner of the copyright in the work or any person authorised by him within the said period of six months or, three months, as the case may be;

(f) the name of the author and the title of the particular edition of the work proposed to be reproduced are printed on all the copies of the reproduction;

(g) the author has not withdrawn from circulation copies of the work; and

(h) an opportunity of being heard is given, wherever practicable, to the owner of the copyright in the work.

(5) No licence to reproduce and publish the translation of a work shall be granted under this section unless such translation has been published by the owner of the right of translation or any person authorised by him and the translation is not in a language in general use in India.

(6) The provisions of this section shall also apply to the reproduction and publication, or translation into a language in general use in India, of any text incorporated in audio- visual fixations prepared and published solely for the purpose of systematic instructional activities.

Explanation : For the purposes of this section," relevant Period" in relation to any work, means a period of—

(a) seven years from the date of the first publication of that work, where the application is for the reproduction and publication of any work of, or relating to, fiction, poetry, drama, music, or art;

(b) three years from the date of the first publication of that work, where the application is for the reproduction and publication of any work of, or relating to, natural science, physical science, mathematics or technology; and

(c) five years from the date of the first publication of that work, in any other case.

32B. Termination of licences issued under this Chapter

(i) If, at any time after the granting of a liccence to produce and publish the translation of a work in any language under sub-section (1A) of section 32 (hereafter in this sub-section referred to as the licenced work), the owner of the copyright in the work or any person authorised by him publishes a translation of such work in the same language and which is substantially the same in content at apprise reasonably related to the price normally charged in India for the translation of works of the same standard on the same or similar subject, the licence so granted shall be terminated:

Provided that no such termination shall take effect until after the expiry of a period of three months from the date of service of a notice in the prescribed manner on the person holding such licence by the owner of the right of translation intimating the publication of the translation as aforesaid:

Provided further that copies of the licenced work produced and published by the person holding such licence before the termination of the licence takes effect may continue to be sold or distributed until the copied already produced and published are exhausted.

(2) If, at any time after the granting of a licence to produce and publish the reproduction or translation of any work under section 32 A, the owner of the right of reproduction or any person authorised by him sells or distributes copies of such work or a translation thereof, as the case may be, in the same language and which is substantially the same in content at a price reasonably related to the price normally charged ij India for works of the same standard on the same or similar subject, the licence so granted shall be terminated:

Provided that no such termination shall take effect until after the expiry of a period of three months from the date of service of a notice in the prescribed manner on the person holding the licence by the owner of the right of reproduction intimating the sale or distribution or the copies of the editions of work as aforesaid:

Provided further that any copies already reproduced by the licence before such termination takes effect may continue to be sold of distributed until the copies already produced are exhausted.}

CHAPTER VII : COPYRIGHT SOCIETIES

33. Registration of Copyright Society

(1) No person or association of persons shall, after coming into force of the Copyright (Amendment Act, 1994 commence or, carry on the business of issuing or granting licences in respect of any work in which copyright subsists or in respect of any other rights conferred by this Act except under or in accordance with the registration granted under sub-section (3):

Provided that an owner of copyright shall, in his individual capacity, continue to have the right to grant licences in respect of his own works consistent with his obligations as a member of the registered copyright society:

Provided further that a performing rights society functioning in accordance with the provisions of section 33 on the date immediately before the coming into force of the copyright (Amendment) act, 1994 shall be deemed to be a copyright society for the purposes of this chapter and every such society shall get itself registered within a period of one year from the date of commencement of the Copyright (Amendment) Act, 1994.

(2) Any association of persons who fulfils such conditions as may be prescribed may apply for permission to do the business specified in sub-section (1) to the Registrar of Copyrights who shall submit the application to the Central Government.

(3) The Central Government may, having regard to the interests of the authors and other owners of rights

under this Act, the interest and convenience of the public and in particular of the groups of persons who are most likely to seek licences in respect of the relevant rights and the ability and professional competence of the applicants, register such association of persons as a copyright society subject to such conditions as may be prescribed:

Provided that the Central Government shall not ordinarily register more than one copyright society to do business in respect of the same class of works.

(4) The Central Government may, if it is satisfied that a copyright society is being managed in a manner detrimental to the interests of the owners of rights concerned, cancel the registration of such society after such inquiry as may be prescribed.

(5) If the Central Government is of the opinion that in the interest of the owners of rights concerned, it is necessary so to do, it may, by order, suspend the registration of such society pending inquiry for such period not exceeding one year as may be specified in such order sub-section (4) and that Government shall appoint an administration to discharge the functions of the copyright society

34 Administration of rights of owner by copyright society

(1) Subject to such conditions as may be prescribed,—

(a) a copyright society may accept from an owner of rights exclusive authorization to administer any right in any work by issue of licenses or collection of license fee or both; and

(b) an owner of rights shall have the right to withdraw such authorisation without prejudice to the rights of the copyright society under any contract.

(2) It shall be competent for a copyright society to enter into agreement with any foreign society or

organisation administration on rights corresponding to rights under this Act, to entrust to such foreign society or organisation the administration in any foreign country of rights administered by the said copyright society in India, or for administering in India the rights administered in a foreign country by such foreign society or organisation:

Provided that no such society or organisation shall permit any discrimination in regard to the terms of license or the distribution of fees collected between rights in Indian and other works.

(3) Subject to such conditions as may be prescribed, a copyright society may—

(i) issue licenses under section 30 in respect of any rights under this Act;

(ii) collect fees in pursuance of such licenses;

(iii) distribute such fees among owners of rights after making deductions for its own expenses;

(iv) perform any other functions consistent with the provisions of section 35.

34A. Payment of remunerations by copyright society

(1) If the Central Government is of the opinion that a copyright society for a class of work is generally administering the rights of the owners or rights in such work throughout India, it shall appoint that society for the purposes of this section.

(2) The copyright society shall, subject to such rules as may be made in this behalf, frame a scheme for determining the quantum of remuneration payable to individual copyright owners having regard to the number of copies of the work in circulation:

Provided that such scheme shall restrict payment to the owners of rights whose works have attained a level of circulation which the copyright society considers reasonable.

35. Control over the copyright society by the owner of rights

(i) Every copyright society shall be subject to the collective control of owners of rights under this Act whose rights it administers (not being owners of rights under this Act administered by a foreign society or organisation referred to in sub- section (2) of section 34) and a shall, in such manners as may be prescribed.-

(a) obtained the approval of such owners of rights for its procedures of collection and distribution of fees;

(b) obtained their approval for the utilisation of any amounts collected as fees for any purpose other than distribution to the owner of rights; and

(c) Provide to such owners regular, full and detailed information concerning all its activities, in relation to the administration of their rights.

(2) All fees distributed among the owners of rights shall. as far as may be, be distributed in proportion to the actual use of their world.

36. Submission of returns and reports

(1) Every copyright society shall submit to the Registrar of Copyrights such returns as may be prescribed.

(2) Any officer duly authorised by the Central Government in this behalf may call for any report and also call for any records of any copyright society for the purpose of satisfying himself that the fees collected by the society in respect of rights administered by it are being utilised or distributed in accordance with the provisions of this Act.

36A. Rights and liabilities of performing rights societies

Nothing in this Chapter shall affect any rights or liabilities in any work in connection with a performing rights society which had accrued or were incurred on or before the day prior to the commencement of the Copyright (Amendment) Act, 1994, Or any legal proceedings in respect of any such rights or liabilities pending on that day.)

CHAPTER VIII : RIGHTS OF BROADCASTING ORGANISATION AND OF PERFORMERS

37. Broadcast reproduction right

(1) Every broadcasting organisation shall have a special right to be known as " broadcast reproduction right" in respect of its broadcasts.

(2) The broadcast reproduction right shall subsist until twenty five years from the beginning of the calendar year next following the year in which the broadcast is made.

(3) During the continuance of a broadcast reproduction right in relation to any broadcast, any person who, without the license of the owner of the right does any of the following acts of the broadcast or any substantial part thereof,-

(a) re-broadcasts the broadcast; or

(b) causes the broadcast to be heard or seen by the public on payment of any charges; or

(c) makes any sound recording or visual recording of the broadcast; or

(d) makes any reproduction of such sound recording or visual recording where such initial recording was done without license or, where it was licensed, for any purpose not envisaged by such license; or

(e) sells or hire to the public, or offers for such sale or hire, any such sound recording or visual recording referred to in clause (c) or clause (d), Shall, subject to the provisions of section 39, be deemed to have infringed the broadcast reproduction right.}

38. Performer's right

(1) Where any performer appears or engages in any performance, he shall have a special right to be known as the " performer's right" in relation to such performance.

(2) The performer's right shall subsist until twenty- five years from the beginning of the calendar year next following the year in which the performance is made.

(3) During the continuance of a performer's right in relation to any performance, any person who, without the consent of the performer, does any of the following acts in respect of the performance or any substantial part thereof, namely:-

(a) makes a sound recording or visual recording of the performance; or

(b) reproduces a sound recording or visual recording of the performance, which sound recording or visual recording was—

(i) made without the performer's consent; or

(ii) made for purposes different from those for which the performer gave his consent; or made for purposes different from those referred to in section 39 from a sound recording or visual recording which was made in accordance with section 39; or

(c) broadcasts the performance except where the broadcast is made from a sound recording or visual recording other than one made in accordance with section 39, or is a re- broadcast by the same broadcasting organisation of an earlier broadcast which did not infringe the performer's right; or communicates the performance to the public otherwise than by broadcast, except where such communication to the public is made from a sound recording or a visual recording or a broadcast, shall, subject to the provisions of section 39, be deemed to have infringed the performer's right.

(4) Once a performer has consented to the incorporation of his performance in a cinematograph film, the provisions of sub- sections (1), (2) and (3) shall have no further application to such performance.}

39. Acts not infringing broadcast reproduction right or performer's right

No broadcast reproduction right or performer's right shall be deemed to be infringed by—

(a) the making of any sound recording or visual recording for the private use of the person making such recording, or solely for purposes of bonafide teaching or research; or

(b) The use, consistent with fair dealing, of experts of a performance or of a broadcast in the reporting of current events or for bonafide review, teaching or research; or

(c) such other acts, with any necessary adaptations and modifications, which do not constitute infringement of copyright under section 52.

39 A. Other provisions applying to broadcast reproduction right and perfor's right

Section 18, 19, 30, 53, 55, 58, 64, 65 and 66 shall, with any necessary adaptations and modifications, apply in relation to the broadcast reproduction right in any broadcast and performer's right in any performance as they apply in relation to copyright in a work:

Provided that where copyright or performer's right subsists in respect of any work or performance that has been broadcast, no license to reproduce such broadcast shall take effect without the consent of the owner of rights or performer, as the case may be, or both of them.}

CHAPTER IX : INTERNATIONAL COPYRIGHT

40. power to extend copyright to foreign works

The Central Government may, by order published in the Official Gazette, direct that all or any provisions of this Act shall apply-

(a) to work first published in any territory outside India to which the order relates in like manner as if they were first published within India;

(b) to unpublished works, or any class thereof, the authors whereof were at the time of the making of the work, subjects or citizens of a foreign country to which the order relates, in like manner as if the authors were citizens of India;

(c) in respect of domicile in any territory outside India to which the order relates in like manner as if such domicile were in India;

(d) to any work of which the author was at the date of the first publication thereof, or, in a case where the author was dead at that date, was at the time of his death, a subject or citizen of a foreign country to which the order relates in like manner as if the author was a citizen of India at that date or time; and thereupon, subject to the provisions of this Chapter and of the order, this Act shall apply accordingly:

Provided that—

(1) before making an order under this section in respect of any foreign country (other than a country with which India has entered into a treaty or which is a party to a convention relating to copyright to which India is also a party), the Central Government shall be satisfied that foreign country has made, or has undertaken to make, such provisions, if any, as it appears to Central Government expedient to require for the protection in that country of works entitled

to copyright under the provisions of this Act;

(ii) the order may provide that the provisions of this Act shall apply either generally or in relation to such classes of works or such classes of cases as may be specified in the order ;

(iii) the order may provide that the term of copyright in India shall no exceed that conferred by the law of the country to which the order relates;

(iii) the order may provide that the enjoyment of the rights conferred by this Act shall be subject to the accomplishment of such conditions and formalities, if any, as may be prescribed by the order;

(iv) in applying the provisions of this Act as to ownership of copyright, the order may make such exceptions and modifications as appear necessary, having regrd to the law of the foreign country;

(v) the order may provide that this Act or any part thereof shall not apply to works made before the commencement of the order or that this Act of any part thereof shall not apply to works first published before the commencement of the order.

41. Provisions as to works of certain international organisations

(1) Where-

(a) any work is made or first published by or under the direction 0r control of any organisation to which this section applies, and

(b) there would, a part from this section, be no copyright in the work in India at the time of the making or, as the case may be, of the first publication thereof, and

(c) either-

(i) the work is published as aforesaid in pursuance of an agreement in that behalf

with the author, being an agreement which does not reserve to the author the copyright, if any, in the work or

(ii) under section 17 any copyright in the work would belong to the organisation; there shall, by virtue of this section, be copyright in the work throughout India.

(2) Any organisation to which this section applies which at the material time had not the legal capacity of a body corporate for the purpose of holding, dealing with and enforcing copyright and in connection with all legal proceedings relating to copyright.

(3) The organisations to which this section applies are such organisations as the Central Government may, by order published in the Official Gazette, declare to be organisations of which one of more sovereign powers or the Government or Governments thereof are members to which it is expedient that this section shall apply.

42. Power to restrict rights in works of foreign authors first published in India

If it appears to the Central Government that a foreign country does not give or has not undertaken to give adequate protection of the works of Indian authors, the Central Government may, by order published in the Official Gazette, direct that such of the provisions of this Act as confer copyright on works first published in India shall not apply to works, published after the that specified in the order, the authors whereof are subjects or citizens of such foreign country and not domiciled in India, and there upon those provisions shall not apply to such works.

43. Orders under this Chapter to be laid before Parliament

Every order made by the Central Government under this Chapter shall, as soon as may be after it is made, be laid before both Houses of Parliament and shall be subject to such modifications as Parliament may make during the session in which it is so laid or the session immediately following.

CHAPTER X : REGISTRATION OF COPYRIGHT

44. Register of Copyrights

There shall be kept at the Copyright Office a register in the prescribed form to be called the Register of Copyrights in which may be entered the names or titles of works and the names and address of author, publishers and owners of copyright and such other particulars as may be prescribed.

45. Entries in register of Copyrights

(1) author or publisher of, or the owner of or other person interested in the copyright in, any work may make an application in the prescribed form accompanied by the prescribed fee to the Registrar of Copyrights for entering particulars of the work in the Register of Copyrights:

{Provided that in respect of an artistic work which is used or is capable of being used in relation to any goods, the application shall include a statement to that effect and shall be accompanied by a certificate from the Registrar if Trade Marks referred to in section 4 of the Trade and Merchandise Marks Act, 1958 (43 of 1958), to the effect that no trade mark identical with or deceptively similar to such artistic work has been registered under that Act in the name of, or that no application has been made under that Act for such registration by, any person other than the applicant.}

(2) On receipt of an application in respect of any work under sub- section (1), the Registrar of Copyrights may, after holding such inquiry as he may deem fit, enter the particulars of the work in the Register of Copyrights.

46. Indexes

There shall be also kept at the Copyright Office such indexes of the Register of Copyrights as may be prescribed.

47. Form and inspection of register

The register of Copyrights and indexes thereof kept under this Act shall at all reasonable times be open to inspection, and any person shall be entitled to take copies of, or make extracts from, such register or indexes on payment of such fee and subject to such conditions as may be prescribed.

48. Register of Copyrights to be prima facile evidence of particulars entered therein

The Register of Copyrights shall be prima facie evidence of the particulars entered therein and documents purporting to be copies of any entries therein, or extracts there from certified by the Registrar of Copyrights and sealed with the seal of the Copyright Office shall be admissible in evidence in all courts without further proof or production of the original.

49. Correction of entries in the Registered of Copyrights

The Registrar of Copyrights may, in the prescribed cases and subject to the prescribed conditions, amend or alter the Register of Copyrights by-

(a) correcting any error in any name, address or particulars; or

(b) correcting any other error which may have arisen therein by accidental slip or omission.

50. Rectification of Register by Copyright Board

The Copyright Board, on application of the Registrar of Copyrights or of any person aggrieved, shall order the rectification of the Register of Copyrights by—

(a) the making of any entry wrongly omitted to be made in the register, or

(b) the expunging of any entry wrongly made in, or remaining on, the register, or

(c) the correction of any error or defect in the register.

50A. Entries in the Register of Copyrights etc., to be published

Every entry made in the Register of Copyrights or the particulars of any work entered under section 45, the correction of every entry made in such register under section 49, and every rectification ordered under section 50, shall be published by the Registrar of Copyrights in the Official Gazette or in such other manner as he may deem fit,}

CHAPTER XI : INFRINGEMENT OF COPYRIGHT

51. When copyright infringed

Copyright in a work shall be deemed to be infringed—

(a) when any person, without a license granted by the owner of the copyright or the Registrar of Copyrights under this Act or in contravention of the conditions of a license so granted or of any condition imposed by a competent authority under this Act—

(i) dose anything, the exclusive right to do which is by this Act conferred upon the owner of the copyright, or

(ii) permits for profit any place to be used for the communication of the work to the public where such communication constitutes an infringement of the copyright in the work, unless he was not aware and had no reasonable ground for believing that such communication to the public would be an infringement of copyright:; or

(b) when any person—

(i) makes for sale or hire, or sells or lets for hire, or be way of trade displays or offers for sale or hire. or

(ii) distributes either for the purpose of trade or to such an extent as to affect prejudicial the owner of the copyright, or

(iii) by way of trade exhibits in public or

(v) imports 1*** into India, any infringing copies of the work: [provided that nothing in sub-clause (iv) shall apply to the import of one copy of any work for the private and domestic use of the importer.]

Explanation : For the purposes of this section the reproduction of a literary, dramatic, musical or artistic work in the form of a cinematographic film shall be deemed to be an " infringing copy".

52. Certain Acts not to be infringement of copyright

(1) The following Acts shall not constitute an infringement of copyright, namely:-

(a) a fair dealing with a literary, dramatic, musical or artistic work {not being a computer programme,} for the purposes of-

(i) private use, including research;

(ii) criticism or review, whether of that work, or of any other work;

[aa) the making of copies or adaptation of a computer programme by the lawful possessor of a copy of such computer programme, from such copy-

(i) in order to utilise the computer programme for the purpose for which it was supplied; or

(ii) to make back –up copies purely as a temporary protection against loss, destruction or damage in order only to utilise the computer programme

for the purpose for which is was supplied;]

(b) a fair dealing with a literary, dramatic, musical or artistic work for the purpose of reporting current events-

(i) in a newspaper, magazine or similar periodical, or

(ii) by {Broadcast} or in a cinematograph film or by means of photographs.

Explanation : The publication of a compilation of addresses or speeches delivered in public is not a fair dealing of such work within the meaning of this clause;

(c) the reproduction of a literary, dramatic, musical or artistic work for the purpose of a judicial proceeding or for the purpose of a report of a judicial proceeding;

(d) the reproduction or publication of a literary, dramatic, musical or artistic work in any work prepared by the Secretariat of a Legislature or where the Legislature consists of two houses, by the Secretariat of either House of the Legislature, exclusively for the use of the members of the Legislature;

(e) the reproduction of ant literary, dramatic or musical work in a certified copy made or supplied in accordance with any law for the time being in force;

(f) the reading or recitation in public of any reasonable extract from a published literary or dramatic work;

(5) the publication in a collection, mainly composed of non-copyright matter, bonafide intended for the use of educational institutions and so described in the title and in any advertisement issued by or on behalf of the publisher, of short passage from published literary or dramatic works not themselves published for the use of educational institutions, in which copyright subsists:

Provided that not more than two such passages from works by the same author are published by the same publisher during any period of five years.

Explanation : In the case of a work of joint authorship, references in this clause to passages from works shall include references to passage from works by any one or more of the authors of those passages or by any one or more of those authors in collaboration with any other person;

(6) the reproduction of a literary, dramatic, musical or artistic work-

(7) by a teacher or a pupil in the course of instruction; or

(i) as part of the questions to be answered in the examination; or

(ii) in answers to such questions;

(iii) the performance, in the course of the activities of an educational institution, of a literary, dramatic or musical work by the staff and students of the institution, or of a cinematograph film or a record, if the audience is limited to such staff and students, the parents and guardians of the students and persons directly connected with the activities of the institution{ or the communication to such an audience of a cinematograph film or sound recording}:

(j) the making of sound recordings in respect of any literary, dramatic or musical work, if—

(i) sound recordings of that work have been made by or with the license or consent of the owner of the right in the work;

(ii) the person making sound recordings has given a notice of his intention to make the sound recordings, has provided copies of all covers or labels with which the sound recordings are to be sold, and has paid in the prescribed manner to the owner of rights in the work royalties in respect of all such sound recordings to be made by him , at the rate fixed by the Copyright Board in this behalf:

Provided that-

(i) no alterations shall be made which have not been made previously by or with the consent of the owner of rights , or which are not reasonably necessary for the adaptation of the work for the purpose of making the sound recordings;

(ii) the sound recordings shall not be issued in any form of packaging or with any label which is likely to mislead or confuse the public as to their identity;

(iii) no such sound recording shall be made until the expiration of two calendar years after the end of the year in which the first sound recordings shall allow the owner of rights or his surly authorised agent or representative to inspect all records and books of account relating to such sound recording:

Provider further that if on a complaint brought before the Copyright Board to the effect that the owner of rights has not been paid in full for any sound recordings purporting to be made in pursuance of this clause, the Copyright Board is, prima facie, satisfied that the complaint is genuine, it may pass an order ex -party directing the person making the sound recording to cease from making further copies and, after holding such inquiry as it considers necessary, make such further order aqs it may deem fit, including an order for payment of royalty;

(k) the causing of a recording to be heard in public by utilising-

(i) in an enclosed room or hall meant for the

common use of residents in any residential premises (not being a hotel or similar commercial establishment) as part of the amenities provided exclusively or mainly for residents therein; or

(ii) as part of the activities of a club or similar organisation which is not established or conducted for profit;)

(l) the performance of literary, dramatic or musical work by an amateur club or society, if the performance is given to a non- paying audience, or for the benefit of a religious institution;

(m) the reproduction of a news paper, magazine or other periodical of an article on current economic, political, social or religious topics, unless the author of such article has expressly reserved to himself the right of such reproduction;

(n) the publication in a newspaper, magazine or other periodical of a report of a lecture delivered in public;

(o) the making of not more than three copies of a book (including a pamphlet, sheet of music, map, chart, or plan) by or under the direction of the person in charge of a public library for the use of the library if such book is not available for sale in India;

(p) the reproduction for the purpose of research or private study or with a view to publication, of an unpublished literary, dramatic or musical work kept in a library, museum or other institution to which the public has access:

Provided that were the identity of the author of any such work or, in the case of a work of joint authorship, of any of the authors is known to the library, museum or other institution, as the case may be, the provisions of this clause shall apply only if such reproduction is made at a time more than fifty years from the date of the death of the authors or, in the case of a work of joint authorship, from the death of the author whose identity is known or , if the identity of more authors than one is known from the death of such of those authors who dies last.

(q) the reproduction or publication of-

(i) any matter which has been published in any Official Gazette except an Act of a legislature;

(ii) any act of a Legislature subject to the condition that such Act is reproduce or published together with any commentary thereon or any other original matter;)

(iii) the report of any committee, commission, council, board or other like body appointed by the Government if such report has been laid on the Table of Legislature, unless the reproduction or publication of such report is prohibited by the Government;

(iv) any judgment or order of a court, tribunal or other judicial authority, unless the reproduction or publication of such judgment or order is prohibited by the court, the tribunal or other judicial authority, as the case may be;

(vii) the production or publication of a translation in any Indian language of an Act of a Legislature and of any rules or orders made there under-

(8) if no translation of such Act or rules or orders in that language has previously been produced or published by the Government; or

(i) where a translation of such Act or rules or orders in that language has been produced or published by the Government, if the translation is not available for sale to the public;

Provided that such translation contains a statement at a prominent place to the effect

that the translation has not been authorised or accepted as authentic by the Government;

(viii) the making or publishing of a painting, drawing, engraving or photograph of a work of architecture or the display of a work of architecture;

(ix) the making or publishing of a painting, drawing, engraving or photograph of a sculpture, or other artistic work falling under sub- clause (iii) of clause (c) of section2, if such work is permanently situate in a public place or any premises to which the public has access;

(x) the inclusion in a cinematograph film of-

(i) any artistic work permanently situate in a public place or any premises to which the public has access; or

(ii) any other artistic work, if such inclusion is only by way of background or is otherwise incidental to the principal matters represented in the film;

(xi) the use by the author of an artistic work, where the author of such work is not the owner of the copyright therein, of any mould, cast, sketch, plan, model or study made by him for the purpose of the work:

Provided that he does not thereby repeat or imitate the main design of the work;

* * * * *

(x) the reconstruction of a building or structure in accordance with the architectural drawings or plans by reference to which the building or structure was originally constructed:

provided that the original construction was made with the consent or license of the owner of the copyright in such drawings and plans;

(y) in relation to a literary, dramatic or musical work recorded or reproduced in any cinematograph film, the exhibition of such film after thee expiration of the term of copyright therein:

Provided that the provisions of sub- clause ii) of clause (a), sub- clause (i) of clause (b) ana clauses (d), (f), (g),(m) and (p) shall not apply as respects any act unless that act is accompanied by an acknowledgement-,

(i) identifying the work by its title or other description; and

(ii) unless the work is anonymous or the author of the work has previously agreed or required that no acknowledgement of his name should be made , also identifying the author.

(z) the making of an ephemeral recording, by a broadcasting organisation using its own facilities for its own broadcast by a broadcasting organisation of a work which it has the right to broadcast; and the retention of such recording for archive purposes on the ground of its exceptional documentary character;

(za) the performance of a literary, dramatic or musical work or the communication to the public of such work or of a sound recording in the course of any bonafide religious ceremony or an official ceremony held by the Central Government or the State Government or any local authority.

Explanation : For the purpose of this clause, religious ceremony including a marriage procession and other social festivities associated with a marriage.

(2) The provisions of sub- section (i) shall apply to the doing of any act in relation to the translation of a literary, dramatic or musical work or the adaptation of a literary, dramatic, musical or artistic work as they apply in relation to the work itself.

[52A.Particulars to be included in records and video films.-

(1) No person shall publish a (sound recording) in respect of any work unless the following particulars are displayed on { the sound recording} and on any container thereof, namely:-

(a) the name and address of the person who has made the record;

(b) the name and address of the owner of the copyright in such work; and

(c) the year of its first publication.

(2) No person shall publish a video film in respect of any work unless the following particulars are displayed in the video film, when exhibited and on the video cassette or other container thereof, namely:-

(a) if such work is a cinematograph film required to be certified for exhibition under the provisions of the Cinematograph Act. 1952 (37 of 1752) a copy of the certificate granted by the Board of Film Certification under section 5A of that Act in respect of such work;

(b) the name and address of the person who has made the video film and a declaration by him that he has obtained the necessary license or consent from the owner of the copyright in such work for making such video film; and

(c) the name and address of the owner of the copyright in such work,]

52B. Accounts and audit

(1) Every copyright society appointed under section 34A shall maintain proper accounts and other relevant records and prepare an annual statement of accounts, in such form and in such manner as may be prescribed by the Central Government in consultation with the **Controller (comptroller)** and

Auditor – General of India.

(2) The accounts of each of the copyright societies in relation to the payments received from the Central Government shall be audited by the comptroller and auditor- General of India at such intervals as may be specified by him and any expenditure incurred in connection with such audit shall be payable by the copyright society to the Comptroller and Auditor-General,

(3) The comptroller and Auditor- General of India or any other person appointed by him in connection with the audit of the accounts ot the copyright society referred to in sub- section (2) shall have the same rights and privileges and authority in connection with such audit as the Comptroller and Auditor- General has in connection with the audit of the Government accounts and, in particular, shall have the right to demand the production of books, accounts and other documents and papers and to inspect any of the offices of the copyright society for the purpose only of such audit.

(4) The accounts of each of the copyright societies as certified by the Comptroller and Auditor- general of India or any other person appointed by him in this behalf together with the audit report thereon shall be forwarded annually to the Central Government and that Government shall cause the same to be laid before each House of the Parliament.]

53. Importation of infringing copies

(1) The Registrar of Copyrights, on application by the owner of the copyright in any work or by his duly authorised agent and on payment of the prescribed fee, may, after making such inquiry as he deems fit, order that copies made out of India of the work which if made in India would infringe copyright shall not be imported.

(2) Subject to any rules made under this Act, the Registrar of Copyrights or any person authorised by him in this behalf may enter any ship, dock or promises where any such copies as are referred to in sub-section (I) may be found and may examine such copies.

(3) All copies to which any order made under sub-section (I) applies shall be deemed to be goods of which the import has been prohibited or restricted (under section II of the Customs Act, 1962 (5) of 1962)] , and all the provisions of that Act shall have effect accordingly:

Provided that all such copies confiscated under the provisions of the said Act shall not vest in the Government but shall be delivered to the owner of the copyright in the work.

53A. Resale share right in original copies

(1) In the case of resale for a price exceeding ten thousand rupees, of the original copy of a publishing, sculpture or drawing, or of the original manuscript of a literary, dramatic or musical work, the author of such work if he was the first owner of rights under section 17 or his legal heirs shall, notwithstanding any assignment of copyright in such work, have a right to share in the price of such original copy or manuscript in accordance with the provisions of this section;

Provided that such right shall cease to exist on the expiration of the term of copyright in the work.

(2) The share referred to in sub-section (1) shall be such as the Copyright Board may fix and the decision of the Copyright Board in this behalf shall be final:

Provided that the Copyright Board may fix different shares for different classes of work:

Provided further that in no case shall the share exceed ten percent, of the resale price.

(3) If any dispute arises regarding the right conferred by this section, it shall be referred to the Copyright Board whose decision shall be final.]

CHAPTER XII : CIVIL REMEDIES

54. Definition

For the purposes of this Chapter, unless the context otherwise requires, the expression "owner of copyright" shall include-

(a) an exclusive licensee;

(b) in the case of anonymous and pseudonymous literary, dramatic, musical or artistic work, the publisher of the work, until the identity of the author or, in the case of an anonymous work of joint authorship, or a work of joint authorship published under names all of which are pseudonyms, the identity of any of the authors, is disclosed publicly by the author and the publisher or is otherwise established to the satisfaction of the Copyright Board by that author or his legal representatives.

55. Civil remedies for infringement of copyright

(1) Where copyright in any work has been infringed, the owner of the copyright shall, except as otherwise provided by this Act, be entitled to all such remedies by way injunction, damages, accounts and otherwise as are or may be conferred by law for the infringement of a right:

Provided that if the defendant proves that at the date of the infringement he was not aware and had no reasonable ground for believing that copyright subsisted in the work, the plaintiff shall not be entitled to any remedy other than an injunction in respect of the infringement and a decree for the whole or part of the profits made by the defendant by the sale of the infringing copies as the court may in the circumstances deem reasonable.

(2) where, in the case of a literary, dramatic, musical or artistic work, a name purposing to be that of the author or the publisher, as the case may be, appears on copies of the work as published, or in the case of an artistic work, appeared on the work when it was made, the person whose name so appears or appeared shall, in any proceeding in respect of infringement of the copyright in such work, be presumed, unless the contrary is proved, to be the author or the publisher or the work, as the case may be,

(3) The costs of all parties in any proceedings in respect of the infringement of copyright shall be in the discretion of the court.

56. Protection of separate rights

Subject to the provisions of this Act, where the several rights comprising the copyright in any work are owned by different persons, the owner of any such right shall, to the extent of that right, be entitled to the remedies provided by this Act and may individually enforce such right by means of any suit, action or other proceeding without making the owner of any other right a party to such suit, action or proceeding.

57. Author's special rights

(1) Independently of the author's copyright and even after the assignment either wholly or partially of the said copyright, the author of a work shall have the right-

(a) to claim authorship of the work ; and

(b) to restrain or claim damages in respect of any distortion, mutilation, modification or other act in relation to the said work which is done before the expiration of the term of copyright if such restoration, mutilation, modification or other act would be prejudicial to his honour or reputation:

Provided that the author shall not have any right to restrain or claim damages in respect of any adaptation, of a computer programme to which clause (aa) of sub-section (1) of section 52 applies.

Explanation : Failure to display a work or to display it to the satisfaction of the author shall not be deemed to be an infringement of the rights conferred by this section.]

(2) The right conferred upon an author of a work by sub–section (1), other than the right to claim authorship of the work, may be exercised by the legal representatives of the author.

58. Rights of owner against persons possessing or dealing with infringing copies

All infringing copies of any work in which copyright subsists, and all plates used or intended to be used for the production of such infringing copies, shall be deemed to be the property of the owner of the copyright, who accordingly may take proceedings for the recovery of possession thereof or in respect of the conversion thereof:

Provided that the owner of the copyright shall not be entitled to any remedy in respect of the conversion of any infringing copies, if the opponent proves-

1. that he was not aware and had no reasonable ground to believe that copyright subsisted in the work of which such copies are alleged to be infringing copies; or
2. that he had reasonable grounds for believing that such copies or plates do not involve infringement of the copyright in any work.

59. Restriction on remedies in the case of works of architecture

(1) Notwithstanding anything contained in [the Specific Relief act, 1963 (47 of 1963), where the construction of a building or other structure which infringes or which, if completed, would infringe the copyright in some other work has been commenced, the owner of the copyright shall not be entitled to obtain an injunction to restrain the construction of such building or structure or order its demolition.

(2) Nothing in section 58 shall apply in respect of the construction of a building or other structure which infringes or which, if completed, would infringe the copyright in some other work.

60. Remedy in the case of groundless threat of legal proceedings

Where any person claiming to be the owner of copyright in any work, by circulars, advertisements or otherwise, threatens any other person with any legal proceedings or liability in respect of an alleged infringement of copyright, any person aggrieved thereby may, notwithstanding anything contained [in section 34 of the Specific Relief Act, 1963 (47 of 1963)] institute a declaratory suit that the alleged infringement to which the threats related was not in fact an infringement of any legal rights of the person making such threats and may in any such suit-

29. obtain an injunction against the continuance of such threats; and

30. recover such damages, if any, as he has sustained by reason of such threats;

Provided that this section shall not apply if the person making such threats, with due diligence, commences and prosecutes an action for infringement of the copyright claimed by him.

61. Owners of copyright to be party to the proceeding

(1) In every civil suit or other proceeding regarding infringement of copyright instituted by an exclusive licensee, the owner of the copyright shall, unless the court otherwise directs, be made a defendant and where such owner is made a defendant, he shall have the right to dispute the claim of the exclusive license.

(2) Where any civil suit or other proceeding regarding infringement of copyright instituted by an exclusive license is successful, no fresh suit or other proceeding in respect of the same cause of action shall lie at the instance of the owner of the copyright.

62. Jurisdiction of court over matters arising under this Chapter

(1) Every suit or other civil proceeding arising under this Chapter in respect of the infringement of copyright in any work or the infringement of any other right conferred by this Act shall be instituted in the district court having jurisdiction.

(2) For the purpose of sub- section (1),a "district court jurisdiction" shall notwithstanding anything contained in the Code of Civil Procedure, 1908 (5) of 1908, or any other law for the time being in force, include a district court within the local limits of whose jurisdiction, at the time of the institution of the suit or other proceeding, the person instituting the suit or other proceeding or, where there are more than one such persons, any of them actually and voluntarily resides or carries on business or personally works for gain.

CHAPTER XIII : OFFENCCES

63. Offence of infringement of copyright or other rights conferred by this Acts

Any person who knowingly infringes or abets the infringement of-

(a) the copyright in a work, or

(b) any other right conferred by this Act.

[shall be punishable with imprisonment for a term which shall not be less than six months but which may extend to three years and with fine which shall not be less than fifty thousand rupees but which may extend to two lak rupees: [except the right conferred by section 53A]

Provided that [where the infringement has not been made for gain in the course of trade or business] the court may, for adequate and special reasons to be mentioned in the judgment, impose a sentence of imprisonment for a term of less than six months or a fine of less than fifty thousand rupees]

Explanation : Construction of a building or other structure which infringes or which, if completed, would infringe the copyright in some other work shall not be an offence under this section.

63A. Enhanced penalty on second and subsequent convictions

Whoever having already been convicted of an offence under section 63 is again convicted of any such offence shall be punishable for the second and for every subsequent offence, with imprisonment for a term which shall not be less than one year but which may extend to three years and with fine which shall not be less than one lak rupees but which may extend to two lak rupees:

Provided that [where the infringement has not been made for gain in the course of trade or business] the court may, for adequate and special reasons to be mentioned in the judgment, impose a sentence of imprisonment for a term of less than one year or a fine of less than one lakh rupees:

Provider further that for the purposes of this section, no cognizance shall be taken of any conviction made before the commencement of the Copyright (Amendment) Act,1984 (65 of 1984.]

63B. Knowing use of infringing copy of computer programme to be an offence

Any person who knowingly makes use on a computer of an infringing for copy of a computer programme shall be punishable with imprisonment for a term which shall not be less than seven days but which may extend to three years and with fine which shall not be less than fifty thousand rupees but which may extend to two lakh rupees:

Provided that where the computer programme has not been used for gain or in the course of trade or business, the court may, for adequate and special reasons to be mentioned in the judgment, not impose any sentence of imprisonment and may impose a fine which may extend to fifty thousand rupees.]

64. Power of police to seize infringing copies

(1) Any police officer, not below the rank of a sub-inspector, may, if he is satisfied that an offence under section 63 in respect of the infringement of copyright in any work has been, is being or is likely to be, committed , seize without warrant, all copies of the work, and all plates used for the purpose of making infringing copies of the work, wherever found and all copies and plates so seized shall, as soon as practicable, be produced before a Magistrate.]

(2) Any person having an interest in any copies of a

work [or plates] seized under sub-section (1) may, within fifteen days of such seizure, make an application to the magistrate for such copies[or plates] being restored to him and the magistrate, after hearing the applicant and the complainant and making such further inquiry as may be necessary, shall make such order on the application as he may deem fit.

65. Possession of plates for purpose of making infringing copies

Any person who knowingly makes, or has in his possession, any plate for the purpose of making infringing copies of any work in which copyright subsists shall be punishable with imprisonment which may extend to [two years and shall also be liable to fine].

66. Disposal of infringing copies or plates for purpose of making infringing copies

The court trying any offence under this Act may, whether the alleged offender, which appear to it to be infringing copies, or plates for the purposes of making infringing copies, be delivered up to the owner of the copyright.

67. Penalty for making false entries in register etc., for producing or tendering false entries

Any person who,——

(a) makes or causes to be made a false entry in the Register of Copyright kept under this Act, or

(b) makes or causes to be made a writing falsely purporting to be a copy of any entry in such register, or

(c) produces or tenders or causes to be produces or tendered as evidence any such entry or writing , knowing the same to be false, shall be punishable with imprison able which may extend to one year, or with fine, or with both.

68. Penalty for making false statements for the purpose of deceiving or influencing any authority or officer

Any person who,—

(a) with a view to deceiving any authority or officer in the execution of the provisions of this Act, or

(b) with a view to procuring or influencing the doing or omission of anything in relation to this Act or any matter there under, makes a false statement or representation knowing the same to be false, shall be punishable with imprisonment which may extend to one year, or with fine, or with both.

68A. Penalty for contravention of section 52A

Any person who publishes a [record] or a video film in contravention of the provisions of section 52A shall be punishable with imprisonment which may extend to three years and shall also be liable to fine.]

69. Offences by companies

(1) Where any offence under this Act has been committed by a company, every person who at the time the offence was committed was in charge of, and was responsible to the company for, the conduct of the business of the company, as well as the company shall be deemed to be guilty of such offence and shall be liable to be proceeded against and punished accordingly:

Provided that nothing contained in this sub-section shall render any person liable to any punishment, if he proves that the offence was committed his knowledge or that he exercised all due diligence to prevent the commission of such offence.

(2) Notwithstanding anything contained in sub-section (1), where an offence under this Act has been committed by a company, and it is proved that the offence was committed with the consent or connivance of, or is attributable to any negligence

on the part of, any direct to, manager, secretary or other officer of the company, such director, manager, secretary or other officer shall also be deemed to be guilty of that offence and shall be liable to be proceeded against and punished accordingly;

Explanation : For the purposes of this section-

1. "company" means any body corporate and includes a firm or other association of persons; and
2. "director" in relation to a firm means a partner in the firm.

70. Cognizance of offences

No court inferior to that of [a Metropolitan Magistrate or Judicial Magistrate of the first class] shall try any offence under this Act.

CHAPTER XIV : APPEALS

71. Appeals against certain orders of Magistrate

Any person aggrieved by an order made under sub-section (2) of section64 or section66 may, within thirty days of the date of such order, appeal to the court to which appeals from the court making the order ordinarily lie and such appellate court may direct that execution of the order be stayed pending disposal of the appeal.

72. Appeals against orders of Registrar of Copyrights and Copyright Board

Any person aggrieved by any final decision or order of the Registrar of Copyrights may, within three months from the date of the order or decision , appeal to the Copyright Board.

(2) Any person aggrieved by any final decision or order of the Copyright Board, not being a decision or order made in an appeal under sub- section (1) may,

within Three months from the date of such decision or order, appeal to the High- Court within whose jurisdiction the appellant actually and voluntarily resides or carries on business or personally works for gain:

Provided that no such appeal shall lie against a decision of the Copyright Board under section 6.

(3) In calculating the period of three months provided for an appeal under this section, the time taken in granting a certified copy of the order or record of the decision appealed against shall be excluded.

73. Procedure for appeals

The High Court may make rules consistent with this Act as to the procedure to be followed in respect of appeals made to it under section 72.

CHAPTER XV : MISCELLANEOUS

74. Registrar of Copyrights and Copyright Board to possess certain powers of civil courts

The Registrar of Copyrights and the Copyright Board shall have the powers of a civil court when trying a suit under the Code of civil Procedure, 1908 (5 of 1908), in respect of the following matters, namely:-

(a) summoning and enforcing the attendance of any person and examining him on oath;

(b) requiring the discovery and production of any document;

(c) receiving evidence on affidavits;

(d) issuing commissions for the examination of witness or documents;

(e) requisitioning any public record or copy thereof from any court or office;

(f) any other matter which may be prescribed.

Explanation : For the purpose of enforcing the

attendance of witness, the local limits of the jurisdiction of the Registrar of Copyrights or the Copyright Board, as the case may be, shall be the limits of the territory of India.

75. Orders for payment of money passed be Registrar of Copyright and Copyright Board to be executable as a decree

Every order made by the Registrar of Copyrights or the Copyright Board under this Act for the payment of money or by the High Court in any appeal against any such order of the Copyright board shall, on a certificate issued by the Registrar of Copyrights, the Copyright Board or the Registrar of the High Court, as the case may be, be deemed to be a decree of a civil court and shall be executable in the same manner as a decree of such court.

76. Protection of action taken in good faith

No suit or other legal proceeding shall lie against any person in respect of anything which is in good faith done or intended to be done in pursuance of this Act.

77. Certain persons to be public servants

Every officer appointed under this Act and every member of the Copyright Board shall be deemed to be a public servant with in the meaning of section 21 of the Indian Penal Code (45 of 1860).

78. Power to make rules

(1) The Central Government may, by notification in the Official Gazette, make rules for carrying out the purposes of this Act.

(2) In particular, and without prejudice to the generality of the foregoing power, the Central Government may make rules to provide for all or any of the following matters, namely:—

(a) the term of office and conditions of service of the Chairman and other members of the Copyright board;

(b) the form of complaints and applications to be made and the licenses to be granted, under this Act;

(c) the procedure to be followed in connection with any proceeding before the Registrar of Copyrights;

[(ca) the conditions for submission of application under sub- section (2) of section 33;

(cb) the conditions subject to which a copyright society may be registered under sub- section (3) of section 33;

(cc) the inquiry for cancellation of registration under sub- section (4) of section 33;

(ed) the conditions subject to which the copyright society may accept authorization under clause (a) of sub- section (1) of section 34 and the conditions subject to which owners or rights have right to withdraw such authorisation under clause (d) of that sub- section;

(ce) the conditions subject to which a copyright society may issue licenses, collect fees and distribute such fees amongst owners of rights under sub- section (3) of section 34;

(cf) the manner in which the approval of the owners of rights regarding collection and distribution of fees, approval for utilization of any amount collected as fees and to provide to such owners information concerning activities in relation to the administration of their rights under sub- section 35;

(cg) the returns to be filed by copyright societies to the Registrar of Copyrights under sub- section (1) of section 36;]

3. the manner of determining any royalties payable under this Act, and the security to be taken for the

payment of such royalties;

(da) the manner of payment of royalty under clause (j) of sub-section (1) of section 52;

(db) the form and the manner in which the copyright society shall maintain accounts and other relevant records and prepare annual statements of accounts and the manner in which the quantum of remuneration is to be paid to individual owner of rights under sub-section (1) of section 52B.]

(e) the form of Register of Copyright to be kept under this Act and the particulars to be entered therein;

(f) the matter of respect of which the Registrar of Copyrights and the Copyright Board shall have powers of a civil court;

(g) the fees which may be payable under this Act;

(h) the regulation of business of the Copyright Office and of all things by this Act placed under the direction or control of the Registrar of Copyrights.

(3) Every rule made under this section shall be laid, a soon as may be after it is made, before each House of Parliament, while it is in session, for a total period of thirty days which may be comprised in one session or in two or more successive sessions, and if before the expiry of the session immediately following the session or the successive sessions aforesaid both Houses agree in making any modification in the rule or both Houses agree that the rule should not be made the rule shall thereafter have effect only in such modified form or be of no effect, as the case may be, so however, that any such modification or annulment shall be without prejudice to the validity of anything previously done under that rule.]

79. Repeals, savings and transitional provisions

(1) The Indian Copyright Act 1914 (3 of 1914) and the Copyright Act of 1911 passed by the Parliament of the United Kingdom as modified in its application to India by the Indian Copyright Act, 1914 are hereby repealed.

(2) Where any person has, before the commencement of this Act, taken any action whereby he has incurred any expenditure or liabilities in connection with the reproduction or performance of any work in a manner which at the time was lawful or for the purpose of or with a view to the reproduction or performance of a work at a time when such reproduction or performance would, but for the coming into force of this Act, have been lawful, nothing in this section shall diminish or prejudice any rights or interests arising from or in connection with such action which are subsisting and valuable at the said date, unless the person who by virtue of this Act, becomes entitled to restrain such reproduction or performance agrees to pay such compensation as ailing agreement, may be determined by the Copyright Board.

(3) Copyright shall not subsist by virtue of this Act in any work in which copyright did not subsist immediately before the commencement of this Act under any Act repealed by sub- section(1).

(4) Where copyright subsisted in any work immediately before the commencement of this Act, the rights comprising such copyright shall, as form the date of such commencement, be the rights specified in section 14 in relation to the class of work to which work belongs and where any new rights are conferred by that section, the owner of such rights shall be —

(a) in any case where copyright in the work was

wholly assigned before the commencement of this Act, the assignee or his successor in interest;

(b) in any other case, the person who was the first owner of the copyright in the work under any Act repealed by sub- section (1) or his legal representatives.

(5) Except as otherwise provided in this Act, where any person is entitled immediately before the commencement of this Act to copyright in any work or any right in such copyright or to an interest in any such right, he shall continue to be entitled to such right or interest for the period for which he would have be entitled thereto if this Act had not come into force.

(6) Nothing contained in this Act, shall be deemed to render any act done before its commencement an infringement of copyright if that act would not otherwise have constituted such as infringement.

(7) Save as otherwise provided in this section, nothing in this section shall be deemed to affect the application of the General Clause Act,1897, (10 of 1897) with respect to the effect of repeals.

APPENDIX II

THE INDIAN CONTRACT (AMENDMENT) ACT,1996
(ACT NO.1 OF 1997)

(8th January,1997)

An Act further to amend the Indian Contract Act,1872.

Be it enacted by parliament in the forty-seventh year of the Republic of India as follows :

1. **Short title :** This Act may be called the Indian Contract (Amendment) Act,1996.
2. Amendment of S.28.- In S.28 of the Indian Contract Act,1872, for the portion beginning with the words "Every agreement" and ending with the words "is void to that extent", the following "Every agreement:- shall be substituted, namely :-
   (a) by which any party thereto is restricted absolutely from enforcing his rights under or in respect of any contract, by the usual legal proceedings in the ordinary tribunals, or which limits the time within which he may thus enforce his rights; or
   (b) which extinguishes the rights of any party thereto, or discharges any party thereto from any liability, under or in respect of any contract on the expiry of a specified period so as to restrict any party from enforcing his right, is void to that extent."

(THE) COPYRIGHT (AMENDMENT)ACT,1992
(ACT NO.13 OF 1992)

(3rd April,1992)

An Act further to amend the Copyright Act,1957.

Be it enacted by parliament in the Forty-third Year of the Republic of India as follows :-

1. Short title and commencement

(This Act may be called the copyright (Amendment) Act,1992.

2. It shall be deemed to have come into force on the 28th day of December,1991.

3. Amendment of Chapter V.- In chapter V of the Copyright Act, 1957 (here in after) referred to as the principal Act), for the words "fifty year", wherever they occur, the words "sixty years" shall be substituted.

4. Copyright not to subsist if term has expired.- For the removal of doubts, it is hereby declared that copyright shall not subsist by virtue of this Act in any work in which copyright did not subsist immediately before the commencement of this Act.

5. Repeal and saving.- (1) The copy right (Amendment) Ordinance, 1991 is hereby repealed.

(2) Not with standing such repeal, anything done or any action taken under the principal Act, as amended by the said ordinance, shall be deemed to have been done or taken under the principal Act, as amended by this Act.

(THE) COPYRIGHT (AMENDMENT) ACT, 1994
(ACT NO. 38 OF 1994)

(9th June,1994)

An Act further to amend the Copyright Act,1957

Be it enacted by parliament in the Forty-fifth year of the Republic of India as :-

1. Short titled and commencement

(1) This act may be called the copyright (Amendment) Act, 1994. (2) It shall come into force on such date as the Central Government may, by notification in the official Gazette, appoint :

Provided that different dates may be appointed for different provision of this Act and any reference in any such provision to the commencement of this Act shall be construed as a reference to the coming into force of that provision.

(a) 10-5-95 - See Gaz.of Ind., 5-5-95, Pt.II, S.3 (ii), Ext, p.2 (No.258).

2. Amendment of section 2.- In section 2 of the copyright Act, 1957 (hereinafter referred to as the principal Act),-

(i) in clause (a),-

(a) in sub-clause (iii), the word "and", occurring at the end, shall be omitted.

(b) in sub-clause (iv), the word "and" shall be inserted at the end.

(c) after sub-clause (iv) as so amended, the following sub-clause shall be inserted, namely:-

"(ii) in relation to any use of such work involving its re-arrangement or alteration;" (ii) in clause (b) and in all other provisions of the principal for the words "architectural work of art", wherever they occur, the words "work of architecture" shall be substituted;

(iii) in clause (d), for sub-clauses (v) and (vi) the following sub-clauses shall be substituted, namely ;-

"(v) in relation to a cinematograph film or sound recording, the produce; and

(vi) in relation to any literary, dramatic, musical or artistic work which is computer-generated, the person who causes the work to be executed;

(iv) for clause (f), the following clause shall be substituted, namely;-

(f) "cinematograph film" means any work of visual recording on any medium produced through a process from which a moving image may be produced by any means and includes a sound recording accompanying such visual recording and "cinematograph" shall be construed as including any work produced by any process analogous to cinematography including video films ;"

(v) for clause (ff), the following clauses shall be substituted, namely:-

(ff) "communication to the public" means making any work available for being seen or heard or otherwise enjoyed by the public directly or by any means of display or diffusion other than by issuing copies of such work regardless of whether any member of the public actually sees, hears or otherwise enjoys the work so made available.

Explanation : For the purpose of this clause, communication through satellite or cable or any other means of simultaneous communication to more than one household or place of residence including residential rooms of any hotel shall be deemed to be communication to the public;

(ffa) "composer", in relation to a musical work, means the person who composes the music regardless of whether he records it in any form of graphical notation;

(ffb) "computer" includes any electronic or similar device having information processing capabilities;

(ffc) "computer programme" means a set of instructions expressed in words, codes schemes or in any other form including a machine readable medium, capable of causing a computer to perform a particular task or achieve a particular result;

(ffd) "copyright society" means a society registered under sub-section(3) of section 33;"

(vi) for clause (m) the following clause shall be substituted, namely:-

(m) "infringing copy" means,-

(i) in relation to a literary, dramatic, musical or artistic work, a reproduction thereof otherwise than in the form of a cinematographic film.

(ii) in relation to a cinematographic film, a copy of the film made on any medium by any means;

(iii) in relation to a sound recording any recording embodying the same sound recording, made by any means;

(iv) in relation to a programme or performance in which such a broadcast reproduction right or a performer's right subsists under the provisions of this Act, the sound recording or a cinematographic film of such programme or performance, if such reproduction, copy or sound recording is made or imported in contravention of the provisions of this Act;'

(vii) for clause (o), the following clause shall be substituted, namely:-

(o) "literary work" includes computer programmes, tables and compilations including computer data basis;"

(viii) for clause (p) the following clause shall be substituted namely:-

'(p) "musical work" means a work consisting of music and includes any graphical notation of such work but does not include any words or any action intended to be sung, spoken or performed with the music;"

(ix) for clause(q) the following clauses shall be substituted namely:-

(q) "performance" in relation to performer's right, means any visual or acoustic presentation made live by one or more performers;"

(x) after clause(q) the following clause shall be inserted, namely:-

(qq) performer includes an actor, singer musician dancer, acrobat, juggler, conjurer, snake charmer, a person delivering a lecture or any other person who makes a performance;"

(xi) clause (r) shall be omitted;

(xii) in clause (t) and in all other provisions of the principal Act, for the word "record" wherever it occurs, the words" sound recording" shall be substituted;

(xiii) after clause(u) the following clause shall be inserted, namely:-

(uu) "producer" in relation to a cinematograph film or sound recording means a person who takes the initiative and responsibility for making the work;"

(xiv) clause (w) shall be omitted:

(xv) for clause (x) the following clauses shall be substituted namely;-

(x) "reprography" means the making of copies of a work, by photocopying or similar means;

(xx) "sound recording" means a recording of sounds from which such sounds maybe produced regardless of the medium on which such recording is made or the method by which the sounds are produced:

3. Substitution of new section for section3.- For section 3 of the principal Act, the following section shall be substituted namely:-

"3. Meaning of publication.- For the purposes of this Act "publication" means making a work available to the public by issue of copies or by communicating the work to the public.'

4. Substitution of new section for section 6.- For section 6 of the principal Act, the following section shall be substituted namely:-

'6. certain disputes to be decided by copyright Board.- If any question arises,-

(a) whether a work has been published or as to the date on which a work was published for the purposes of chapter V, or

(b) whether the term of copyright for any work is shorter in any other country than that provided in respect of that work under this Act, it shall be referred to the copyright board constituted under section 11 whose decision thereon shall be final:

Provided that if in the opinion of the copyright board the issue of copies or communication to the public referred to in section 3 was of an in significant nature it shall not be deemed to be publication for the purposes of that section.

5. Amendment of section11.- In section 11 of the principal Act,-

(a) in sub-section (1) for the word "eight" the word "fourteen" shall be substituted;

(b) in sub-section (3) the words "the supreme court or" shall be omitted;

6. Amendment of section12.- In section 12of the principal Act,-

(a) after sub-section (2) the following proviso shall be inserted namely;-

" Provident that, if the chairman is of opinion that any matter of importance is required to be heard by a larger bench, he may refer the matter to a special bench consisting of five members";

(b) in sub-section(3) for the proviso, the following proviso shall be substituted namely:-

"Provided that where there is no such majority, the opinion of the chairman" shall be substituted.

7. Substitution of new section for section 14.- For section 14 of the principal Act, the following section shall be substituted, namely:-

"14.Meaning of copyright.- For the purposes of this Act," copyright" means the exclusive right subject to the provisions of this Act, to do or authorise the doing of any of the following acts in respect of a work or any substantial part thereof, namely :-

(a) in the case of literary, dramatic or musical work, not being computer programme,-

(i) to reproduce the work in any material form including the storing of it in any medium by electronic means;

(ii) to issue copies of the work to the public not being copies already in circulation;

(iii) to perform the work in public, or communicate it to the public;

(iv) to make any cinematograph film or sound recording in respect of the work;

(v) to make any translation of the work;

(vi) to make any adaptation of the work;

(vii) to do in relation to a translation or an adaptation of the work, any of the acts specified in relation to the work in sub-clauses (i) to (vi);

(b) in the case of a computer programme-

(i) to do any of the acts specified in clause(a);

(ii) to sell or give on hire or offer for sale or hire any copy of the computer programme, regardless of whether such copy has been sold or given on hire on earlier occasions;

(c) in the case of an artistic work-

(i) to reproduce the work in any material from including depiction in three dimensions of a two dimensional work or in two dimensions of a three dimensional work;

(ii) to communicate the work to the public;

(iii) to issue copies of the work to the public not being copies already in circulation;

(iv) to include the work in any cinematograph film;

(v) to make any adaptation of the work;

(vi) to do in relation to an adaptation of the work any of the acts specified in relation to the work in sub-clauses(i) to (iv);

(d) in the case of a cinematograph film-

(i) to make a copy of the film including a photograph of any image forming part thereof;

(ii) to sell or give on hire or offer for sale or hire any copy of the film, regardless of whether such copy has been sold or given on hire on earlier occasions;

(iii) to communicate the film to the public;

(e) in the case of a sound recording-

(i) to make any other sound recording embodying it;

(ii) to sell or give on hire, or offer for sale or hire any copy of the sound recording regardless of whether such copy has been sold or given on hire on earlier occasion;

(iii) to communicate the sound recording to the public.

Explanation : For the purpose of this section, a copy which has been sold once shall be deemed to be a copy already in circulation.'

8. Amendment of section 19.- In section 19 of the principal Act, for sub-section(2), the following sub-section shall be substituted, namely:-

"(2) The assignment of copyright in any work shall identify such work, and shall specify the rights assigned and the duration and territorial extent of such assignment.

(3) The assignment of copyright at any work shall also specify the amount of royalty payable, if any, to the author or his legal heirs during the currency of the assignment and the assignment shall be subject to revision, extension or termination terms mutually agreed upon by the parties.

(4) Where the assignee does not exercise the rights assigned to him under any of the other sub-sections of this section within a period of one year from the date of assignment the assignment in respect of such rights shall be deemed to have lapsed after the expiry of the said period unless otherwise specified in the assignment.

(5) If the period of assignment is not stated, it shall be deemed to be five years from the date of assignment.

(6) If the territorial extent of assignment of the rights is not specified it shall be presumed to extend within India.

(7) Nothing in sub-section(2) or sub-section (3) or sub-section (4) or sub-section (5) or sub-section(6) shall be applicable to assignments made before the coming into force of the copyright(Amendment)Act, 1994."

9. Substitution of new section for section 19A.- For section 19A of the following section shall be substituted namely:-

"19A. Disputes with respect to assignment of copyright.- (1) If an assignee fails to make sufficient exercise of the rights assigned to him and such failure is not attributable to any act or omission of the assignor then the copyright board may on receipt of a complaint from the assignor and after holding such inquiry as it may deem necessary revoke such assignment.

(2) if any dispute arises with respect to the assignment of any copyright board may, on receipt of a complaint from the aggrieved party and after holding such

inquiry as it considers necessary, pass such order as it may deem fit including an order for the recovery of any royalty payable:

Provided that the copyright board shall not pass any order under this sub-section to revoke the assignment unless it is satisfied that the terms of assignment are harsh to the assignor in case the assignor is also the author:

Provided further that no order of revocation of assignment under this sub-section shall be made within a period of five years from the date of such assignment."

10. Insertion of new section 30A.- After section 30 of the principal Act, the following section shall be inserted namely:-

"30A. Application of section 19 and 19A.- The provisions of section 19 and 19A shall, with any necessary adaptation and modifications, apply in relation to a licence under section 30 as they apply in relation to assignment of copyright in a work."

11. Substitution of new chapter for chapter VII.- For chapter VII of the principal Act, the following chapter shall be substituted namely:-

APPENDIX III

CHAPTER VII : COPYRIGHT SOCIETIES

33. (1) No person or association of person shall after coming into force of the copyright (Amendment) Act, 1994 commence or carry on the business of the issuing or granting licences in respect of any work in which copyright subsists or in respect of any other rights conferred by this Act except under or in accordance with the registration granted under sub-section (3):

Provided that an owner of copyright shall, in his individual capacity, continue to have the right to grant licences in respect of his own works consistent with his obligations as member of the registered copyright society:

Provided further that a performing rights society functioning in accordance with the provisions of section 33 on the date immediately before the coming into force of copyright (Amendment) Act, 1994 shall be deemed to be copyright society for the purpose of this chapter and every such society shall get itself registered within a period of one year from the date of the commencement of the copyright (Amendment)Act,1994.

(2) Any association of persons who fulfils such conditions as may be prescribed may apply for permission to do the business specified in sub-section (1) to the Registrar of copyright who shall submit the application to the Central Government.

(3) The Central Government may having regard to the interest of the authors and other owners of rights under this Act, the interest and convenience of the public and in particular of the groups of persons who are most likely to seek licences in respect of the relevant rights and ability and professional competence of the applicants register such association of persons as a copyright society subject to such conditions as may be prescribed:

Provided that the Central Government shall not ordinarily registers more than one copyright society to do business in respect of the same class of works.

(4) The Central Government may, if it is satisfied that a copyright society is being managed in manner detrimental to the interests of the owners of rights concerned, cancel the registration of such society after such inquiry as may be prescribed.

(5) If the Central Government is of the opinion that in the interest of the owners of rights concerned, it is necessary so to do, it may, by order, suspend the registration of such society pending inquiry for such period not exceeding one year as may be specified in such order under -section (4) and that Government shall appoint an administrator to discharge the functions of the copyright society.

34. Administration of rights of owner by copyright society

(1) Subject to such conditions as may be prescribed.-

(a) a copyright society may accept from an owner of rights exclusive authorization to administer any right in any work by issue of licencess or collection of licence fees or both: and

(b) an owner of rights shall have the right to withdraw such authorisation without prejudice to the rights of the copyright society under any contract.

(2) It shall be competent for a copyright society to enter agreement with any foreign society or organisation administering rights corresponding to rights under this Act, to entrust to such foreign society or organisation the administration in any foreign country by such foreign society or organisation:

Provided that no such society or organisation shall permit any discrimination in regard to the terms of licence or the distribution of fees collected between rights in Indian and other works.

(3) Subject to such conditions as may be prescribed, a copyright society may-

(i) issue licences under section 30 in respect of any rights under this Act;

(ii) collect fees in pursuance of such licences;

(iii) distribute such fees among owners of rights after making deductions for its own expenses;

(iv) perform any other functions consistent with provisions of section 35.

34A. Payment of remunerations by copyright society

(1) If the Central Government is of the opinion that a copyright society for a class of work is generally administering the rights of the owners of rights in such work throughout India, it shall appoint that society for the purposes of this section.

(2) The copyright society shall, subject to such rules as may be made in this behalf frame a scheme for determining the quantum of remuneration payable to individual copyright owners having regard to the number of copies of the work in circulation:

Provided that such scheme shall restrict payment to the owners of rights whose works have attained a level of circulation which the copyright society considers reasonable.

35. Control over the copyright society by the owner of rights

(1) Every copyright society shall be subject to the collective control of the owners of rights under this Act whose rights it administers (not being owners of rights under this Act administered by a foreign society or organization referred to in sub-section (2) of section 34 and shall in such manner as maybe prescribed,-

(a) obtain the approval of such owners of rights for its procedures of collection and distribution of fees;

(b) obtain their approval for the utilization of any amounts collected as fees for any purpose other than distribution to the owner of rights; and

(c) provide to such owners regular, full and detailed information concerning all its activities, in relation to the administration of their rights.

(2) All fees distributed among the owners of rights shall as far as may be distributed in proportion to the actual use of their works.

36. Submission of returns and reports

(1) Every copyright society shall submit to the Registrar of copyrights such returns as may be prescribed.

(2) Any officer duly authorized by the Central Government in this behalf may call for any report and also call for any records of any copyright society for the purpose of satisfying himself that the fees collected by the society in respect of rights administered by it are being utilized or distributed in accordance with the provisions of this Act.

36A. Rights and liabilities of performing rights societies

Nothing in this chapter shall affect any rights or liabilities in any work in connection with a performing rights society which had accrued or were incurred on or before the day prior to the commencement of the copyright (Amendment) Act, 1994, or any legal proceedings in respect of any such rights or liabilities pending on that day."

12. Amendment of Chapter VIII.- In chapter VIII of the principal Act, for the heading RIGHTS OR BROADCASTING AUTHORITIES", the heading "RIGHTS OF BROADCASTING ORDGANISATION AND OR PERFORMERS " shall be substituted.

13. Substitution of new section for section 37.- For section 37 of the principal Act, the following section shall be substituted namely:-

37. Broadcast reproduction right

(1) Every broadcasting organisation shall have a special right to be known as "broadcast reproduction right" in respect of its broad casts.

(2) The broadcast reproduction right shall subsist until twenty five years from the beginning of the calendar year next following the year in which the broadcast is made.

(3) During the continuance of a broadcast reproduction right in relation to any broadcast, any person who, without the licence of the owner of the right does any of the following acts of the broadcast or any substantial part thereof-

(a) re-broadcasts the broadcast; or

(b) causes the broadcast to be heard or seen by the public on payment of any charges; or

(c) makes any sound recording or visual recording of the broadcast; or

(d) makes any reproduction of such sound recording or visual recording where such initial recording was done without licence or, where it was licensed, for any purpose not envisaged by such licence; or

(e) sells or hires to the public or offers for such sale or hire, any such sound recording or visual recording referred to in clause (c) or clause- (4) shall subject to the provisions of section 39, be deemed to have infringed the broadcast reproduction right.

14. Substitution of new section for section 38.- For section 38 of the principal Act the following section shall be substituted namely:-

38. Performer's right

(1) Where any performer appears or engages in any performance, he shall have a special right to be known as the "performer's right" in relation to such performance.

(2) The performer's right shall subsist until twenty five years from the beginning of the calendar year next following the year in which the performance is made.

(3) During the continuance of a performer's right in relation to any performance any person who without the consent of the performer does any of the following acts in respect of the performance or any substantial part thereof, namely:-

(a) makes a sound recording or visual recording of the performance; or

(b) reproduce a sound recording or visual recording of the performance which sound recording or visual recording was-

(i) made without the performer's consent; or

(ii) made for purposes different from those for which the performer gave his consent; or

(iii) made for purposes different from those referred to in section 39 from a sound recording or visual recording which was made in accordance with section 39; or

(c) broadcasts the performance except where the broadcast is made from a sound recording or visual recording other than one made in accordance with section 39, or is a re-broadcast by the same broadcasting organisation of an earlier broadcast which did not infringe the performer's right; or

(d) communicates the performance to the public otherwise than by broadcast except where such communication to the public is made from a sound recording or a visual recording or a broadcast, shall subject to the provisions of section 39, be deemed to have infringed the performer's right.

(4) Once a performer has consented to the incorporation of his performance in cinematograph film, the provisions of sub-sections (1), (2) and 3 shall have no further application to such performance.'

15. Substitution of new section for section 39.- For section 39 of the principal Act, the following sections shall be substituted namely:-

39. Acts not infringing broadcast reproduction right or performer's right

No broadcast reproduction right or performer's right shall be deemed to be infringed by-

(a) the making of any sound recording or visual recording for the private use of the person making such recording or solely for purposes of bona fide teaching or research; or

(b) the use, consistent with fair dealing, of excerpts of a performance or of a broadcast in the reporting of current events or for bona fide review teaching or research; or

(c) such other acts, with any necessary adaptations and modifications, which do not constitute infringement of copyright under section 52.

39A. Other provisions applying to broadcast reproduction right and performer's right

Sections 18, 19, 30, 53, 64, 65 and 66 shall with any necessary adaptations and modifications, apply in relation to the broadcast reproduction right in any broadcast and the performer's right in any performance as they apply in relation to copyright in a work:

Provided that where copyright or performer's right

subsists in respect of any work or performance that has been broadcast, no licence to reproduce such broadcast shall take effect without the consent of the owner of rights or performer as the case may be or both of them."

16. Amendment of section 51.- In section 51 of the principal Act

(1) in clause (a) for sub-clause (ii) the following sub-clause shall be substituted namely:- "(ii) permits for profits any place to be used for the communication of the work to the public where such communication constitutes an infringement of the copyright in the work unless he was not aware and had no reasonable ground for believing that such communication to the public would be an infringement of copyright; or"

(2) for the proviso, the following proviso shall be substituted namely:- "Provided the nothing in sub-clause (iv) shall apply to the import of one copy of any work for the private and domestic use of the importer."

17. Amendment of section 52.- In section 52 of the principal Act, in sub-section (1)

(1) in clause (a),-

(i) after the words " artistic work"' the words, "not being a computer programme", shall be inserter;

(ii) for sub-clause (i) the following sub-clause shall be substituted, namely:- "(i) private use, including research;"

(2) after clause (a) the following clause shall be inserted namely:-

"(aa)the making of copies or adaptation of a computer programme by the lawful possessor of a copy of such computer programme from such copy-

(i) in order to utilize the computer programme for the purpose for with it was supplied; or

(ii) to make back-up copies purely as a temporary protection against loss, destruction or damage in order only to utilise the computer programme for the purpose for which it was supplied;"

(3) in clause (i) the words "or the communication to such an audience of a cinematograph film or sound recording" shall be inserted at the end;

(4) for clause (j) and (k), the following clauses shall be substituted, namely:-

"(i) the making of sound recordings in respect of any literary, dramatic or musical work, if,- (i) sound recordings of that work have been made by or with the licence or consent of the owner of the right in the work;

(ii) the person making the sound recordings has given a notice of his intention to make the sound recordings, has provided copies of all covers or labels with which the sound recordings are to be sold and has paid the prescribed manner to the owner of rights in the work royalties in respect of all such sound recordings to be made by him, at the rate fixed by the copyright board in this behalf:

Provided that-

(i) no alterations shall be made which have not been made previously by or with the consent of the owner of rights or which are not reasonably necessary for the adaptation of the work for the purpose of making the sound recordings;

(ii) the sound recordings shall not be issued in any form of packaging or with any label which is likely to mislead or confuse the public as to their identity;

(iii) no such sound recording shall be made until the expiration of two calendar years after the end of the year in which the first sound recording of the work was made; and

(iv) the person making such sound recordings shall allow the owner of rights or his duly authorised agent or representative to inspect all records and books of account relating to such sound recording:

Provided further that if on a complaint brought before the copyright board to the effect that the owner of rights has not been paid in full for any sound recordings purporting to be made in pursuance of this clause, the copyright board is, prima facie, satisfied that the complaint is genuine, it may pass an order ex party directing the person making the sound recording to cease from making further copies and, after holding such inquiry as it considers necessary, make such further order as it may deem fit, including an order for payment of royalty;

(k) the causing of a recording to be heard in public by utilising it,-

(i) in an enclosed room or hall meant for the common use of residents in any residential premises (not being a hotel or similar commercial establishment) as part of the amenities provided exclusively or mainly for residents therein; or

(ii) as part of the activities of a club or similar organisation which is not established or conducted for profit;"

(5) for clause (s) the following clause shall be substituted namely:-

"(s) the making or publishing of a painting, drawing, engraving or photograph of a work of architecture or the display of a work of architecture;"

(6) clause (w) shall be omitted;

(7) after clause (y) the following clauses shall be inserted, namely:-

"(z) the making of an ephemeral recording, by a broadcasting organisation using its own facilities for its own broadcast by a broadcasting organisation of a work which it has the right to broadcast; and the retention of such recording for archival purposes on the ground of its exceptional documentary character;

(za) the performance of a literary, dramatic or musical work or the communication to the public of such work or of a sound recording in the course of any bona fide religious ceremony or an official ceremony held by the Central Government or the State Government or any local authority.

Explanation : For the purpose of this clause, religious ceremony including a marriage procession and other social festivities associated with a marriage."

18. Insertion of new section 52B.- After section 52A of the principal Act, the following section be inserted namely:-

52B. Accounts and audit

(1) Every copyright society appointed under section 34A shall maintain proper accounts and other relevant records and prepare an annual statement of accounts in such form and in such manner as may be prescribed by the Central Government in consultation with the comptroller and Auditor-General of India.

(2) The accounts of each of the copyright societies in relation to the payments received from the Central Government shall be audited by the Comptroller

and Auditor-General of India at such intervals as may be specified by him and any expenditure incurred in connection with such audit shall be payable by the copyright society to the Comptroller and Auditor-General.

(3) The comptroller and Auditor-General of India or any other person appointed by him in connection with the audit of the accounts of the copyright society referred to in sub-section (2) shall have the same rights and privileges and authority in connection with such audit as the comptroller and Auditor-General has in connection with the audit of the Government accounts and, in particular, shall have the right to demand the production of books, accounts and other documents and papers and to inspect any of the offices of the copyright society for the purpose only of such audit.

(4) The accounts of each of the copyright societies as certified by the comptroller and Auditor-General of India or any other person appointed by him in this behalf together with the audit report thereon shall be forwarded annually to the Central Government and that Government shall cause the same to be laid before each House of Parliament."

19. Insertion of new section 53A

In chapter XI after section 53 of the principal Act, the following section shall be inserted namely:-

53A. Resale share right in original copies

(1) in the case of resale for a price exceeding ten thousand rupees, of the original copy of a painting, sculpture or drawing, or of the original manuscript of a literary or dramatic work or musical work, the author of such work if he was the first owner of rights under section 17 or his legal heirs shall, notwithstanding any assignment of copyright in

such work, have a right to share in the resale price of such original copy of manuscript in accordance with the provisions of this section:

Provided that such right shall cease to exist on expiration of the term of copyright in the work.

(2) The share referred to in sub-section (1), shall be such as the copyright board may fix and the decision of the copyright board in this behalf shall be final:

Provided that the copyright board may fix different classes of work.

Provided further that in no case shall the share exceed ten per cent of the resale price.

(3) if any dispute arises regarding the right conferred by this section, it shall be referred to the copyright board whose decision shall be final."

20. Amendment of section 57

In section 57 of the principal Act, for sub-section (1), the following sub-section shall be substituted, namely:-

"(1) Independently of the author's copyright and even after the assignment either wholly or partially of the said copyright, the author of a work shall have the right-

(a) to claim authorship of the work; and

(b) to restrain or claim damages in respect of any distortion, mutilation, modification or the act in relation to the said work which is done before the expiration of the term of copyright if such distortion, mutilation, modification or other act would be prejudicial to his honor or reputation:

Provided that the author shall not have any right to restrain or claim damages in respect of any adaptation of a computer programme to which clause (aa) of sub-section (1) of section 52 applies.

Explanation : Failure to display a work or to display it to the satisfaction of the author shall not be deemed to be an infringement of the rights conferred by this section."

21. Amendment of section 63

In section 63 of the principal Act,-

(1) in clause (b) the words, figures and letter "except the right conferred by section 53A" shall be inserted at the end;

(2) in the proviso, after the words "Provided that," where the infringements has not been made for gain in the course of trade or business" shall be inserted.

22. Amendment of section 63A

In the first proviso to section 63A of the principal Act, after the words "Provided that" the words "where the infringement has not been made for gain in the course of trade or business" shall be inserted.

23. Insertion of new section 63B

After section 63A of the principal Act, the following section shall be inserted namely:-

"63B. Knowing use of infringing copy of computer programme to be an offence.- Any person who knowingly makes use on a computer of an infringing copy of a computer programme shall be punishable with imprisonment for a term which shall not be less than seven days but which may extend to three years and with fine which shall not be less than fifty thousand rupees but which may extend to two lac rupees:

Provided that where the computer programme has not been used for gain or in the course of trade or business the court may, for adequate and special reasons to be mentioned in the judgment not impose any sentence of imprisonment and may impose a fine which may extend to fifty thousand rupees."

24. Amendment of section 78

In section 78 of the principal Act, in sub-section(2),-

(i) after clause (c) the following clauses shall be inserted, namely:-

"(ca) the conditions for submission of application under sub-section(2) of section33;

(cb) the conditions subject to which a copyright society may be registered under sub-section (3) of section 33,

(cc) the inquiry for cancellation of registration under sub-section (4) of section 33;

(cd) the conditions subject to which the copyright society may accept authorisation under clause (a) of sub-section (3) of section 34 and the conditions subject to which owners of rights have right to withdraw such authorisation uder clause (a) of that sub-section;

(ce) the conditions subject to which a copyright society may issue licences, collect fees and distribute such fees amongst owners of rights under sub-section (3) of section 34;

(cf) the manner in which the approval of the owners of rights regarding collection and distribution of fees, approval for utilisation of any amount collected as fees and to provide to such owners information concerning activities in relation to the administration of their rights under sub-section (1) of section 35;

(cg) the returns to be filed by copyright societies to the Registrar of copyrights under sub-section (1) of section 36;"

(ii) after clause (d) the following clauses shall be inserted, namely :-

(da) the manner of payment of royalty under clause (j) of sub-section (1) of section 52;

(db) the form and the manner in which the copyright society shall maintain accounts and other relevant records and prepare annual statements of accounts and the manner in which the quantum of remuneration is to be paid to individual owner of rights under sub-section (1) of section 52B".

APPENDIX IV

THE DIGITAL MILLENNIUM COPYRIGHT ACT OF 1998
U.S. COPYRIGHT OFFICE SUMMARY
DECEMBER 1998

INTRODUCTION

The Digital Millennium Copyright Act (D.M.C.A.) was signed into law by Clinton on October 28,1998. The legislation implements two 1996 World Intellectual Property Organization (WIPO) treaties : the WIPO Copyright Treaty and the WIPO Performances and Phonograms Treaty. The DMCA also addresses a number of other significant copyright related issues.

The DMCA is divided into five titles:

- Title I, the "WIPO Copyright and Performances and Phonograms Treaties Implementation Act of 1998," implements the WIPO treaties.
- Title II, the "Online Copyright Infringement Liability Limitation Act," creates limitations on the liability of online service providers for copyright infringement when engaging in certain types of activities.
- Title III , the "Computer maintenance Competition Assurance Act" creates an exemption for making a copy of a computer program by activating a computer for purposes of maintenance or repair.
- Title IV contains six miscellaneous provisions, relating to the functions of the Copyright Office, distance education, the exceptions in the Copyright Act for libraries and for making ephemeral recordings, "web casting" of sound recordings on the Internet, and the applicability of collective bargaining agreement obligations in the case of transfers of rights in motion pictures.
- Title V , the " Vessel Hull Design Protection Act, " creates a new form of protection for the design of vessel hulls.

This memorandum summarizes briefly each title of the DMCA. It provides merely an overview of the law's provisions; for purposes of length and readability a significant amount of detail has been omitted. *A complete understanding of any provision of the DMCA requires reference to the text of the legislation itself*

TITLE I : WIPO TREATY IMPLEMENTATION

Title I Implements the WIPO treaties. First, it makes technical amendments to U.S. law, in order to provide appropriate references and links to the treaties. Second, it creates two new prohibitions in Title 17 of the U.S. Code- one on circumvention of technological measures used by copyright owners to protect their works and one on tampering with copyright management information- and adds civil remedies and criminal penalties for violating the prohibitions. In addition, Title I requires the U.S. Copyright Office to perform two joint studies with the National Telecommunications and Information Administration of the Department of Commerce (NTIA).

Technical Amendments

National Eligibility

The WIPO Copyright Treaty (WCT) and the WIPO Performances and Phonograms Treaty (WPPT) each require member countries to provide protection to certain works from other member countries or created by nationals of other member countries. That protection must be no less favorable than that accorded to domestic works.

Section 104 of the Copyright Act establishes the conditions of eligibility for protection under U.S. law for works from other countries. Section 102 (b) of the DMCA amends section 104 of the Copyright Act and adds new definitions to section 101 of the Copyright Act in order to extend the protection of U.S. law to those woks requires to be protected under the WCT and the WPPT.

Restoration of Copyright Protection

Both treaties require parties to protect preexisting works from other member countries that have not fallen into the public domain in the country of origin through the expiry of the term of protection. A similar obligation is contained in both the Berne Convention and the Trips Agreement. In 1955 this obligation was implemented in the Uruguay Round Agreements Act, creating a new Section 101A in the Copyright Act to restore protection to works from Berne or WTO member countries that are still protected in the country of origin, but fell into the public domain the United States in the past because of a failure to comply with formalities that then existed in U.S. law, or due to a lack of treaty relations .Section 102 (c) of the DMCA amends section 104A to restore copyright protection in the same circumstances to work from WCT and WPPT member countries.

Registration as a Prerequisite to Suit

The remaining technical amendment relates to the prohibition in both treaties against conditioning the exercise or enjoyment of rights on the fulfillment of formalities. Section 411 (a) of the Copyright Act requires claims to copyright to be registered with the Copyright Office before a law suit can be initiated by the copyright owner, but exempts many foreign works in order to comply with existing treaty obligations under the Berne Convention . Section 102(d) of the DMCA amends section 411 (a) by broadening the exemption to cover all foreign works.

Technological Protection and Copyright Management Systems

Each of the WIPO treaties contains virtually identical language obligating member states to prevent circumvention of technological measures used to protect copyrighted works, and to prevent tampering with the integrity of copyright management information. These obligations serve as technological adjuncts to the exclusive rights granted by copyright law. They provide legal protection that the international copyright community deemed critical to the safe and efficient exploitation of works on digital networks.

Circumvention of Technological Protection Measures

General approach

Article 11 of the WCT states :

Contracting Parties shall provide adequate legal protection and effective legal remedies against the circumvention of effective technological measures that are used by authors in connection with the exercise of their rights under this Treaty or the Berne Convention and that restrict acts, in respect of their works, which are not authorized by the authors concerned or permitted by law.

Article 18 of the WPPT contains nearly identical language

Section 103of the DMCA adds a new chapter 12 to Title 17 of the U.S. Code. New section 1201 implements the obligation to provide ade3quate and effective protection against circumvention of technological measures used by copyright owners to protect their works.

Section 1201 divides technological measures into two categories: measures that prevent unauthorized copying of a copyright work. Making or selling devices or services that are used to circumvent either category of technological measure is prohibited in certain circumstances, described below. As to the act of circumvention in itself, the provision prohibits circumventing the first category of technological measures, but not the second. This distinction was employed to assure that the public will have the continued ability to make fair; use of copyrighted works, Since copying of a work may be a fair use under appropriate circumstances, Section 1201 does not prohibit the act of circumventing a technological measure that prevents copying. By contrast, since the fair use doctrine is not defiance to the act of gaining unauthorized access to a work, the act of circumventing a technological measure in order to gain access is prohibited.

Section 1201 prescribes devices or services that fall within any one of the following three categories:

- they are primarily designed or produced to circumvent ;
- they have only limited commercially significant purpose or use other than to circumvent; or
- they are marketed for use in circumventing.

No mandate

Section 1201 contains language clarifying that the prohibition on circumvention devices does not require manufactures of consumer electronics, telecommunications or computing equipment to design their products affirmatively to respond to any particular technological measure. (Section 1201 (c) (3) . Despite this general 'no mandate 'rule, section 1201 (k) does mandate an affirmative response for one particular type of technology : within 18 months of enactment, all analog videocassette records must be designed to conform to certain defined technologies, commonly known as Macro vision, currently in use for preventing unauthorized copying of analog videocassettes and certain analog signals. The provision prohibits right- holders from applying these specified technologies to free television and basic and extended basic tier cable broadcasts.

Savings clause

Section 1201 contains two general savings clauses. First, section 1201 (c) (1)states that nothing in section 1201 affects rights, remedies, limitations or defenses to copyright infringement including fair use. Second, section

1201 (c) (2) states that nothing in section 1201 enlarges or diminishes vicarious contributory copyright infringement.

Exceptions

Finally , the prohibitions contained in section 1201 are subject to a number of exceptions. One is an exception to the operation of the entire section for law enforcement, intelligence and other government activities.

(Section 1201 (e)). The others relate to section 1201 (a), the provision dealing with the category of technological measures that control access to works.

The broadest of these exceptions, section 1201 (a) (1) (B)- (E), establishes an ongoing administrative rule-making proceeding to evaluate the impact of the prohibition against the act of circumventing such access-control measures. This conduct prohibition does not take effect for two years. Once it does, it is subject to an exception for users of a work which is in a particular class of works if; they are or are likely to be adversely affected by virtue of the prohibition in making non infringing uses. The applicability of the exemption is determined though a periodic rulemaking by the Librarian Congress, on the recommendation of the Register of Copyrights, who is to consult with the Assistant Secretary of Commerce for Communications and Information.

The six additional exceptions are as follows :

1. Nonprofit library, archive and educational institution exception : (Section 1201(d)). The prohibition on the act of circumvention of access control measures is subject to an exception that permits nonprofit libraries, archives and educational institutions to circumvent solely for the purpose of making a good faith determination as to whether they wish to obtain authorized access to the work.

2. Reverse engineering (section 1201 (f)). This exception permits circumvention, and the development of technological means for such circumvention, by a person who has lawfully obtained a right to use a copy of a computer program for the sole purpose of identifying and analyzing elements of the program necessary to achieve interoperability with other programs, to the extent that such acts are permitted ;under copyright law.

3. Encryption research (section 1201 (g)). An exception for encryption research permits circumvention of access control measures, and the development of the technological means to do so, in order to identify flaws and vulnerabilities of encryption technologies.

4. Protection of minors (section 1201 (h)). This exception allows a court applying the prohibition to a component or part to consider the necessity for its incorporation in technology that prevents access of minors to material on the Internet .

5. Personal privacy (section 1201(i)). This exception permits circumvention when the technological measure, or the work it protects, is cable of collecting or disseminating personally identifying about the online activities of a natural person.

6. Security testing (section 1201 (j)). This exception permits circumvention of access control measures, and the development of technological means for such circumvention, for the purpose of testing the security of a computer, computer system or computer network, with the authorization of its owner or operator.

Each of the exceptions has its own set of conditions on its applicability, which are beyond the scope of this summary.

Integrity of Copyright Management Information

Article 12 of the WCT provides in relevant part:

Contracting Parties shall provide adequate and

effective legal remedies against any person knowingly performing any of the following acts knowing, or with respect to civil remedies having reasonable grounds to know, that it will induce, enable, facilitate an infringement of any right covered by this Treaty or the Berne Convention :

(i) to remove or alter any electronic rights management information without authority ;

(ii) to distribute, import for distribution, broadcast or communicate to the public, without authority, works or copies of works knowing that electronic rights management information has been removed or altered without authority.

Article 19 of the WPPT contains nearly identical language.

New section 1202 is the provision implementing this obligation to protect the integrity of copyright management information (CMI). The scope of the protection is set out in two separate paragraphs, the first dealing with false CMI and the second with removal or alteration of CMI. Subsection (a) prohibits the knowing provision or distribution of false CMI. If done with the intent to induce, enable, facilitate or conceal infringement. Subsection (b) bars the international removal or alteration of CMI without authority, as well as the dissemination of CMI or copies of works, knowing that the CMI has been removed or altered without authority. Liability under subsection (b) requires that the act be done with knowledge or with respect to civil remedies, with reasonable grounds to know that it will induce, enable, facilitate or conceal an infringement.

Subsection (c) defines CMI as identifying information about the work, the author, the copyright owner and in certain cases, the performer, writer or director of the work, as well as the terms and conditions for uses of the work and such other information as the Register of Copyrights may prescribe by regulation. Information concerning users of works is explicitly excluded.

Section 1202 is subject to a general exemption for law information, intelligence and other governmental activities. (Section1202(d)). It also contains limitations on the liability of broadcast stations and cable systems for removal or alteration of CMI in certain circumstances where there is no intent to induce, enable, facilitate or conceal an infringement. (Section 1202(e)).

Remedies

Any person injured by a violation of section 1201or 1202 may bring a civil action on Federal court. Section 1203 gives courts the power to grant a range of equitable and monetary remedies similar to those available under Copyright Act, including statutory damages. The court has discretion to reduce or remit damages in cases of innocent violations, where the violator proves that it was not aware and had no reason to believe its acts constituted a violation. ((Section 1203(C)(5)(A). Special protection is given to nonprofit libraries, archives and educational institutions which are entitled to a complete remission of damages in these circumstances. (Section1203(C)(5)(B)).

In addition, it is a criminal offense to violate section 1201 or 1202 with fully and for purposes of commercial advantage or private financial gain. Under section 1204 penalties range up to a $ 500=00 fine or up to five years imprisonment for a first offense and up to a $1000,000 fine or up to 10 years imprisonment for subsequent offenses. Nonprofit libraries, archives and educational institutions are entirely exempted from criminal liability. (Section 1204 (b)).

Copyright Office and NTIA Studies Relating to Technological Development

Title I of the DMCA requires the Copyright Office to conduct two studies jointly with NTIA, one dealing with encryption and the other with the effect of technological developments on two existing exceptions in the Copyright Act. New section 1201(g)(5) of the Title 17 of the U.S. Code requires the Register of Copyrights and the Assistant Secretary of Commerce for Communications and information to report to the Congress no later than one year from enactment on the effect that the exemption for encryption research (new section 1201(g)) has had on encryption research, the development of encryption technology, the adequacy and effectiveness of technological means designed to protect copyrighted works and the protection of copyright owners against unauthorized access to their encrypted copyrighted works.

Section 104 of the DMCA requires the Register of Copyrights and the Assistant Secretary of Commerce for Communications and Information to jointly evaluate (1) the effects of Title I of the DMCA and the development of electronic commerce and associated technology on the operation of sections 109 (first sale doctrine) and 117 (exemption allowing owners of copies of computer programs to reproduce and adapt them for use on a computer). and (2) the relationship between existing and emergent technology and the operation of those sections. This study is due 24 months after the date of enactment of the DMCA.

TITLE II: ONLINE COPYRIGHT INFRINGEMENT LIABILITY LIMITATION

Title II of the DMCA adds new section 512 of the Copyright Act to create four new limitations on liability for copyright infringement by online service providers. The limitations are based on the following four categories of conduct by a service provider:

1. Transitory communications;
2. System caching;

3. Storage of information on systems or networks at direction of users; and
4. Information location tools.

New section 512 also includes special rules concerning the application of these limitations to nonprofit educational institutions.

Each limitation entails a complete bar on monetary damages and restricts the availability of injunctive relief in various respects. (section 512(j)). Each limitation relates to a separate and distinct function and a determination of whether a service provider qualifies for one of the limitations does not bear upon a determination of whether the provider qualifies for any of the other three.(section 512(n)).

The failure of service provider to qualify for any of the limitations in section 512 does not necessarily make it liable for copyright infringement. The copyright owner must still demonstrate that the provider has infringed and the provider may still avail itself of any of the defenses, such as fair use, that are available to copyright defendants generally. (section 512(i)).

In addition to limiting the liability of service providers, Title ii establishes a procedure by which a copyright owner can obtain a subpoena from a federal court ordering a service provider to disclose the identity of a subscriber who is allegedly engaging in infringing activities. (Section 512(h)).

Section 512 also contains a provision to ensure that service providers are not placed in the position of choosing between limitations on liability on the one hand and preserving the privacy of their subscribers, on the other. Subsection (m) explicitly states that nothing in section 512 requires a service provider to monitor its service or access material in violation of law (Such as the Electronic Communications Privacy Act) in order to be eligible for any of the liability limitations.

Eligibility for Limitations Generally

A party seeking the benefit of the limitations on liability in Title II must qualify as a "service provider." For purposes of the first limitations, relating to transitory communications, "service provider" is defined in section 512(k)(i)(A) as "an entity offering the transmission, routing or providing of connections for digital online communications, between or among points specified by a user, of material of the user's choosing, without modification to the content of the material as sent or received." For purposes of the other three limitations, "service provider" is more broadly defined in section 512(k)(i)(B) as "a provider of online services or network access, or the operator of facilities thereof."

In addition, to be eligible for any of the limitations, a service provider must meet two overall conditions: (i) it must adopt and reasonably implement a policy of terminating in appropriate circumstances the accounts of subscribers who are repeat infringers: and (2) it must accommodate and not interfere with " standard technical measures." (Section 51`2(i)). " Standard technical measures" are defined as measures that copyright owners use to identify or protect copyrighted works, that have been developed pursuant to a broad consensus of copyright owners and service providers in an open, fair and voluntary multi- industry process, are available to anyone on reasonable nondiscriminatory terms and do not impose substantial costs or burdens on service providers.

Limitation for Transitory Communications

In general terms, section 512(a) limits the liability of service providers in circumstances where the provider merely acts as a data conduit, transmitting digital information from one point on a network to another at someone else's request. This limitation covers acts of transmission, routing or providing connections for the information, as well as the intermediate and transient copies that are made automatically in the operation of a network.

In order to qualify for this limitation, the service provider's activities must meet the following conditions:

- The transmission must be initiated by a person other than the provider.
- The transmission, routing, provision of connections or copying must be carried out by an automatic technical process without selection of material by the service provider.
- The service provider must not determine the recipients of the material.
- Any intermediate copies must not ordinarily be accessible to anyone other than anticipated recipients and must not be retained for longer than reasonably necessary.
- The material must be transmitted with no modification to its content.

Limitation for System Caching

Section 512(b) limits the liability of service providers for the practice of retaining copies, for a limited time, of material that has been made available online by a person other than the provider, and then transmitted to a subscriber at his or her direction. The service provider retains the material so that subsequent requests for the same material can be fulfilled by transmitting the retained copy, rather than retrieving the material from the original source on the network.

The benefit of this practice is that it reduces the service provider's bandwith requirements and reduces the waiting time on subsequent requests for the same information. On the other hand, It can result in the delivery of outdated information to subscribers and can deprive website operators of accurate "hit" information –

information about the number of requests for particular material on a website- from which advertising revenue is frequently calculated. For this reason, the person making the material available online may establish rules about updating it, and may utilize technological means to track the number of "hit".

The limitation applies to acts of intermediate and temporary storage, when carried out through an automatic technical process for the purpose of making the material available to subscribers who subsequently request it. It is subject to the following conditions.

- The content of the retained material must not be modified.
- The provider must comply with rules about "refreshing" material- replacing retained copies of material with material from the original location- when specified in accordance with a generally accepted industry standard data communication protocol.
- The provider must not interfere with technology that returns "hit" information to the person who posted the material, where such technology meets certain requirements.
- The provider must limit users access to the material in accordance with conditions on access (e.g. password protection) imposed by the person who posted the material.
- Any material that was posted without the copyright owner's authorization must be removed or blocked promptly once the service provider has been notified that it has been removed, blocked or ordered to be removed or blocked, at the originating site.

Limitation for Information Residing On Systems or Networks at the Direction of users

Section 512(C) limits the liability of service providers

for infringing material on website (or other information repositories) hosted on their systems. It applies to storage at the direction of a user. In order to be eligible for the limitation., the following conditions must be met:

- The provider must not have the requisite level of knowledge of the infringing activity, as described below.
- If the provider has the right and ability to control the infringing activity, it must not receive a financial benefit directly attributable to the infringing activity.
- Upon receiving proper notification of claimed infringement, the provider must expeditiously take down or block access to the material.

In addition a service provider must have filed with the Copyright Office a designation of an agent to receive notifications of claimed infringement. The Office provides a suggested form for the purpose of designating an agent (http://www.loc.gov/copyright.onlinesp/) and maintains a list of agents on the Copyright Office website (*http://www.loc.gov/copyright/onlinesp/list/*).

Under the knowledge standard, a service provider is eligible for the limitation on liability only if it does not have actual knowledge of the infringement, is not aware of facts or circumstances from which infringing activity is apparent or upon gaining such knowledge or awareness, responds expeditiously to take the material down or block access to it.

The statute also establishes procedures for proper notification and rules as to its effect. (Section 512(c)(3)). Under the notice and takedown procedure, a copyright owner submits a notification under penalty of perjury, including a list of specified elements, to the service provider's designated agent. Failure to comply substantially with the statutory requirements means that the notification will not be considered in determining the requisite level of knowledge by the service provider. If, upon receiving a proper notification, the service provider promptly removes or blocks access to the material identified in the notification, the provider is exempt from monetary liability. In addition, the provider is protected from any liability to any person for claims based on its having taken down the material. (Section 512(g)(i)).

In order to protect against the possibility of erroneous or fraudulent notifications, certain safeguards are built into section 512. Subsection (g)i) gives the subscriber the opportunity to respond to the notice and takedown by filing a counter notification. In order to qualify for the protection against liability for taking down material, the service provider must promptly notify the subscriber that it has removed or disabled access to the material. If the subscriber serves a counter notification complying with statutory requirements, including a statement under penalty of perjury that the material was removed or disabled through mistake or misidentification, then unless the copyright owner files an action seeking a court order against the subscriber, the service provider must put the material back up within 10-14 business days after receiving the counter notification.

Penalties are provided for knowing material misrepresentations in either a notice or a counter notice. Any person who knowingly materially misrepresents, that material is infringing, or that it was removed or blocked through mistake or misidentification, is liable for any resulting damages (including costs and attorney's fees) incurred by the alleged infringer, the copyright owner or its licensee, or the service provider,(Section 512(f).

Limitation for Information Location Tools

Section 512(d) relates to hyperlinks, online directories, search engines and the like, it limits liability for the acts of referring or linking users to assisted that contains infringing material by using such information location tools, if the following conditions are met:

- The provider must have the requisite level of knowledge that the material is infringing. The knowledge standard is the same as under the limitation for information residing on systems or networks.
- If the provider has the right and ability to control the infringing activity, the provider must not receive a financial benefit directly attributable to the activity.
- Upon receiving a notification of claimed infringement, the provider must expeditiously take down or block access to the material.

These are essentially the same conditions that apply under the previous limitation, with some differences in the notification requirements. The provisions establishing safeguards against the possibility of erroneous or fraudulent notifications, as discussed above, as well as those protecting the provider against claims based on having taken down the material apply to this limitation. (Sections 512(f)-(g)).

Special Rules Regarding Liability of Nonprofit Educational Institutions

Section 512 (e) determines when the actions or knowledge of a faculty member or graduate student employee who is performing a teaching or research function may affect the eligibility of a nonprofit educational institution for one of the four limitations on liability. As to the limitations for transitory communications or system caching, the faculty member or student shall be considered a "person other than the provider," so as to avoid a disqualifying the institution from eligibility .As to the other limitations, the knowledge or awareness of the faculty member or student will not be attributed to the institution. The following conditions must be met:

- the faculty member or graduate student's infringing activities do not involve providing online access to course materials that were required or recommended during the past three years;

- the institution has not received more than two notifications over the past three years that the faculty member or graduate student was infringing; and
- the institution provides all of its users with informational materials describing and promoting and promoting compliance with copyright law.

Title III: Computer Maintenance or Repair

Title iii expands the existing exemption relating to computer programs in section 117 of the Copyright Act, which allows the owner of a copy of a program to make reproductions or adaptations when necessary to use the program in conjunction with a computer. the amendment permits the owner or lessee of a computer program in the course of maintaining or repairing that computer. The exemption only permits a copy that is made automatically when a computer is activated, and only if the computer already lawfully contains an authorized copy of the program. The new copy cannot be used in any other manner and must be destroyed immediately after the maintenance or repair is completed.

Title IV: Miscellaneous Provisions

Clarification of the Authority of the Copyright office

Section 401(b),adds language to section 701 of the Copyright Act confirming the Copyright Office's authority to continue to perform the policy and international functions that it has carried out for decades under its, existing general authority.

Ephemeral Recordings for Broadcasters

Section 112 of the Copyright Act grants an exemption for the making of "ephemeral recordings." These are recordings made in order to facilitate a transmission. Under this exemption, for example, a radio station can record a set of songs and broadcast from the new recording rather than from the original CDs (which would have to be changed "on the fly" during the course of a broadcast).

As it existed prior to enactment of the DMCA, section 112 permitted a transmitting organization to make and retain for up to six months (hence the term "ephemeral") no more than one copy of a work if it was entitled to transmit a public performance or display of the work, either under a license or by virtue of the fact that there is no general public performance right in sound recordings (as distinguished from musical works).

The Digital Performance Right in Sound Recording Act of 1995 (DPRA) created, for the first time in U.S. copyright law, a limited public performance right in sound recordings. The right only covers public performances by means of digital transmission and is subject to an exemption for digital broadcasts (i.e., transmissions by FCC licensed terrestrial broadcast stations) and a statutory license for certain subscription transmissions that are not made on demand (i.e. in response to the specific request of a recipient).

Section 402 of the DMCA expands the section 112 exemption to include recordings that are made to facilitate the digital transmission of a sound recording where the transmission is made under the DPRA exemption for digital broadcasts or statutory license. As amended, section 112 also permits in some circumstances the circumvention of access control technologies in order to enable an organization to make an ephemeral recording.

Distance Education Study

In the course of consideration of the DMCA, legislators expressed an interest in amending the Copyright Act to promote distance education, possibly through an expansion of the existing exception for instructional broadcasting in section110(2). Section 403 of the DMCA directs the Copyright Office to consult with affected parties and make recommendations to Congress on how to promote distance education through digital technologies. The Office must report to Congress within six months of enactment.

The Copyright Office is directed to consider the following issues:

- The need for a new exemption;
- Categories of works to be included in any exemption;
- Appropriate quantitative limitations on the portion of works that may be used under any exemption;
- Which parties should be eligible for any exemption;
- Which parties should be eligible recipients of distance education material under ant exemption;
- The extent to which use of technological protection measures should be mandated as a condition of eligibility for any exemption;
- The extent to which the availability of licenses should be considered in assessing eligibility for any exemption; and other issues as appropriate.

Exemption for Nonprofit Libraries and Archives

Section 404 of the DMCA amends the exemption for nonprofit libraries and archives in section 108 of the Copyright Act to accommodate digital technologies and evolving preservation practices. Prior to enactment of the DMCA, section 108 permitted such libraries and archives to make a single facsimile (i.e., not digital) copy of a work for purposes of preservation or interlibrary loan. As amended, section 108 permits up to the public outside the library premises. In addition, the amended section permits such a library or archive to copy a work into a new format if the original format becomes obsolete- that is, the machine or device used to render the work perceptible is no longer manufactured or is no longer reasonably available in the commercial marketplace.

Webcasting Amendments to the Digital Performance Right in Sound Recordings

As discussed above, in 1995 Congress enacted the DPRA, creating a performance right in sound recordings that is limited to digital transmissions. Under that legislation, three categories of digital transmissions were addressed: broadcast transmissions, which were exempted from the performance right; subscription transmissions, which were generally subject to a statutory license; and on—demand transmissions, which were subject to the full exclusive right. Broadcast transmissions under the DPRA are transmissions made by FCC- licensed terrestrial broadcast stations.

In the past several years, a number of entities have begun making digital transmission of sound recordings over the internet using streaming audio technologies. This activity does not fall squarely within any of the three categories that were addressed in the DPRA. Section 405 of the DMCA amends the DPRA, expanding the statutory license for subscription transmissions to include web casting as a new category of "eligible non subscription transmissions."

In addition, to expanding the scope of the statutory license, the DMCA revises the criteria that any entity must meet in order to be eligible for the license (Other than those who are subject to a grandfather clause, leaving the existing criteria intact). It revises the considerations for setting rates as well (again, subject to a grandfather clauses)., directing arbitration panels convened under the law to set the royalty rates at fair market value.

This provision of the DMCA also creates a new statutory license for making ephemeral recordings. As indicated above, section 402 of the DMCA amends section 112 of the Copyright Act to permit the making of a single ephemeral recording to facilitate the digital transmission of sound recording that is permitted either under the

DPRA's broadcasting exemption or statutory license. Transmitting organizations that wish to make more that the single ephemeral recording of a sound recording that is permitted under the outright exemption in section 112 are now eligible for a statutory license applies to the making of ephemeral recordings. In addition, the new statutory license applies to the making of ephemeral recordings by transmitting organizations other that broadcasters who are exempt from digital performance right, who are not covered by the expanded exemption in section 402 of the DMCA.

Assumption of Contractual Obligations upon Transfers of Rights in Motion Pictures

Section 416 addresses concerns about the ability of writers, directors and screen actors to obtain residual payments for the exploitation of motion pictures in situations where the producer is no longer able to make these payments. The guild's collective bargaining agreements currently require producers to obtain assumption agreements from distributors in certain circumstances, by which the distributor assumes the producer's obligation to make such residual payments. Some production companies apparently do not always do so, leaving the guilds without contractual privities enabling them to seek recourse from the distributor.

The DMCA adds a new chapter to Title 28 of the U.S. Code imposes on transferees those obligations to make residual payments that the producer would be required to have the transferee assume under the relevant collective bargaining agreement. The obligations attach only if the distributor knew or had reason to know that the motion picture was produced subject to a collective bargaining agreement or in the event of a court order confirming an arbitration award under the collective bargaining agreement that the producer cannot satisfy within ninety days. there are two classes of transfers that are excluded from the scope of this provision. The first is transfers limited to public performance rights and the second is grants of security interests, along with any subsequent transfers from the security interest holder.

The provision also directs the Comptroller General, in consultation with the Register of Copyrights to conduct a study on the conditions in the motion picture industry that gave rise to this provision and the impact of the provision oin the industry. The study is due two years from enactment.

Title V: Protection of Certain Original Designs

Title V of the DMCA, entitled the Vessel Hull Design Protection Act (VHDPA), adds a new chapter 13 to Title 17 of the U.S. Code. It creates a new system for protecting original designs of certain useful articles that make the article attractive or distinctive in appearance. For purposes of the VHDPA, " useful articles" are limited to the hulls (including the decks) of vessels no longer than 200 feet.

A design is protected under the VHDPA as soon as a useful article embodying the design is made public or a registration for the design is published. Protection is lost if an application for registration is not made within two years after a design is first made public, but a design is not registrable if it has been made public more than one year before the date of the application for registration. Once registered, protection continues for ten years from the date protection begins,

The VHDPA is subject to a legislative sunset: the Act expires two years from enactment (October 28, 2000). The Copyright Office is directed to conduct two joint studies with the Patent and Trademark Office—the first by October 28, 1999 and the second by October 28, 2000-evaluating the impact of the VHDPA.

Effective Dates

Most provisions of the DMCA are effective on the date of enactment. There are, however, several exceptions. The Technical amendments in Title I that relate to eligibility of works for protection under U.S. copyright law by virtue of the new WIPO treaties do not takes effect until the relevant treaty comes into force. Similarly, restoration of copyright protection for such works does not become effective until the relevant treaty comes into force. The prohibition on the act of circumvention of access control measures does not take effect until two years from enactment (October 28.2000).

APPENDIX V

FORM IV- APPLICATION FOR REGISTRATION OF COPYRIGHT

To

The Registrar of Copyrights
Copyright Office
New- Delhi- 110001.

Sir,

In accordance with Section 45 of the Copyright Act, 1957 (14 if 1957), i hereby apply for registration of Copyright and request you that entries may be made in the Register of Copyrights in the enclosed Statement pf Particulars sent herewith in triplicate.

1. I also send herewith completed the statement of Further Particulars relating to the work. (For Literary, Dramatic, Musical and Artistic works only)
2. In accordance with Rule 16 of the Copyright Rules, 1958, I have sent by prepaid registered post copies of this letter and of the enclosed Statement(s) to other parties concerned, as shown below:

Name and addresses of the parties	Date of dispatch
(1)	(2)

See columns 7,11,12 and 13 of the Statement of Particulars and the party referred in Col.2 (e) of the Statement of further particulars.)

3. The prescribed fee has been paid, as per details below.

4. Communications on this subject may be addresses to:
5. I hereby declare that to the best of my knowledge and belief, no person, other than to whom a notice has been sent to as per paragraph 2 above has any claim or interest or dispute to my copyright of this work or to its use by me.
6. I hereby verify that the particulars given in this form and in the Statement of Particulars and Statement of Further Particulars are True to the best of my knowledge belief and information and nothing has been concealed there from.

List of enclosures: Yours faithfully,

Place: Signature by the applicant

Date:

APPENDIX VI

STATEMENT OF PARTICULARS

(To be sent in Triplicate)

1. Registration No. — (to be filled in by the Copyright Office)
2. Name, address & nationality of the Applicant—
3. Nature of the Applicant's interest in the Copyright of the work—
4. Class & Description of the work—
5. Title of the work—
6. Language of the work—
7. Name, Address & Nationality of the Author and if the author is deceased, the date of decease—
8. Whether the work is published or unpublished—
9. Year & Country of first publication—
10. Years and Countries of subsequent publications if any, and name, address and nationalities of the publishers
11. Names, address and nationalities of the owners of various rights comprising the copyright in the work and the extent of rights held by each, together with the particulars of assignments and license, if any-
12. Names, addresses and nationalities of other persons if any, authorised to assign or license the rights comprising the copyrights—
13. If the work is ' Artistic' the location of the original work, including name and address and nationality of person in possession of the work, (in case of an architectural work, the year of completion of the work should also be shown).
14. If the work is an Artistic work which is used or is capable of being used in relation to any goods, the application should include a certification from the

Registrar of Trade Marks in terms of the proviso to sub- Section (I) of section 45 of the Copyright Act, 1957.

15. Remarks , if any—

Place: Signature of the Applicant

Date :

APPENDIX VI (I)

STATEMENT OF FURTHER PARTICULARS

(To be sent in Triplicate)

(For Literary, Dramatic, Musical and Artistic works only)

1. Is the work to be registered
   - an original work?
   - a translation of a work in the public domain?
   - a translation of a work in which Copyright subsists?
   - an adaptation of a work in the public domain?
   - an adaptation of a work in which Copyright subsists?
2. If the work is a translation or adaptation of a work in which Copyright subsists:
   - Title of the original work
   - Language of the original work
   - Name, address and nationality of the author of the original work and if the author is deceased, the date of decease.
   - Name, address and nationality of the publisher, if any, of the original work
   - Particulars of the authorization for a translation or adaptation including the name, address and nationality of the party authorizing:
3. Remarks, if any.

Place: Signature

Date:

APPENDIX VIITH

Second schedule to the copyright Rules, 1958 (As amended from the time to time) enlisting various fee payable under Copyright Act, 1957.

1. For a license to republish a Literary, Dramatic, Musical Rs. 400/- per work or Artistic work (Section 31,31-A and 32-A)
2. For license to republish a Cinematograph Film (Section31) Rs.600/- per work
3. For a license to republish a sound recording (Section 31) Rs.400/- per work
4. For a license to perform an Indian work in public or to communicate the work to the public by Broadcast (Section31) Rs.200/- per work
5. For an application for a license to produce and publish a translation of a Literary, Dramatic work in any Language (Section 32 & 32-A) Rs. 200/- per work
6. For an application for registration or copyright in a: Rs.50/- per work
   (a) Literary, Dramatic, Musical or Artistic work
   (b) Provided that in respect of a Literary or artistic work which is used or is capable of being used in relation to any goods (Section 45) Rs.400/- per work
7. For an application for change in particulars of copyright entered in the Register of Copyrights in respect of a :-
   (a) Literary, Dramatic, Musical or Artistic work Rs.50/= per work
   (b) Provided that in respect of a literary or Artistic work which is used or is capable of being used in relation to any goods (Section 45) Rs.200/=
8. For an application for registration of copyright in a

Cinematograph Film (Section 45) Rs. 600/= per work

9. For an application for registration of change in particulars of copyright entered in the Register of Copyrights in respect of Cinematograph Film (Section 45) Rs. 400/= per work
10. For an application for registration of copyright in a Sound Recording (Section 45) Rs.400/= per work
11. For an application for registration of changes in particulars of copyright entered in the Registered of Copyrights in respect of Sound Recording (Section 45) Rs. 200/= per work.
12. For taking extracts from the indexes (Section 47) Rs.20/= per work
13. For taking extracts from the Register of Copyrights (Section 47) Rs. 20/= per work
14. For a certified copy of an extract from the Register of Copyrights of the indexes (Section 47) Rs. 20/= per work
15. For a certified copy of any other public document in the custody of the Register of Copyright or the Copyright Board. Rs. 20/= per work
16. For an application for prevention of importation of infringing copies (Section 53) Rs. 400/= per work.

Composition of Copyright Enforcement Advisory Council

1. Chiarman : Additional Secretary, Department of Education, Ministry of Human Resource Department (Ex-officio).

2. Vice-Chairman : Joint Secretary in- charge of Book Promotion and Copyright Division, Department of Education (Ex-officio).

Members

3. Joint-Secretary (Films), Ministry of Information & Broadcasting(Ex-officio).

4. Joint Secretary, Department of Electronics (Ex-officio).
5. Director General of Police ,Government of Uttar-Pradesh.
6. Director General of Police, Government of Andhra Pradesh.
7. Director General of Police, Government of Gujarat .
8. Director General of Police, Government of Punjab.
9. Director General of Police, Administration of Chandigarh.
10. Representative of the Federation of Indian Publishers, New Delhi.
11. Representative of Authors Guild of India, New Delhi.
12. Representative of the Federation of Publishers and Booksellers Associations in India, New Delhi.
13. Representative of Film Federation of India, Mumbai.
14. Representative of National Association of Software Service Companies, New- Delhi.
15. Representative of Phonographic performance limited, Mumbai.
16. Representative of Indian Performing Right Society Ltd., Mumbai.
17. Representative of Cine Artistes Association, Mumbai

Composition of Copyright Board

1.	Shri S. Ramaiah Former Law Secretary to the Government of India.	Chairman
2.	Joint-Secretary of in-charge of Copyrights Ministry of Human Resource Development Department of Education Government of India.	Member
3.	Joint Secretary and Legal Adviser in	Member

the Ministry of law, Justice and company Affairs, dealing with Department of Education, Government of India.

4.	Law Secretary, Govt. of Kerala.	Member
5.	Law Secretary, Govt. of Karnataka	Member
6.	Law Secretary, Govt. of Rajasthan	Member
7.	Law Secretary, Govt. of West Bengal	Member
8.	Law Secretary, Govt. of Maharashtra	Member
9.	Law Secretary, Govt. of Uttar-Pradesh	Member
10	Law Secretary, Govt. of Meghalaya	Member
11.	LawSecretary, Govt. of Madhya Pradesh	Member

APPENDIX XI

ROLE OF JUDICIARY IN THE EFFECTIVE PROTECTION OF INTELLECTUAL PROPERTY RIGHT JUSTICE R. K. ABICHANDANI, JUDGE, HIGH COURT OF GUJARAT

GENERAL

The importance of judiciary in a democratic set up for protection of personal and proprietary rights can hardly be over estimated. The principal function of Judiciary is to provide legal remedies against infringement of personal and property rights of persons.

The Intellectual Property Rights for their effectiveness depends upon the speed with which they can be enforces by the courts. The statutory provisions provide only a modicum of direction as regards the nature of remedies and the procedure for safeguarding them, leaving a large extent of free play within the province of judge.

Infringement of intellectual property rights is a tortuous invasion of property. The common law developed several heads of liability constituting the economic tort." Their general characteristics are that the defendant must be acting intentionally or recklessly; that the plaintiff must suffer or be about to suffer damage; and that they will not apply if some ground of justification is open to the defendant" (Intellectual Property: Patents, Copyright, Trade Marks and Allied Rights, (Second edition) page 28 by W.R. Cornish.). Before statutory provisions in respect of these rights were enacted are remedy was award of damages by the common law courts and remedy by way of injunction was developed by the equity courts.

Intellectual Property is inchoate property when manifested in a legally recognizable way. Property Right was, till the deletion of Article19(1)(f) of the Constitution of India, a fundamental right for citizens, but now under Article 300-A it is separately notified as a Constitutional right ensuring that no person can be deprived of his property save by the authority of law.

II. Equality – A Constitutional Promise

Even though certain important fundamental rights including right to carry on any trade or business are guaranteed only to citizens, all persons including non-citizens can claim equality before the law and equal protection of the laws (Article 14). Therefore any arbitrary discrimination against a person who is a non- citizen qua his claim to be treated equality as others before the law, can be challenged before the courts.

Recourse of court by law is a well recognized concept world over and firmly entrenched in the Constitutional and other laws of India. Therefore, any person can claim a statutorily or customarily recognized right to property. In case of infringement of a legally recognized right recourse to law cannot be denied and the rule of law enshrined in Article 14 of the Constitution will enable any person including a non- citizen to approach the legal forum of the country for redressal of his grievances. In India, as otherwise residing in India or in a foreign Country shall not sue in any such Court without the permission of the Central Government.

Ordinarily, violation of Intellectual Property Rights has a private dimension in as much as it affects the proprietary rights of individuals and may causes financial loss and loss of credit to the owner. Therefore, the questions of national or public interest would rarely arise when redressal is sought by a non-citizen for violation of such proprietary rights by the infringer. The judiciary is bound to implement the laws and redress grievances of all persons including aliens to uphold their common law or statutorily recognized rights.

III. Constitutional directive to respect treaty obligation

As provided by Article 51(c) of the Constitution of

India, the state is under a constitutional directive to endeavor to foster respect for international law and treaty obligations in the dealings of the organized peoples with one another. Though the directive principles of State Policy cannot be enforced in the Municipal Courts, they are nonetheless fundamental in the governance of the Country. The definition of 'State' given in Article 12 for part III of the constitution relating to Fundamental Rights and incorporated in Article 36 for Part IV which contains the Directive Principles of State Policy; is very wide and includes judicial and quasi- judicial authorities also. Therefore, the courts in India are obliged to endeavor to foster respect for international law and obligations under the international treaties.

The constitutional concern for respecting international law including international treaties and conventions is also reflected in Article 253 which, not with standing the distribution of legislative powers between the Federal Union and the States, empowers the Parliament to make law for the whole or any part of the territory of India for implementing any treaty, agreement or convention with any other Country or Countries or any decision made at any international Conference, association or other body. The Parliament is under Article 246 read with entry 14 of the Union List of subjects on which it can legislate contained in Schedule VII of the Constitution, empowered to legislate with respect to the subject entering into treaties and agreements with foreign countries and implementing of treaties, agreements and conventions with foreign countries. However, barring treaties which require legislation to be made, the international agreements entered into by the Union in exercise of its executive power under Article 73 which are not contrary to law are required to be recognized by the Municipal Courts. For entering into treaty or bringing it in force for India, It is not a Constitutional requirement that the executive should have the support of Parliamentary legislation. (Maganbhai V. Union of India, AIR 1969 SC 783). The subject of patents inventions and designs; copyright; trademarks and merchandise marks is assigned to the Parliament under entry 49 of the Union List for the purpose of legislation.

IV. Developed judicial system

India has a highly developed judicial system with the Supreme Court having plenary powers (Article 142) to make any order for doing complete justice in any cause or matter and a mandate in the Constitution (Article 144), to all authorities, Civil and judicial, in the territory of India to act in aide of the Supreme Court. The scope of Writ Jurisdiction of the High Court (Article226) is wiser than traditionally understood and the judiciary is separate and independent of the executive to ensure impartiality in administration of justice. The judiciary has a central role to play in this thriving democracy and shuns arbitrary executive action. The higher judiciary has been empowered to pronoun upon the legislative competence of the law making bodies and the validity of a legal provision. The range of judicial review recognized in the higher judiciary in India is the widest and most extensive known to any democratic set up in the world.

The civil court have jurisdiction to try all suits of a civil nature excepting suits of which their cognizance is either expressly or impliedly barred. (Section 9 of the Code of Civil Procedure).The exclusion of Jurisdiction of a civil court to entertain civil causes is not readily inferred and there is a presumption in favour of the jurisdiction of a civil court. As noted above aliens may sue in any court as if they were citizens of India (Section 83 of Code of Civil Producer). Therefore, in respect of violation of any property rights including intellectual property rights any aggrieved person can resort to remedies available under the Indian law in any court which has jurisdiction in the matter. Aliens and foreign corporation can invoke the principle of equality before the law enshrined in Article 14 of the Constitution of India which applies to 'any person' and is not limited to citizens. This should allay any doubt in the international Community about the protection of the legitimate interests of their nationals who may have to seek redressal in this country, of their grievance against violation of their legal rights.

V. Recognition of Intellectual Property Rights not new to Indian Courts

Even before India became independent there were intellectual property laws viz. the Indian Patent and Designs Act, 1911; The Indian Copyright Act,1914; The Indian Merchandise Market Act, 1889 and the Trade Marks Acts, 1940 which though repealed by the corresponding laws namely Patent Act,1970 (Section 162 repealing Patents and Designs Act, 1911 in so far as it related to Patents), The Copyright Act ,1957 (Section 79) and Trade and Merchandise Market Act,1958 (Section 136), the existing rights and liabilities as also the decisions taken under the repealed laws were saved. The valuable private proprietary rights of the owners of intellectual property or their assignees enjoyed previously to the governmental changes cannot be swept clean out of existence by some malign magic. The Constitutional change bringing India into existence as a sovereign power (Indian Independence Act, 1947 since repealed by Article 395 of the Constitution of India) which was supposed to have affected public rights and national status, was not intended to interfere with private rights of property, whether real or personal, whether based on common law or the statute law and whether owned by persons residing inside or outside the territory which may even affect the citizens of India who may have acquired sub-interests in the property in question by way of lien, assignment or trust. All the existing laws were to continue in force subject to the provisions of the constitution (See Article 372).

The on us that the plaintiff's existing rights in the intellectual property have been confiscated or extinguished, expressly or by necessary implication as a result of political changes would clearly be on the defendant. Emergence of a new state or change of sovereignty within State does not bring about any change in the private rughts of its citizens or the laws governing such rights. Law once established continues to operate until changed by a competent legislative power. It is not changed merely by change of Sovereignty. Therefore, the Courts have with them while dealing with infringement of Intellectual Property Rights a wealth of past experiences and judicial approaches in such matters to draw upon and to view these proprietary rights in their proper perspective.

V. Court's powers under the present Intellectual Property Laws.

The Courts in India are empowered under the municipal laws to grant relief's against violation of intellectual property rights and the parameters reflected in part III of the TRIPS agreement are already adopted enabling the courts to protect these private rights. This can be briefly outlined:

(A) Copyrights

The Civil proceedings in respect of the infringement of Copyright or any other right conferred by the copyright Act can be instituted in the District Court having jurisdiction (Section 62). The civil remedies available for the infringement of the copyright are by way of injunction, damages accounts and otherwise as are or may be provided by law for such infringements (Section 55). There is a rebuttable presumption that the person who name appears on the work or the copies of the work as published, is the author or the publisher of the work, as the case may be (Section 55(2). Independently of his copyright, the author of a work has a special right to claim authorship of the work and to restrain or claim damages in respect of any distortion, mutilation, modification or other act which is done before the expiration of the term of copyright if such deviation would be prejudicial to the honour or reputation of the author (Section 57). The infringing material (copies and plates) will be deemed to be the property of the owner of the copyright (Section 58). Remedy in the case of groundless threat of legal proceedings is by way of a declaratory suit the infringement alleged was in fact not any infringement of any legal; rights of the person making such threats and the court can grant an injunction against continuance of groundless threats and award damages sustained by the owner by reason of such threats, except where the person making such threats, with due diligence commences and prosecutes an action for infringement of the copyright claimed by him. (Section 60). Though no copyright can be claimed except as provided by the Act it is specially provided that there will be no abrogation of any right or jurisdiction to restrain a breach of trust or confidence. (Section 16).

The Central Government by Section 40 is empowered to direct that all or any of the provisions of the copyright Act shall apply to foreign works. The Government has made the International Copyright Order, 1991 applying the provisions of the copyright Act as indicated in paragraph 3 of the order, except those of chapter VIII relating to rights and broadcasting organisation and of performers and the provisions which apply exclusively to Indian works to the Bern Conventions Countries and the Universal Copyright Conventions Countries.

(B) Patents And Designs

The suits for a declaration as the non- infringement (Section 105 of the Patents Act).or for any relief in cases of groundless threats of infringement proceedings (Section

106), or for infringement of a patent (Section 107,108), shall be instituted in a District Court having jurisdiction (Section 104). However if there is a counter claim for revocation of patent, the suit and the counter claim shall be transferred to the High-Court for decision. The Court in cases of groundless threats of unjustifiable, issue injunction against their discontinuance and award damages, if any as he has sustained (Section 106). In any suit for infringement a court may grant an injunction (subject to such terms as the court thinks fit).and at the option of the plaintiff either damages or an account of profit (Section 108) appeal Lies to the High-Court against the decision, order to direction of the Controlled as provided by section 116(2).

For piracy of any registered design by a person he will be liable for every contravention of Section 53 of the Design Act, 1911 to pay to the registered proprietor of the design a sum not exceeding Rs.500/= (but not exceeding in all Rs.1000/= in respect of any one design) as a contract debt or if the proprietor elects to bring a suit for recovery of damages for such contravention and for an injunction against repetition thereof, to pay damages as may be awarded and to be restrained by injunction (Section53(2) of the Design Act, 1911). Remedy in case of groundless threats of legal proceedings by a patentee will mutates mutandis apply in the case of registered designs (Section 54 of Design Act, 1911).

(C) Trade Marks

Suits for the infringement of a registered trade mark or relating to any right in such trade mark or for passing off are to be instituted in a court not inferior to a District Court (Section 106 of the Trade and Merchandise Market Act,1958). The court is empowered to grant in such suit an injunction subject to such terms, as the court think fit, and at the option of the plaintiff, either damages or an account of profits. (Section 106).

VII. Statutory interpretation and treaties

In interpreting a statute, the courts in India would, so far as its language permits, construe it so as not to be inconsistent with the comity of nations or the established rule of International law. If the terms of the legislation are not clear and are reasonably capable of more than one meaning, the international agreements or conventions on the points become relevant, for there is a prima facie presumption that Parliament does not intend to act in breach of International law, including there in specific treaty obligations; and if one of the meaning which can meanings which can reasonably be ascribed to the legislation is consonant is to be preferred. (Kubic Dariusz V. Union of India AIR 1990 SC 605, 615, Saloman V. Commissioner of customs & Excise (1966)3 ALL ER 871 (CA)). Where an International agreement is incorporated in an Indian Statute, the statute should be construed with a view to attaining uniformity in the different jurisdictions in which the agreement operates. This would ordinarily be the approach of the courts in India while dealing with the matters relating to intellectual property rights which is warranted by the Constitutional directive to the State of foster respect for International law and treaty obligations (Article 51).

Outside certain exceptional cases, such as a treaty providing for a money to a foreign power which must be with drawn from the consolidated fund of India a treaty affecting the justifiable rights of a citizen or affecting life or liberty or the imposition of a tax which can be done only by legislation, it is competent for the executive to enter into treaties binding on India. Where the treaties envisage enactment or change of municipal law the courts will not be in a position to directly implement the treaty provision until it gets incorporated in the municipal law. Therefore, while it would be obligatory on the part of the State under the International law to make provisions in its laws as agreed to under a treaty, the obligation cannot be enforced in municipal court. However, where the municipal law on the subject is not in any way in consistent with the treaty obligations undertaken by the Executive, while implementing the municipal law, that aspect will assume great significance and its implementation will be done by the municipal courts in furtherance of the fulfillment of the obligations undertaken by the Executive which do not require to be followed up by any legislative action.

VIII. Court's discretionary powers and treaties

In the field where the law courts enjoy discretion such as while granting interlocutory relief's or imposing conditions while making discretionary orders, the courts can and should keep in view the treaty obligations which bind the State and make orders and impose conditions which are supported by the provisions of binding treaties and conventions. The extent to which rights and obligations of the owners of the intellectual property rights and infringers would get affected in the jurisdictions other than its own can also be one of the parameters to be kept in mind by the municipal court for the sound exercise of its discretionary powers. Therefore, while the role of judiciary is confined to the four corners of the statutory provisions governing the intellectual property rights, its discretionary powers enable it to legitimately take into account the ramifications that its discretionary orders would have in the context of the wider horizons of the intellectual property rights.

India has been party to important treaties and conventions on Intellectual Property, though due to certain internal compulsions, its approach has been somewhat cautions in certain fields. As a member of the WIPO it has important role to play for encouraging creative activity and promoting the protection of intellectual property throughout the world. As member of the WTO and TRIPS Agreement binds it under Article II 2 of the

WTO Agreement. It is therefore under a treaty obligation to give effect to the provisions of the TRIPS Agreement for adequate protection of intellectual property rights. The Courts exercising jurisdiction under the Intellectual Property Laws have to provide effective and expeditious remedies against any act the infringement of intellectual property rights keeping in view the treaty obligations undertaken by the State in the process of interpretation of the statutory provisions, exercise of its discretion and granting adequate relief's against the infringements of the Intellectual Property Rights.

IX. Judicial review of administrative and quasi-Judicial orders

Against the orders of the administrative or quasi-judicial authorities empowered to take decisions interalia on the question of registration, recognition, revocation, cancellation or imposition of conditions under the intellectual property laws, judicial review is permissible as an effective check on any arbitrary or illegal action. The writ jurisdiction of the High-court is effectively invoked for ensuring that the authorities act within the bounds of their powers, do not take any biased attitude; do not act arbitrarily, do not deny equality before the law to the concerned person, observe principles of natural justice and fair play in making orders or taking action, pass reasoned orders and communicate their decisions to the affected party to enable them to challenge any adverse decision. Due to the rapid growth of the administrative law, requirement of making a reasoned order has emerged as a basic principle of natural justice in addition to the two traditionally recognized principles of natural justice namely' No man shall be a judge of his own cause' and that ' no on should be condemned unheard' (See Siemens Engineering V. Union of India, AIR 1976 SC 1785=(1976)2 SCC 981; M.P. Industries V. Union if India AIR 1966 S.C. 671:(1966) 1 SCR466).

5. Injunctions

The statutory safeguards against infringement of the intellectual property rights in form of injunction and damages are university recognized. Apart from the specific provisions of empowering the Courts to issue injunction contained in the intellectual property laws as noted above, there are provisions in the Specific Relief Act for grant of preventive relief by injunction, temporary or perpetual, at the discretion of the court (Section 36, 37, 38). a perpetual injunction can only be granted by the decree made at the hearing and upon the merits of the suit and the defendant is thereby perpetually enjoyed from the assertion of a right or from the commission of an act, which would be contrary to the rights of the plaintiff. (Section 37(2) of the Specific Relief Act).Temporary injunctions can be granted during the tendency of the suit and are regulated by the code of Civil Procedure (O.XXXIX).

In the field of intellectual property, injunction is almost always prohibitory in nature. Till the infringement of a right is established at the trial interlocutory injunction would constitute a temporary redress to be granted at the discretion of the court and has great deal of practical efficacy. The interim period is sometimes very long because of the delays in the disposal of the trial. It would therefore be important for the courts to invariably impose a condition on the plaintiff to undertake to make good any damage suffered by any defendant from the injunction, should the plaintiff fail at the trial. (See Harmen Pictures V. Osborne (1967)2 All E, R, 324).This principal of indemnification is incorporated in Article 48 of the TRIPS Agreement and ought to be specifically incorporated in the provisions of O.XXXIX of the Code of Civil Procedure, relating to temporary injunction and interlocutory orders as a Specific rule. There is of course a general provision under section 144 of the code for applying for restitution; where the orders are vacated.

The courts, however, have amply discretion to impose terms and conditions while granting interlocutory orders or taking provisional measures to ensure appropriate compensation being paid to the defendant who ultimately is found not to have done any infringement. The experience however has shown that though the courts have discretion to impose such conditions, by and large it is not imposed leaving scope for the unscrupulous plaintiff to act with impunity. The courts are empowered to make interlocutory orders under O.XXXIX Rule 7 of the Code for detention inspection or preservation of any property which is the subject matter of the suit and for this purpose to authorize any person to enter upon or into any premises in possession of any other party and authorize samples to be taken. Experts orders of this nature can be made under Rule 8 (3). Thus it was already within the jurisdiction of the Indian Courts to make orders under the procedural rules contained in the Code like Anton Pillar order or the Mareva injunction. Where no specific provision is made it has inherent jurisdiction under Section 151 of the Code to make orders necessary for the ends of justice.

XI. Damages

Damages can be assessed on the basis of loss caused to the plaintiff or profit to the infringer. In "economic" torts, damages should be assessed so as to put the injured party in the position he would have been in, if he had not sustained the wrong. Reasonable royalty or licence analogy can be applied and rates customary in the royalty or licence agreements can be taken as the basis for assessing damages (See General Tire V. Firestone, 1976)- R.P.C.197,212 (H.L.). In competitive infringements, where the anticipated profits are the same in the same market, the defendant's gain will be the plaintiff's loss. In such cases the plaintiff's loss will also include the extent of loss caused due to his being placed in a disadvantageous position by the defendants getting a foot hold in the market in other competitive lines. The judicial precedents provide general guidelines for assessing damages and the judges can have their own approach to deal with a particular assessment with a view to provide adequate and just compensation for the loss suffered by the plaintiff.

XII. Criminal procedure

In the Indian Legal System, Civil and Criminal modes of redress are largely kept separate. In the field of intellectual property stringent punishments are prescribed in respect of the offences of infringement (See chapter XIII of the Copyright Act, 1957; Chapter X of the Trade and Merchandise Marks Act, 1958; Chapter XX of the Patents Act 1970).In criminal proceedings there would be no possibility of securing an interlocutory order to stop further infringement pending the trial and the burden of proof would be higher than in civil action. Therefore, most claimants resort to civil remedies which are more useful to them than punishment in the name of the state. Prosecutions would however have a great deterrent effect against infringement of the intellectual property rights.

XIII. Conclusions

The Courts while considering the question of grant of relief's where parameters are not laid down in the statutory provisions will be guided by the norms accepts by the international community and would be justified in seeking guidance from the treaties and conventions on the subject so long they are not in consistent with the municipal laws. The courts undoubtedly will be bound by the constitutional mandates and the law, and will have to strike a delicate balance between public welfare and private interests so that an atmosphere conductive to respect for the intellectual property rights of the nationals of the member states is created which would help in increased international trade and encourage the citizens to strive for excellence to produce intellectual property which will be recognized and inforced by all the courts of the member States.

In India there is a highly mature and developed legal system firmly imbedded in rule of law and approach of judiciary in safeguarding the basic human rights and the majesty of law is amply reflected in the decisions of the Apex Court and the High Courts. The courts have frowned upon arbitrary actions of the administrative authorities or unfair and arbitrary approach of the authorities in their decision making process. There is judicial insistence on following the principles of natural justice and fair play by the authorities who make orders that may have an adverse impact on the right of a person. As a safeguard against arbitraries, the authorities are required to make reasoned orders and their decisions are required to be communicated to the concerned parties. The proceedings of courts are normally held in the open. With its independence secured against any arm twisting by outside forces the role that the Indian judiciary can play in safeguarding the legally recognized rights including the intellectual property rights can put to envy any enlightened judicial system of any developed country. The fairness of the procedures reflected in our laws and recognition of equality rights of even aliens by virtue of Article 14 ad their fundamental rights should generate sufficient confidence in our legal system to encourage the entrepreneurs to be sure of the protection of their intellectual property rights which are recognized by the municipal laws. The role that judiciary can play in protection of private and other rights will ultimately depend upon the perceptions of those who have to play it. It is therefore important that they thoroughly understand the natural of the rights recognized by law, the need for their protection, the steps required to be taken as also the urgency of the matter. The establishment of Judicial Academy for providing periodic training and refreshers can keep the decision makes abreast of the needs of time and situations and be aware of the important role that may have to play.

PATENT APPLICATION

A patent application is a request pending at a patent office for the grant of a patent for the invention described and claimed by that application. An application consists of a description of the invention (the patent specification), together with official forms and correspondence relating to the application. The term patent application is also used to refer to the process of applying for a patent, or to the patent specification itself.

In order to obtain the grant of a patent, a person, either legal or natural, must file an application at a patent office with jurisdiction to grant a patent in the geographic area over which coverage is required. This will often be a national patent office, such as the United Kingdom Patent Office of the United States Patent and Trademark Office (USPTO), but could be a regional body, such as the European Patent Office, Once the patent specification complies with the laws of the office concerned, a patent may be granted for the invention described and claimed by the specification.

The process of "negotiating" or "arguing" with a patent office for the grant of a patent, and interaction with a patent office with regard to a patent after its grant, is known as patent prosecution . Patent prosecution is distinct from patent litigation which relates to legal proceedings for infringement of a patent after it is granted.

The History of Patent Law

The history of patents and patent laws is generally considered to have started in Itly with a Venetian Statute of 1474 which was issued by the Republic of Venice. They issued a decree by which new and inventive device, once they had been put into practice, had to be communicated to the Republic in order to obtain legal protection against potential infringers. The period of protection was 10 years.

Patents, however, existed before the law. The first Italian patent was actually awarded by the Republic of Florence in1421, (1) and there is evidence suggesting that something like patents was used among some *ancient Greek Cities.*

What is a Patent?

A patent is a grant from the Government, which confers on the grantee for a limited period of time the exclusive privilege of making, selling and using the invention for which a patent has been granted and also of authorizing others to do so. The grant of patents for inventions in India is governed by the Patents Act, 1970 and the Patents Rules 1972 as amended from time to time.

A patent granted under the Act confers upon the patentee where the patent is for an article or a substance, the exclusive right by himself, his agents or licenses to make use, exercise sell or distribute such article or substance in India and where the patent is for a method or process of manufacturing an article or substance, the exclusive right by himself, his agents or licenses to use or exercise the method or process in India. The patents granted under the Act are operative in the whole of India.

2. The Patent Office

The Patent Office has been established by the Government of India for granting patents for inventions under the Patents Act, 1970 and for the registration of industrial design under the Designs Act, 1911. The head office of the patent office is located at Calcutta. At present the patent office has Branch Offices at Mumbai.,Chennai and Delhi.

3. Varieties of patent

Three kinds of patents are granted under the provision of the Act, namely.

(i) An ordinary Patent.

(ii) A patent of addition for infringement in or modification of an invention for which invention a patent has already been applied for a granted. A patent of addition remains in force only as long as the patent for the original invention remain in force and no renewal fees are payable in respect thereof. In case the original patent is revoked, the patent of addition may be made as independent patent by the authority ordering the revocation and it will be continue there after for the unexpired terms of original patent subject to the payment of the prescribed renewal fees.

(iii) A patent will be granted in respect of a convention application filed under section 135 of the Act is based on an application made in a convention country. The convention application has to be made within one year from the date of the first application made in a convention country in respect of that invention.

(iv) Who may apply for a patent?

(a) An application for an ordinary patent for an invention may be made by any person, whether a Citizen of India, or not, claiming to be true and first inventor of the invention or his assignee. The first importer of an invention into India or the first communicator of an invention from outside India cannot be considered as the 'true and first inventor' The term 'person' includes the government.

(b) An application for a patent of addition may be made only by the applicant for the original patent to which it is an addition, if the application for the main patent is pending; or by the patentee of such main patent, if it has been granted.

(c) A convention application may be made by any person who has made an application for a patent in respect of that invention in a convention country or by his assignee or his legal representative.

(V) What may be patented?

Any invention which satisfies the definition of the 'invention' give in the Act may be patented.

(a) As defined in Section 2 of the Act; am invention, means any new and useful:

(i) art, process, method or manner of manufacture,

(ii) machine, apparatus or other article;

(iii) substance produced by manufacture and includes any new, any useful improvement of any of them and an alleged invention.

(b) The following inventions are **not patentable** within the meaning of the Act.

(i) an invention which is frivolous or which claims anything obviously contrary to well established natural laws;

(ii) an invention the primary intended use of which would be contrary to law or morality or injurious to public health;

(iii) the mere discovery of a scientific principle or the formulation of an abstract theory;

(iv) the mere discovery of any new property or new use for a known substance or of the mere use a known process, machine or apparatus unless such known process results in a new product or employs at least one new reactant;

(v) a substance obtained by a mere admixture resulting only in the aggregation of the properties of the components thereof or a process for producing such substance;

(vi) the mere arrangement or rearrangement or duplication of known devices each functioning independently of one another in known way;

(vii) a method or process of testing applicable during the process of manufacture for rendering the machine, apparatus or other equipment more efficient or for the improvement or restoration of the existing machine, apparatus or other equipment or for the improvement or control of manufacture;

(viii) a method of agriculture or horticulture;

(ix) any process medicinal, surgical, curative, prophylactic, or other treatment of human being or any process for a similar treatment of animals of plants to render them free of disease or to increase their economic value or that or their products.

(c) Certain invention not patentable as provided in Section4 of Act, no patent shall be granted in respect of invention relating to Atomic energy falling within sub-section (1) of section 20 of the Atomic energy act, 1962.

(d) Inventions in respect of which only processes of manufacture are patentable in respect of inventions.

(i) claiming substance intended for use or capable of being used, as food or as medicine or drug, or

(ii) relating to substance prepared or produced by chemical processes (including alloys; optical glass, semi-conductors and inter-metallic compounds); no patent shall be granted in respect of claims for the substances themselves, but claims for the methods or processes of manufacture shall be patentable.

The terms 'medicine or drug' includes insecticide, germicides fungicides and the like.

(VI) Term of the Patent

Subject to the payment or prescribed renewal fee within the precribed period, the term of every patent granted shall be as follows;

(a) In respect of any other invention claiming process or method of manufacture of a substance intended for use or capable of being used as food, or as a medicine or drug 5 years from the date of sealing of the patent or 7 years from the date of the patent whichever period is shorter; this has been amended to a uniform period 20 years.

(b) In respect of any other invention, 14 years from the date of the patent; subsequently amended to 20 years.

(VII) Date of the Patent

Subject to the provisions of the Act in respect of the post dating of patent applications, every patent granted under the Act shall be dated as of the date on which the complete specification was filed.

(VIII) General procedure for obtaining a patent

The following are the successive stages of the procedure for obtaining a patent.

(i) Filling an application for a patent accompanied by either a provisional specification or a complete specification;

(ii) Filling the complete specification if a provisional specification accompanied the application;

(iii) Examination of the application;

(iv) Acceptance of the application and advertisement of

such acceptance in the official Gazette.

(v) Overcoming opposition, if any, to the grant of a patent; (over coming by applicant for Patent).

(vi) Sealing or grant of the patent (to be done by HO at Calcutta).

(IX) Filing application for patents outside India

In case a person resident in India desires to make an application for patent outside, he should either (I) apply for a patent at the appropriate office in India and thereafter apply for a patent outside after the expiry of six weeks from the date of filing in India, provided no secrecy orders have been imposed by the controller under section 35 of the Act, or (II) seek permission of the Central Government for applying outside of India by making an application to the controller in Form 21 with prescribed fee before filing an application for patent outside India. Failure to comply with prescribed fee before filing an application for patent outside India. Failure of comply with these requirements will attract the provisions of Section 40 and 118 of the Patent Act, 1970.

(X) General

All applications for patents are kept secret up to the stage of the advertisement of their acceptance. The correspondence with the applicants for Patents is also treated as confidential.

JAYANT BHATT- LAW STUDENT

1. Patent, is a legal document granted by the government giving an inventor the exclusive right to make, use and sell an invention for a specified number of years. Patents are also available for significant improvements on previously invented items.

The goal of the patent system is to encourage inventors to advance the state of technology by awarding them special rights to benefit from their inventions. Books, movies and works of art cannot be patented, but protection is available for such items under the law of copyright. Patent law is one branch of the larger legal field known as intellectual property, which also includes trademark and copyright law.

Patent law centers round the concept of novelty and inventive step (or lack of obviousness). The right which they accord is to prevent all others, not just imitators but even independent devisors of the same idea from using the invention for the duration of the patent. The special potential of a patent is accordingly that it may be used to prevent all others from including any from of invention in their product and services. A patent thus poses serious difficulties for its competitors. This is why patents are not freely available for all industrial improvements but only what is judged to qualify as a patentable invention.

What is patentable ?

To qualify for a patent, the invention must meet three basic tests. First, it must be novel, meaning that the invention did not previously exist. Second, the invention must be non- obvious, which means that the invention must be a significant improvement to existing technology. Simple changes to previously known devices do not comprise a patentable invention. Finally, the proposed invention must be useful. Legal experts commonly interpret this to mean that no patent will be granted for inventions that can only be used for an illegal or immoral purpose.

Some types of discoveries are not patentable. No one can obtain a patent on a law of nature or a scientific principle even if he or she is the first one to discover it. For example, Isaac Newton could not have obtained a patent on the laws of gravity, and Albert Einstein could not have patented his formula for relativity, $E=mc^2$.

Under the law of the European patent Convention (EPC), patents area only granted for inventions which are capable of industrial application, which are new and which innvolve an inventive step.An invention may be defined as a proposal for the practical implementation of an idea for solving a technical problem. An invention is capable of industrial application if it can be made or used in any kind of industry, including agriculture , as distinct from purely intellectual or aesthetic activity.

An invention is said to be new if, prior to the date of filing or to the priority date accorded to the application from an earlier application for the same invention, it was not already known to the public in any form (written oral or through use), i e it did not from part of the state of the art . An invention is said to involve an inventive step if, in the light of what is already known to the public, it is not obvious to a so- called skilled person, ie someone with good knowledge and experience of the field.

Under the Indian patent law a patent can be obtained only for an invention which is new and useful. The invention must relate to a machine, article or substance produced by manufacture or the process of manufacture of an article. A patent may also be obtained for an improvement of an article or of a process of manufacture. In regard to medicine or drug and certain classes of chemicals no patent is granted for the substance itself even if new, but a process of manufacturing and substance is patentable. The application for a patent must be true and the first inventor or the person who has derived title from him, the right to apply for a patent being assignable.

Patentability of Biotechnological Inventions

In view of the office instructions of the Controller General of Patents, Designs & Trademarks dated 15th July,1991, view point regarding patentability of biotechnological inventions in India is:

(1) Inventions relating to organisms or biological material per se viz.-

a. Living entities of natural or artificial origin such as animals, plants and microorganisms, biological material such as plasmids, virusses, gene, recombinant DNA, bacteria, fungi, algae and other material having self replicating properties and parts thereof,

b. Naturally occurring substances from living entities, biological materials and also process for their production, are not Patentable under the Act. Hence no claim is allowable for such inventions.

(2) Inventions relating to process or methods of production of tangible and nonliving substances like enzymes, antibiotics, insulin, hormones, interferon, alcohols, vaccines etc. by bioconversion or using such microorganisms or by utilizing the above referred biologically active substances as well as chemical substances produced by using genetically engineered organisms or such existing substances made more economically by use of biotechnology and or microbiology are patentable under the Patent Act, 1970.

(3) While claiming the invention in respect of above subject where strain/ bacteria have been used and deposited in depositing authorities and allotted their accession number, such depositions or accession number should be followed by the characteristics of such strain or bacteria.

Under U.S. law, the person who first invented the item receives the patent. If it is unclear who invented the item first, the PTO decides who gets the patent in a proceeding known as an interference. The losing party may then appeal the PTOs decision at the Court of Appeals for the Federal Circuit, a specialized court in Washington, D.C., established to deal with patent matters.

Under the United States law 4 types of patents can

be issued viz., utility, design, plant and provisional :-

Utility patents may be granted to anyone who invents or discovers any new and useful process, machine, article of manufacture, or compositions of matters, or any new useful improvement thereof. Design patents may be granted to anyone who invents a new, original and or an a mental design for an article of manufacture. The term of a design patent is 14 years. Plant patents may be granted to anyone who invents or discovers and a sexually reproduces any distinct and new variety of plant. Plant utility patent protection is available for biotechnology process, genes, seeds, plant parts, cultivates and hybrids. Utility patents may also be obtained on plants if the invention is new, useful, and not obvious.

Provisional patents allow applicants to inexpensively establish an early filing date, or constructive reduction to practice for an invention describer in the provisional application without starting the 20 year patent term clock. It can provide up to twelve months to further develop the invention, determine marketability, acquire funding or capital, seek licensing or manufacturing.

What is not patentable?

Some inventions cannot be patented Under the law of the European Patent Convention (EPC) the list of non-patentable subject- matter includes methods of medical treatment or diagnosis, and new plant or animal varieties. Further information on such fields can be obtained from a patent attorney. Nor may patents be granted for inventions whose exploitation would be contrary to public order or morality (obvious examples being land mines or letter- bombs). The following are not regarded as inventions: discoveries; scientific theories and mathematical methods; aesthetic creations, such as works of art or literature; presentations of information; computer software.

Under the Indian law the following are non patentable (as mentioned under section 3 and 5 of Indian Patents Act, 1970) : An invention which is frivolous or which claims anything obvious contrary to well established natural laws. An invention the primary or intended use of which would be contrary to law or morality or injurious to public health. The mere discovery of a scientific principle or the formulation of an abstract theory.

The mere discovery of any new property or new use for a known substance or of the mere use of a known process, machine or apparatus unless such known process results in a new product or employs at least one new reactant.

A substance obtained by a mere admixture resulting only in the aggregation of the properties of the components thereof or a process for producing such substance. The mere arrangement or rearrangement or duplication of known devices each functioning independently of one another in a known way. A method or a process of testing applicable during the process of manufacture for rendering the machine, apparatus or other equipment more efficient or for the improvement or restoration of the existing machine, apparatus or other equipment more efficient or for the improvement or control of manufacture.

A method of agriculture or horticulture. Any process for the medicinal, surgical, curative, prophylactic or other treatment, of human being or any process for a similar treatment of animals or plants to render them free of disease or to increase their economic value or that of their products.

No patents shall be granted in respect of an invention relating to Atomic energy. Claiming substances intended for use, or capable of being used, as food or as medicine or drug relating to substance prepared or produced by chemical processes (including Alloys, optical glass, semiconductor and inter- metallic compounds), no patent shall be granted in respect of claims for the substances themselves, but claims for the methods or processes of manufacture shall be patentable. The criteria under the US laws are also quite similar as above. Books, Moves and works of art cannot be patented but protection is available for such items under the law of copyright.

History of Patents

The first patent law was passed by the city of Venice in 1474. It protected the interests of inventors by assuring them the right to their inventions and prohibiting unauthorised copying. In 1624, the Statute of Monopolies was enacted in England. This allowed patents to be granted for a limited period to the true and first inventor. The increasing number of national patent laws led in 1883 to the conclusion of the Paris convention, providing a guarantee of equal treatment for patent applicants in all its member states. It was originally adopted by 20 countries from around the world and has since been adopted by most others.

In addition, most of the worlds nations have signed several other treaties dealing with patent issues during the 20th century. For example, more than 120 countries have signed the 1994 Agreement on Trade Related Aspects of Intellectual Pr oper ty Rights (TRIPS). This treaty strengthened legal protection for patents worldwide.

In the United States, patent law dates to 1641, when the first patents for inventions were issued by the Massachusetts Bay Colony for the manufacture of salt. The Constitution of the United States, which became effective in 1789, gave Congress the power to enact federal patent laws. Congress adopted the first patent law in 1790 as one of its first actions. It has frequently amended U.S. patent law since then. The current patent law was adopted in 1952 and is administered by the U.S. Patent and Trademark Office (PTO), an agency within the Department of Commerce. Despite the early development of patent law in the United States, there was no central administrative office to determine the validity of U.S. patents until the PTO was established in1836. Since then, the PTO has examined all applications for patents to decide whether they meet the requirements of the patent laws.

The Patent Act, 1970 came into force on 20-4-1972 replacing Indian Patents and designs Act, 1911. The Patent Act, 1970 in comparison with Indian Patents and Design Acts, 1911 has far more reaching effect in some areas such as food, Drug and Medicines where all the patents granted under this category and deemed to be endorsed with the words License of Right. India has become a member of the Paris Convention ant PCT W.e.f. 7-12-1998 and by virtue of this, the Head Office of Patent Office & Branch offices have become receiving offices for the purpose of international applications filed under PCT.

In view of these developments, the Patents Rules,1972 have been amended by incorporating a new chapter IIA dealing with international application which can be filed at Head office of the Patent Office at Calcutta or Branch Offices at Delhi, Chennai & Mumbai w.e.f. 17-11-99 as applicable. The present Act under Chapter IVA provides specific provisions for the grant of EMR (Exclusive Marketing Rights) with a view to fulfill its international obligation under the provisions of article 70.9 of TRIPs agreement which are in force w.e.f. 1-1-1995.

India : In India as per the patent Act of 1970, an application for a patent may be made by the actual inventor of the invention, or an assignee of the right to make an application or a legal representative of either. It is the person who first applies for a patent who is entitled to the grant. A prior inventor of the invention who applies subsequently will not get the patent as against the first applicant. A person who has merely communicated the idea to another, who actually gave practical shape to the idea and developed the invention, cannot claim to be the first and true inventor. A foreign national resident abroad is not prohibited from making an application and obtaining a Patent of India.

An application for a patent in the prescribed form along with the prescribed fee should be filed in appropriate office of the patent office. An application is required to be filed according to the territorial limits where the applicant or the first mentioned applicant in case of joint applicants for a patent normally resides or has domicile or has a place of business or the place from where the invention actually originated. It the applicant for the patent or party in a proceeding having no business places or domicile in India, the appropriate office will be according to the address of service in India given by the applicant or party in a proceeding.

Patent Office Branch, Mumbai : The state of Gujarat, Goa, Maharashtra, Madhya Pradesh and the Union Territories of Daman and Diu and Dadra and Nagar Haveli.

Patent Office Branch, New Delhi : The State of Haryana, Himachal Pradesh, Jammu & Kashmir, Punjab, Rajasthan, Uttar-Pradesh and Delhi and the Union Territory of Chandigarh.

Patent Office Branch, Chennai : The States of Andhra Pradesh Karnataka, Kerala, Tamilnadu and Pondicherry and the Union Territories of Laccadive, Minicoy and Amandive Islands.

Patent Office (Head Office), Kolkata : Rest of India.

The application should be accompanied by a provisional or complete specification. A provisional specification should describe the invention only briefly and need not contain the claims. Where the application is accompanied by a provisional specification, a complete specification should be filed within 12 months from the date of filing the application. If this is not done, the application will deemed to be abandoned.

The complete specification should fully and particularly describe the invention and the method by which it is to be carried out. It should disclose the best method of performing the invention for which protection is claimed. The claim should relate to single invention. They should be clear and be fairly based on the matter disclosed in the specification. The specification should be accompanied by drawings where appropriate and necessary. The specification should relate to single invention.

The application is examined by examiners of patents to see whether it complies with the requirements of the Act and the Rules, whether there is any lawful ground of objection to the grant of patent and whether the invention has already been published or claimed by any other person. The examiner makes a search in publications available in the patent Office and specification of prior applications and Patents to see whether the same invention has already been published or claimed or is the subject matter of existing or expired patents.

After examination of the application, the Patent Office will communicate to the applicant, the objections if any to grant of a patent. The objections generally relate to the drafting of the specifications and claims, anticipation of any of the claims in prior publication of any specification or claims, or documents,. In many cases these objections can be overcome by suitably amending the description of the invention and the claims and in some cases by insertion of the reference to the prior specification number. If the objections are not satisfactorily met, the Controller of patents, after giving an opportunity of hearing to the applicant will refuse the application.

Where the application has satisfactorily removed the official objections the controller will accept the complete specification and advertise it in the Official Gazette. From the date of acceptance to the date of selling of the patent the application will get the benefits of the grant except that he will not be entitled to institute infringement proceedings until the patents is sealed. Any person interested may give notice of opposition within three months from the date of advertisement in the Official Gazette. The Controller will forward the copy a copy of the notice of opposition to the applicant who may file their evidence in support of their respective cases and the matter will be heard and decided.

Where an application is accepted either without opposition, a patent will be granted if a request for sealing is made by the applicant. An inventor, if he so desires, may make a request for mentioning his name in the patent. The Controller, if satisfied, will cause his name to be mentioned as inventor in the patent granted, in the complete satisfaction and in the register of patents. The mention of the inventors name in the patent will not confer or derogate from any rights under the patent.

Under Indian law the term of patent is not the same for all kinds of invention as in most of other developed countries. In respect of process patents relating to drugs and fruits, the term is five years from the date of sealing the patents or seven years from the date of patent i.e. the date of filing the complete specifications which ever is shorter. In respect of all other patents the term is 14 years from the date of patent.

A patent can be kept alive only by paying the renewal fee from time to time. Also in case of any improvement in or modification of a previous invention already patented, a patent called patent of addition may be obtained. The term of the patent of addition will run concurrently and terminate with the main patent. No renewal fee is payable so long as the main patent remains in force.

APPENDIX IXTH

REGISTERED NO . DL- 33004/99

THE GAZETTE OF INDIA

EXTRAORDINARY

PART II—SESCTION I

PUBLISHED BY AUTHORITHY

No. 621 NEW-DELHI, THRUSDAY, DECEMBER 30, 1999/ PAUSA9,1921

Separate paging is given to this Part in order that it may be filed as a separate compilation.

MINISTRY OF LAW, JUSTICE AND COMPANY AFFAIRS

(Legislative Department)

New Delhi, the 30th December,1999
Pausa 9, 1921 (Saka)

The following Act of Parliament received the assent of the President on the 30th December, 1999 and is hereby published for general information:—

THE COPYRIGHT (AMENDMENT) ACT, 1999 No. 49 OF 1999

[30TH December,1999]

An Act further to amend the Copyright Act, 1957

BE it enacted by Parliament in the Fifteenth year of the Republic of India as following:-

1. (1) This Act may be called the Copyright (Amendment) Act, 1999.(Short title and commencement)

(2) It shall come into force on such date as the Central Government may, by notification in the Official Gazette, appoint. **(Amendment of section 2)**

In section 2 of the Copyright Act,,1957 (here in after referred to as the principal Act). in section

3. In section 14 of the principal Act, in clause (b), for sub-clause (ii), the following shall be substituted,

namely:——

"(ii) to sell or give on commercial rental or offer for sale or for commercial rental any copy of the computer programme;

Provided that such commercial rental does not apply in respect of computer programmes where the programme itself is not the essential object of the rental."

2. In section 38 of the principal Act, in sub- section (2), for the words " twenty- five years", the words "fifty years" shall be substituted.

3. After section 40 of the principal Act, the following section shall be inserted, namely:—

"40A. (i) If the Central Government is satisfied that a foreign country (other than a country with which India has entered into a treaty or which is a party to a convention relating to rights of broadcasting organizations and performers to which India is also a party) has made or has undertaken to in the such provisions, if any, as it appears to the Central Government expedient to require, for the protection in that foreign country, of the rights of broadcasting organisations and performers as is available under this Act, it may, by order published in the Official Gazette, direct that the provisions of Chapter VIII shall apply—

(a) to broadcasting organisations whose headquarters is situated in a country to which the order relates or the broadcast was transmitted from a transmitter situated in a country to which the order relates as if the headquarters of such organisation were situated in India or such broadcast were made from India;

(b) to performances that took place outside India to which the order relates in like manner as if they took place in India;

(c) to performances that are incorporated in a sound

recording published in a country to which the order relates as if it were published in India;

(d) to performances not fixed on a sound recording broadcast by a broadcasting organisation the headquarters of which is located in a country to which the order relates or where the broadcast is transmitted from a transmitter which is situated in a country to which the order relates as if the headquarters of such organisation were situated in India or such broadcast were may from India.

(2) Every order made under sub- section (I) may provide that—

(i) the provisions of Chapter VIII shall apply either generally or in relation to such class or classes of broadcasts or performances or such other class or classes of cases as may be specified in the order;

(ii) the term of the rights of broadcasting organisations and performance and performers in India shall not exceed such term as is conferred by the law of the country to which the order relates;

(iii) the enjoyment of the rights conferred by Chapter VIII shall be subject to the accomplishment of such conditions and formalities, if any, as may be specified in that order,

(iv) Chapter VIII or any part thereof shall not apply to broadcast and performances made before the commencement of the order or that Chapter VIII or any part thereof shall not apply to broadcasts and performances broadcast or performed before the commencement of the order;

(v) in case of ownership of rights of broadcasting organisations and performers, the provisions of Chapter VIII shall apply with such exceptions and modifications as the Central Government may, having regard to the law of the foreign country, consider necessary."

4. After section 42 of the principal Act, the following section shall be inserted, Insertion of new section 42A power to restrict rights of foreign broadcasting organisations and performers.

"42A. If it appears to the Central Government that a foreign country does not give or has not undertaken to give adequate protection to rights of broadcasting organisations or performers, the Central Government may, by order published in the Official Gazette, direct that of the provisions of this Act as confer right to broadcasting organisations or performers as the case may be, shall not apply to broadcasting organisations or performers whereof are based or incorporated in such foreign country or are subjects or citizens of such foreign country and are not incorporated or domicile] in India and thereupon those provisions shall not apply in such broadcasting, organisations or performers."

5. In section 52 of the principal Act, in sub- section (1),—

Amendment of section 52

(a) after clause (aa) . the following clauses shall be inserted, namely:-

"(ab) the doing of any act necessary to obtain information essential for operating inter operability of an independently computer programme with other programmes by a lawful possessor of a computer programme provided that such information is not otherwise readily available;

(ac) the observation study or test of functioning of the computer programme in order to determine the ideas and principles which underline any elements of the programme while performing such acts necessary for the functions for which the computer programme was supplied;

(ad) the making of copies or adaptation of the computer programme from a personality legally obtained copy for non commercial personal use;"

(b) in the proviso to clause (p) for the words "fifty years," the words "Sixty years" shall be substituted.

RAGHUBIR SINGH

Secretary to the Govt. of India.

APPENDIX XTH

THE GAZETTE OF INDIA

EXTRAORDINARY

PART II –SECTION I

PUBLISHED BY AUTHORITY

No. 29 New Delhi, Friday, June 8, 2012

Ministry Of Law And Justice

(Legislative Department)

New Delhi, 8 June,2012

The following Act of Parliament received the assent of the President on the 7th June, 2012 And is hereby published for general information:—

The Copyright (Amendment) Act, 2012

No. 27 Of 2012

An Act further to amend the Copyright Act, 1957

[7th June, 2012]

BE it enacted by Parliament in the Six1y-third Year of the Republic of lndia as follows:-

(1) This Act may be called the Copyright (Amendment)Act, 2012.

(2) It shall come into force on such date as the Central Government may, by notification in the Official Gazette, appoint.

2. In section 2 of the Copyright Act, 1957 (hereinafter referred to as the principal Act),-

Amendment of Section 2.

(1) in clause (/),the portion beginning with the words "on any medium" and ending with the words "produced by any means" shall be omitted;

(i1) after clause(/), the following clause shall be inserted, namely:-

'*(fa)* "commercial rental" does not include the rental, lease or lending of a lawfully acquired copy of a compnter programme, sound recording, visual recording or cinematograph film for non-profit purposes by a non-profit library or non-profit educational institution.';

Explanation : For the purposes of this clause, a "non-profit library or nonprofit educational institution" means a library or educational institution which receives grants from the Government or exempted from payment of tax under the Income-tax Act, 1961. **43 of 1961**

(iii) for clause (ff), the following shall be substituted, namely:-

'*(ff)* "communication to the public" means making any work or performance available for being seen or heard or otherwise enjoyed by the public directly or by any means of display or diffusion other than by issuing physical copies of it, whether simultaneously or at places and times chosen individually, regardless of whether any member of the public actually sees, hears or otherwise enjoys the work or performance so made available.

Explanation : For the purposes of this clause, communication through satellite or cable or any other means of simultaneous communication to more than one household or place of residence including residential rooms of any hotel or hostel shall be deemed to be communication to the public;

(iv) in clause *(qq)*, the following proviso shall be inserted, namely:-

"Provided that in a cinematograph film a person whose performance is casual or incidental in nature and, in the normal course of the practice of the industry, is not acknowledged anywhere including in the credits of the film shall not be treated as a performer except for the purpose of clause (b) of section 38B;";

(v) after clause (x), the following clause shall be inserted, namely:-

'(xo) "Rights Management Information" means,-

(a) the title or other information identifying the work or performance;

(b) the name of the author or performer;

(c) the name and address of the owner of rights;

(d) terms and conditions regarding the use of the rights; and

(e) any number or code that represents the information referred to in sub-clauses (a) to (d), Amendment but does not include any device or procedure intended to identify the user;';

(w) after clause *(xx);* the following clause shall be inserted, namely:-

'(:o:a) "visual recording" means the recording in any medium, by any method including the storing of it by any electronic means, of moving images or of the representations thereof; from which they can be perceived, reproduced or communicated by any method;';

3. In section 11 of the principal Act,- Amendment of section II.

(a) in sub-section (I), for the words "not less than two nor more than fourteen other members", the words "two other members" shall be substituted;

(c) for sub-section (2), the following sub-section shall be substituted, namely:"

(2) The salaries and allowances payable to and the other terms and conditions of service of the Chairman and other members of the Copyright Board shall be such as may be prescribed:

Provided that neither the salary and allowances nor the other terms and conditions of service of the Chairman or any other member shall be varied to his disadvantage after appointment.";

(c) for sub-section (4), the following sub-section shall

be substituted, namely:-

"(4) The Central Government may,.after consultation with the Chairman of the Copyright Board, appoint a Secretary to the Copyright Board and such **Amendment** other officers and employees as may be considered necessary for the efficient **of section** discharge of the functions of the Copyright Board.". **12**

4. In section 12 of the principal Act, in sub-section *(2),* for the words "members, each Bench consisting of not less than three members", the word "members" shall be substituted.

5. In section 14 of the principal Act,- Amendment of (t) in clause (c). for sub-clause (l), the following sub-clause shall be substituted, section 14 namely:-

"(l) to reproduce the work in any material form including-

(A) the storing of it in any medium by electronic or other means; or

(B) depiction in three dimensions of a two-dimensional work; or

(C) depiction in two-dimensions of a three-dimensional work;"; (it) in clause *(d),-*

(a) for sub-clause (1), the following sub-clause shall be substituted, namely:"— to make a copy of the film, including-

(A) a photograph of any image forming pan thereof; or

(B) storing of it in any medium by electronic or other means;";

(b) for sub-clause (ii), the following sub-clause shall be substituted, namely:-

"(ii) to sell or give on commercial rental or offer for sale or for such rental, any copy of the film;";

(ii1) in clause (e),-

(a) in sub-clause (1), after the words "embodying if', the words "including storing of it in any medium by electronic or other means" shall be inserted;

(b) for sub-clause (i1), the following sub-clause shall be substituted, namely:-

"(il) to sell or give on commercial rental or offer for sale or for such rental, any copy of the sound recording;"

2 of 1911. 6. In section 15 of the principal Act, for the words and figures, "Designs Act, 1911",

16 of 2000. wherever they occur, the words and figures "Designs Act, 2000" shall be substituted. **Amendment of section 15.**

7. In section 17 of the principal Act, in clause (e), the following proviso shall be inserted at the end, namely:- **Amendment of section 17.**

Provided that in case of any work incorporated in a cinematograph work, nothing contained in clauses (b) and (c) shall affect the right of the author in the work referred to in clause *(a)* of sub-section(/) of section 13;".

8. In section 18 of the principal Act, in sub-section (J), after the proviso, the following provisos shall be inserted, namely:- Amendment of section 18

"Provided further that no such assignment shall be applied to any medium or mode of exploitation of the work which did not exist or was not in commercial use at the time when the assignment was made, unless the assignment specifically referred to such medium or mode of exploitation of the work:

Provided also that the author of the literary or musical work included in a cinematograph film shall not assign or waive the right to receive royalties to be shared on an equal basis with the assignee of copyright for the utilisation of such work in any form other than for the communication to the public of the work along with the cinematograph film in a cinema hal, except to the legal heirs of the authors or to a copyright society for collection and distribution and any agreement to contrary shall be void:

Provided also that the author of the literary or musical work included in thesound recording but not forming part of any cinematograph film shall not assign or waive the right to receive royalties to be shared on an equal basis with the assignee of copyright for any utilisation of such work except to the legal heirs of the authors or to a collecting society for collection and distribution and any assignment to the contrary shall be void.".

9.1n section 19 of the principal Act,- Amendment of section 19.

(i) -in sub-section (3), for the words "royalty payable, if aoy", the words "royalty and any other consideration payable" shall be substituted;

(iz) after sub-section (7), the following sub-sections shall be inserted, namely:"

(8) The assignment of copyright in any work contrary to the terms and conditions of the rights already assigned to a copyright society in which the author of the work is a member shall be void.

(9) No assignment of copyright in any work to make a cinematograph film shall affect the right of the author of the work to claim an equal share of royalties and consideration payable in case of utilisation of the work in any form other than for the communication to the public of the work, along with the cinematograph film in a cinema hall.

(10) No assignment of the copyright in any work to make a sound recording which does not form part of any cinematograph film shall affect the right of the author of the work to claim an equal share of royalties and consideration payable for any utilisation of such work in any form."

10..In section I9A of the principal Act,- Amendment of section 19 A (z) in sub-section (2), in the second proviso, for the words "Provided further that", the following shall be substituted, namely:-

"Provided further that, pending the disposal of an application for revocation of assignment under this sub-section, the Copyright Board may pass such order, as it deems fit regarding implementation of the terms and conditions of assignment including any consideration to be paid for the enjoyment of the rights assigned:-

Provided also that";

(iz) after sub-section (2), the following sub-section shall be inserted, namely:-

"(3) Every complaint received under sub-section (2) shall be dealt with by the Copyright Board as far as possible and efforts shall be made to pass the final order in the matter within a period of six months from the date of receipt of the complaint and any delay in compliance of the same, the Copyright Board shall record the reasons thereof.".

11. In section 21 of the principal Act,- Amendment of section 21.

(i) in sub-section (1), for the words "the Registrar of Copyrights", the words "the Registrar of Copyrights or by way of public notice" shall be substituted;

(ii) after sub-section (2), the following sub-section shall be inserted, namely:-

"(2A) The Registrar of Copyrights shall, within fourteen days from the publication of the notice in the Official Gazette, post the notice on the official website of the Copyright Office so as to remain in 1he public domain for a period of not less than three years.".

12. In section 22 of the principal Act, the brackets and words ~(other than a photograph)" shall be omitted. Amendment of section 22.

13. Section 25 of the principal Act shall be omitted. Omission of section 25.

14.1n section 30 of the principal Act, for the words "writing signed by him", the words "writing by him" shall be substituted. Amendment of section 30.

15. In section 30A of the principal Act and in its marginal heading, for the words, Amendment 30A. figures and letter, "section 19 and 19A ",the word and figures "section 19" shall be substituted. of section

16. In section 31 of the principal Act, Amendment of section 31.

(i) in sub-section (1),-

(a) for the words "any Indian work", the words "any work" shall be substituted;

(b) for the words "licence to the complainant" the words "licence to such person or persons who, in the opinion of the Copyright Board, is or are qualified to do so" shall be substituted;

(c) the Explanation shall be omitted;

(ii) sub-section (2) shall be omitted.

17.1n section 31A of the principal Act,- Amendment of section 31A.

(i) in the marginal heading, for the words "Indian works", the words "or published works" shall be substituted;

(ii) for sub-section (1), the following sub-section shall be substituted, namely:-

"(J) Where, in the case of any unpublished work or any work published or communicated to the public and the work is withheld from the public in India, the author is dead or unknown or cannot be traced, or the owner of the copyright in such work cannot be found, any person may apply to the Copyright Board for a licence to publish or communicate to the public such work or a translation thereof in any language.".

18. After section 3JA of the principal Act, the following sections shall be inserted, namely:- Insertion of New Sections 31B, 31C and 31D. '31B. (I) Any person working for the benefit of persons with disability on a profit basis or for business may apply to the Copyright Board, in such form and manner and accompanied by such fee as may be prescribed, for a compulsory licence to publish any work in which copyright subsists for the benefit -of such persons, in a case to which clause (zb) of sub-section (/) of section 52 does not apply and the Copyright Board shall dispose of such application as expeditiously as possible and endeavor shall be made to dispose of such application within a period of two months from the date of receipt of the application. Compulsory licence for benefit of disabled.

(2) The Copyright Board may, on receipt of an application under sub-section (/), inquire, or direct such inquiry as it considers necessary to establish the credentials of the applicant and satisfy itself that the application has been made in good faith.

(3) If the Copyright Board is satisfied, after giving to the owners of rights in the work a reasonable opportunity of being beard and after holding such inquiry as it may deem necessary, that a compulsory licence needs to be issued to make the work available to the disabled, it may direct the Registrar of Copyrights to grant to the applicant such a licence to publish the work

(4) Every compulsory licence issued under this section shall specify the means and format of publication, the period during which the compulsory licence may be exercised and, in the case of issue of copies, the number of copies that may be issued including the rate or royalty:

Provided that where the Copyright Board has issued such a compulsory licence it may, on a fur1her application and after giving reasonable opportunity to the owners of rights, extend the period of such compulsory licence and allow the issue of more copies as it may deem fit.

31 C. (1). Any person desirous of making a cover version, being a sound Statutory licence for cover versions. recording in respect of any literal)', dramatic or musical work, where sound recordings of that work have been made by or with the licence or consent of the owner of the right in the work, may do so subject to the provisions of this section:

Provided that such sound recordings shall be in the same medium as the last recording, unless the medium of the last recording is no longer in current commercial use.

(2) The person making the sound recordings shall give prior notice of his intention to make the sound recordings in the manner as may be prescribed, and provide in advance copies of all covers or labels with which the sound recordings are to be sold, and pay in advance, to the owner of rights in each work royalties in respect of all copies to be made by him, at the rate fixed by the Copyright Board in this behalf:

Provided that such sound recordings shall not be sold or issued in any form of packing or with any cover or label which is likely to mislead or confuse the public as to their identity, and in particular shall not contain the name or depict in any way any performer of an earlier sound recording of the same work or any cinematograph film in which such sound recording was incorporated and, further, shall state on the cover that it is a cover version made under this section.

(3) The person making such sound recordings shall not make any alteration in the literal)' or musical work which has not been made previously by or with the consent of the owner of rights, or which is not technically necessary for the purpose of making the sound recordings:

Provided that such sound recordings shall not be made until the expiration of five calendar years after the end of the year in which the first sound recordings of the work was made.

(4) One royalty in respect of such sound recordings shall be paid for a minimum of Fifty thousand copies of each work during each calendar year in which copies of it are made:

Provided that the Copyright Board may, by general order, fix a lower minimum in respect of works in a particular language or dialect having regard to the potential circulation of such works.

(5) The person making such sound recordings shall maintain such registers and books of account in respect thereof; including full details of existing stock as may be prescribed and shall allow the owner of rights or his duly authorized agent or representative to inspect all records and books of account relating to such sound recording:

Provided that if on a complaint brought before the Copyright Board to the effect that the owner of rights has not been paid in full for any sound recordings purporting to be made in pursuance of this section, the Copyright Board is, prima facie, satisfied that the complaint is genuine, it may pass an order ex parte directing the person making the sound recording to cease from making further copies and, after holding such inquiry as it considers necessary, make such further order as it may deem fit, including an order for payment of royalty.

Explanation : For the purposes of this section "cover version" means a sound recording made in accordance with this section.

31D. (I) Any broadcasting organisation desirous of communicating to the public by way of a broadcast or by way of performance of a literary or musical work and sound recording which has already been published may do so subject to the provisions of this section. Statutory licence for broadcasting of literary and musical works and sound recording.

(2) The broadcasting organisation shall give prior notice, in such manner as may he prescribed, of its intention to broadcast the work stating the duration and territorial coverage of the broadcast, and shall pay to the owner of rights in each work royalties in the manner and at the rate fixed by the Copyright Board.

(3) The rates of royalty for radio broadcasting shall he different from television broadcasting and the Copyright Board shall fix separate rates for radio broadcasting and television broadcasting.

(4) In fixing the manner and the rate of royalty under sub-section (2), the Copyright Board may require the broadcasting organisation to pay an advance to the owners of rights.

(5) The names of the authors and the principal performers of the work shall, except in case of the broadcasting organisation communicating such work by way of performance, he announced with the broadcast

(6) No fresh alteration to any literary or musical work, which is not technically necessary for the purpose of broadcasting, other than shortening the work for convenience of broadcast, shall he made without the consent of the owners of rights.

(7) The broadcasting organisation shall-

(a) maintain such records and books of account, and render to the owners of rights such reports and accounts; and

(b) allow the owner of rights or his duly authorised agent or representative to inspect all records and books of account relating to such broadcast, in such manner as may he prescribed.

(8) Nothing in this section shall affect the operation of any licence issued or any agreement entered into before the commencement of the Copyright (Amendment) Act, 2012.

19.1n section 33 of the principal Act,- Amendment of section 33.

(1) in sub-section (1), for the words "provided further", the following shall he substituted, namely:-

"Provided further that the business of issuing or granting license in respect of literary, dramatic, musical and artistic works incorporated in a cinematograph films or sound recordings shall he carried out only through a copyright society duly registered under this Act:

Provided also";

(ii) after sub-section (3), the following shall he inserted, namely:-

"(3A) The registration granted to a copyright society under sub-section

(3)shall be for a period of five years and may he renewed from time to time before the end of every five years on a request in the prescribed form and the Central Government may renew the registration after considering the report of Registrar of Copyrights on the working of the copyright society under section 36:

Provided that the renewal of the registration of a copyright society shall he subject to the continued collective control of the copyright society being shared with the authors of works in their capacity as owners of copyright or of the right to receive royalty:

Provided further that every copyright society already registered before the coming into force of the copyright (Amendment) Act, 2012 shall get itself registered under this Chapter within a period of one year from the date of commencement of the Copyright (Amendment) Act,2012.";

(iii) in sub-sections (4) and (5), for the words "owners of rights", the words "authors and other owners of right" shall be substituted; ·

(iv) in sub-section (5), after the word "concerned" the words "or for non-compliance of sections 33A, sub-section (3) of section 35 and section 36 or any change carried out in the instrument by which the copyright society is established or incorporated and registered by the Central Government without prior notice to it" shall be inserted.

20. After section33 of the principal Act, the following section shall be inserted, namely:-

"33A. (J) Every copyright society shall publish its tariff scheme in such manner as may be prescribed Insertion of new section 33A.

Tariff Scheme by copyright societies.

(2) Any person who is aggrieved by the tariff scheme may appeal to the Copyright Board and the Board may, if satisfied after holding such inquiry as it may consider necessary, make such orders as may be required to remove any unreasonable element, anomaly or inconsistency therein:

Provided that the aggrieved person shall pay to the copyright society any fee as may be prescribed that has fallen due before making an appeal to the Copyright

Board and shall continue to pay such fee until the appeal is decided, and the Board shall not issue any order staying the collection of such fee pending disposal of the appeal:

Provided further that the Copyright Board may after hearing the parties fix an interim tariff and direct the aggrieved parties to make the payment accordingly pending disposal of the appeal.".

21. In section 34 of the principal Act, for the words "owner of rights", wherever they occur, the words "author and other owners of right" shall be substituted

22. Section 34A of the principal Act shall be omitted. Amendment of section 34.

23..ln section 35 of the principal Act and its marginal beading,- Omission of section 34A.

(a) for the words "owners of rights", wherever they occur, the words "author and other owners of right" shall be substituted; Amendment of section 35.

(b) after sub-section (2), the following sub-sections shall be inserted, namely:-

(3) Every copyright society shall have a governing body with such number of persons elected from among the members of the society consisting of equal number of authors and owners of work for the purpose of the administration of the society as may be specified.

(4) All members of copyrights society shall enjoy equal membership rights and there shall be no discrimination between authors and owners of rights in the distribution of royalties.

24. In section 36A of the principal Act,- Amendment of section 36A.

(a) for the words "performing rights society", the words "copyright society" shall be substituted;

(b) for the words, brackets and figures "the Copyright (Amendment) Act, 1994", the words, brackets and figures "the Copyright (Amendment) Act, 2012". 38 of 1994 shall be substituted

25. .ln section 37 of the principal Act, in sub-section (3), for clause (e), the following clause shall be substituted, namely:- Amendment of section 37

"(e) sells or gives on commercial rental or offer for sale or for such rental, any such sound recording or visual recording referred to in clause (c) or clause (d).".

26. 1n section 38 of the principal Act, sub-sections (J) and (4) shall be omitted.

27. After section 38 of the principal Act, the following sections shall be inserted, namely:-

Amendment of section 38~38A. (I) Without prejudice to the rights conferred on authors, the performer's Insertion right which is an exclusive right subject to the provisions of this Act to do or authorize of for doing any of the following acts in respect of the performance or any substantial new part thereof, namely:- section 38 A and 38 B

(a) to make a sound recording or a visual recording of the performance, including- Exclusive right of performers.

(i) reproduction of it in any material form including the storing of it in any medium by electronic or any other means;

(ii) issuance of copies of it to the public not being copies already in circulation;

(iii) communication of it to the public;

(iv) selling or giving it on commercial rental or offer for sale or for commercial rental any copy of the recording;

(b) to broadcast or communicate the performance to the public except where the performance is already broadcast.

(2) Once a performer has, by written agreement, consented to the incorporation of his performance in a cinematograph film he shall not, in the absence of any contract to the contrary, object to the enjoyment by the producer of the film of the performer's right in the same film:

Provided that, notwithstanding anything contained in this sub-section, the performer shall be entitled for royalties in case of making of the performances for commercial.

38B.The performer of a performance shall, independently of his right after Moral rights of assignment, either wholly or partially of his right, have the right,- the performer.

(a) to claim to be identified as the performer of his performance except where omission is dictated by the manner of the ~ of the performance; and

(b) to restrain or claim damages in respect of any distortion, mutilation or other modification ofbis performance that would be prejudicial to his reputation.

Explanation : For the purposes of this clause, it is hereby clarified that mere removal of any portion of a performance for the purpose of editing, or to fit the recording within a limited duration, or any other modification required for purely technical reasons shall not be deemed to be prejudicial to the performer's reputation.

28. For section 39A of the principal Act, the following section shall be substituted, Substitution of a new section for section 39A. namely:-

"39A. (I) Sections 18,19, 30, 30A, 33, 33A,.34, 35, 36, 53, 55, 58, 63, 64, 65, 65A, 65B and 66 shall, with necessary adaptations and modifications, apply in relation to the broadcast reproduction right in any broadcast and the performer's right in any performance as they apply in relation to copyright in a work:

Provided that where copyright or performer's right subsists in respect of any work or performance that has been broadcast, no licence to reproduce such broadcast, shall be given without the consent of the owner of right or performer, as the case may be, or both of them:

Provided further that the broadcast reproduction right or performer's right shall not subsist in any broadcast or performance if that broadcast or performance is an infringement of the copyright in any work. Certain provisions to apply in case of broadcast reproduction right and performer's rights.

Amendment of section 40.

Amendment of section 40A.

Amendment of section 45.

Amendment of section 52.

(2) The broadcast reproduction right or the performer's right shall not affect the separate copyright in any work in respect of which, the broadcast or the performance, as the case may be, is made.".

29. In section 40 of the principal Act, in the proviso, in clause (iiz), after the words "the order relates", the words "but such a term of copyright shall not exceed the term of copyright provided under this Act" shall be inserted.

30. In section 40A of the principal Act, in sub-section (2), in clause (iz), the following proviso shall be inserted, namely:-

"Provided that it does not exceed the period provided under this Act;".

31. In section 45 of the principal Act, in sub-section (1), in the provison (z) for the words "relation to any goods", the words "relation to any goods or services" shall be substituted;

(iz) for the words and figures "section 4 of the Trade and Merchandise Marks Act, !958" the words and figures "section 3 of the Trade Marks Act, 1999" shall be 43 of 1958. substituted. 47 of 1999.

32. In section 52 of the principal Act, in sub-section (I),- (z) for clause (a), the following clause shall be substituted, namely:-

(a) a fair dealing with any work, not being a computer programme, for the purposes of-

(i) private or personal use, including research;

(ii) criticism or review, whether of that work or of any other work;

(iii) the reporting of current events and current affairs, including the reporting of a lecture delivered in public.

Explanation : The storing of any work in any electronic medium for the purposes mentioned in this clause, including the incidental storage of any computer programme which is not itself an infringing copy for the said purposes, shall not constitute infringement of copyright";

(iz) for clauses (b), (c), (d), (e), (/), (g), (h), (z) and (J), the following shall be substituted, namely:-

"(b) the transient or incidental storage of a work or performance purely in the technical process of electronic transmission or communication to the public;

(c) transient or incidental storage of a work or performance for the purpose of providing electronic links, access or integration, where such links, access or integration bas not been expressly prohibited by the right bolder, unless the person responsible is aware or bas reasonable grounds for believing that such storage is of an infringing copy:

Provided that if the person responsible for the storage of the copy bas received a written complaint from the owner of copyright in the work, complaining that such transient or incidental storage is an infringement, such person responsible for the storage shall refrain from facilitating such access for a period of twenty-one days or till be receives an order from the complete of court refraining from facilitating access and in case no such order is received before the expiry of such period of twenty-one days, be may continue to provide the facility of such access;

(d) the reproduction of any work for the purpose of a judicial proceeding or for the purpose of a report of a judicial proceeding;

(e) the reproduction or publication of any work prepared by the Secretariat of a Legislature or, where the Legislature consists of two Houses, by the Secretariat of either House of the. Legislature, exclusively for the use of the members of that Legislature;"

(e) the reproduction of any work in a certified copy made or supplied in accordance with any law for the time being in force;

(g) the reading or recitation in public of reasonable extracts from a published literacy or dramatic work;

(h) the publication in a collection, mainly composed of non-copyright matter, bona fide intended for instructional use, and so described in the title and in any advertisement issued by or on behalf of the publisher, of short passages from published literary or dramatic works, not themselves published for such use in which copyright subsists:

Provided that not more than two such passages from works by the same author are published by the same publisher during any period of five years.

Explanation : In the case of a work of joint authorship, references in this clause to passages from works shall include references to passages from works by any one or more of the authors of those passages or by any one or more of those authors in collaboration wilh any other person;

(1) the reproduction of any work-

(i) by a teacher or a pupil in the course of instruction; or

(ii) as part of the questions to be answered in an examination; or

(iii) in answers to such questions;

(J) the performance, in the course of the activities of an educational institution, of a literary, dramatic or musical work by the staff and students of the institution, or of a cinematograph film or a sound recording if the audience is limited to such staff and students, the parents and guardians of the students and persons connected with the activities of the institution or the communication to such an audience of a cinematograph film or sound recording;"

(iii) for clause (n), the following clause shall be

substituted, namely:-

"(n) the storing of a work in any medium by electronic means by a noncommercial public library, for preservation if the library already possesses a non-digital copy of the work;";

(iv) in clause (o), for the words "public library", the words, "non-commercial public library" shall be substituted;

(v) after clause (v), the following clause shall be inserted, namely:-

"(w) the making of a three-dimensional object from a two-dimensional artistic work, such as a technical drawing, for the purposes of industrial application of any purely functional part of a useful device;

(vi) in clause (y), for the words "dramatic or", the words "dramatic, artistic or" shall the substituted;

(vii) after clause (za) and the Explanation there under, the following shall be inserted, namely:-

"(zb) the adaptation, reproduction, issue of copies or communication to the public of any work in any accessible format, by-

(l) any person to facilitate persons with disability to access to works including sharing with any person wilh disability of such accessible format for private or personal use, educational purpose or research; or

(ii) any organisation working for the benefit of the persons with disabilities in case the normal format prevents the enjoyment of such works by such persons:

Provided that the copies of the works in such accessible format are made available to the persons with disabilities on a non-profit basis but to recover only the cost of production:

Provided further that the organisation shall ensure that the copies of works in such accessible format are used only by persons with disabilities and takes reasonable steps to prevent its entry into ordinary channels of. business.

Explanation : For the purposes of this sub-clause, "any organisation" includes and organisation registered under section 12A of the Income-tax Act, 1961 and working for the benefit of persons with disability or recognised under Chapter X of 43 of 1961. the Persons with Disabilities (Equal Opportunities, Protection or Rights and full Participation)

Act, 1995 or receiving grants from the government for facilitating access 1 of 1996. to persons with disabilities or an educational institution or library or archives recognised by the Government".

(zc) the importation of copies of any literary or artistic work, such as labels, company logos or promotional or explanatory material, that is purely incidental to other goods or products being imported lawfully.".

33. Section 52B of the principal Act shall be omitted. Omission of section 52B

34. For section 53 of the principal Act, the following section shall be substituted, namely:- Substitution of new section for section 53.

"53. (J) The owner of any right conferred by this Act in respect of any work or any performance embodied in such work or his duly authorised agent, may give notice in writing to the Commissioner of Customs, or to any other officer authorised in this behalf by the Central Board of Excise and Customs,- Importation of infringing copies.

(a) that he is the owner of the said right, with proof thereof; and

(b) that he requesters the Commissioner for a period specified in the notice, which shall not exceed one year, to treat infringing copies of the work as prohibited goods, and that infringing copies of the work are expected to arrive in India at a time and a place specified in the notice.

(2) The Commissioner, after scrutiny of the evidence furnished by the owner of the right and on being satisfied may, subject to the provisions of sub-section (J), treat infringing copies of the work as prohibited goods that have been imported into India, excluding goods in transit:

Provided that the owner of the work deposits such amount as the Commissioner may require as security having regard to the likely expenses on demurrage, cost of storage and compensation to the importer in case it is found that the works are not infringing copies.

(3) When any goods treated as prohibited under sub-section (2) have been detained, the Customs Officer detaining them shall inform the importer as well as the person who gave notice under sub-section(I) of the detention of such goods within forty-eight hours of their detention.

(4) The Customs Officer shall release the goods, and they shall no longer be treated as prohibited goods, if the person who gave notice under sub-section (J) does not produce any order from a court having jurisdiction as to the temporary or permanent disposal of such goods within fourteen days from the date of their detention.".

(35) In section 55 of the principal Act, in sub-section (2), for the portion beginning Amendment of section 55 with the words "a name purporting to be" and ending with the words "as the case may be, appears", the following shall be substituted, namely:- "or, subject to the provisions of sub-section (3) of section 13, a cinematograph film or sound recording. a name purporting to be that of the author, or the publisher, as the case may be, of that work, appears".

36. In section 57 of the principal Act,- Amendment of section 57 (r) in sub-section (1), in clause (b), the words "which is done before the expiration of the term of copyright" shall be omitted;

37. After section 65 of the principal Act, the following sections shall be inserted, namely:- Insertion of new sections 65A and 65B

"65A. (1) Any person who circumvents an effective technological measure applied for the purpose of protecting any of the rights conferred by this Act, with the intention of infringing such rights, shall be punishable with imprisonment which may extend to two years and shall also be liable to fine. Protection of technological measures.

(2) Nothing in sub-section (1) shall prevent any person from,-

(a) doing anything referred to therein for ·a purpose not expressly prohibited by this Act:

Provided that any person facilitating circumvention by another person of a technological measure for such a purpose shall maintain a complete record of such other person including his name, address and all relevant particulars necessary to identify him and the purpose for which he has been facilitated; or

(b) doing anything necessary to conduct encryption research using a lawfully obtained encrypted copy; or

(c) conducting any lawful investigation; or

(d) doing anything necessary for the purpose of testing the security of a computer system or a computer network with the authorisation of its owner; or

(e) operator; or

(f) doing anything necessary to circumvent technological measures intended for identification or surveillance of a user; or

(g) taking measures necessary in the interest of national security.

65B.Any person, who knowingly,- Protection of Rights

(z) removes or alters any rights management information without Management authority, or Information.

(iz) distributes, imports for distribution, broadcasts or communicates to the public, without authority, copies of any work, or performance knowing that electronic rights management information has been removed or altered without authority, shall be punishable with imprisonment which may extend to two years and shall also be liable to fine:

Provided that if the rights management information has been tampered with in any work, the owner of copyright in such work may also avail of civil remedies provided under

Chapter XII against the persons indulging in such acts.". .

Amendment of section 66.

38. In section 66 of the principal Act, after the words "delivered up to the owner of the copyright," the words "or may make such order as it may deem fit regarding the disposal of such copies or plates" shall be inserted.

39. In section 78 of the principal Act, in Sub.-section (2),- Amendment of Section 78(1) for clause (a), the following clause shall be substituted, namely:-

(a) the salaries and allowances payable to and the other terms and conditions of service of the chairman and other members of the Copyright Board under sub-section (2) of section II;

(ii) after clause (c), the following clauses shall be inserted, namely:-

"(cA) the form and manner in which an Organisation may apply to the Copyright Board for compulsory licence for disabled and the fee which may accompany such application under sub-section (J) of section 31B;

(cB) the manner in which a person making sound recording may give prior notice of his intention to make Sound recording under sub-section (2) of section 31 C;

(cC) the register and books of account and the details of existing stock which a person making sound recording may maintain under sub-section (5) of section 31 C;

(cD) the manner in which prior notice may be given by a broadcasting organisation under sub-section (2) of section 31D;

(cE) the reports and accounts which may be maintained under clause (a), and the inspection of records and books of account which may be made under clause (b) of sub-section (7) of section 31D;";

(iii) after clause (cc), the following clauses shall be inserted, namely:-

"(ccA) the manner in which a copyright society may publish its Tariff Scheme under sub-section (J) of section 33A;

(ccB) the fee which is to be paid before filing an appeal to the Copyright Board under sub-section (2) of section 33A;"

(ccC) the form of application for renewal of registration of a copyright society and the fee which may accompany such application under sub-section

(3A) ofsection33; .

(iv) clause (db) shall be omitted.

V.K.BHASIN

Secretary to the Govt. of India.